PRAISE FOR *FUNCTIONAL TRAINING AND BEYOND*

"Adam has an extraordinary and unquenchable thirst for knowledge that draws the reader in and opens up a whole new world of functional fitness. He doesn't just think outside the box; he breaks the box right down, giving anyone and everyone an inspiring and motivating view on health and fitness for the mind and body. This is a must-read book. Adam has an unbelievable depth of knowledge stemming from a very genuine passion and fascination in his subject. If anyone needs to find something to motivate them to get fit and find a different way of looking at health and fitness, look no further!"

—Alex Gregory, English rower and a two-time Olympic Gold medalist

"Adam on The Bioneer is one of the most intellectual and informative people I've ever had the pleasure of watching. Each video leaves you blessed with new knowledge quite helpful for everyday life. He's a great creator and I respect his work."

—Jordan "JaxBlade" Downs

T0266666

"Adam is the new breed of educator and has loaded *Functional Training and Beyond* with a ton of information not contained in any one text—not even mine. Adam covers definitions, physiological processes, cognitive and neural mechanisms of movement, different training perspectives, and ties all in with historical accounts and applications. I recommend this book to all personal trainers, training geeks, and people who just want to learn about different training methods and philosophies."

—**JC Santana,** author of *Functional Training*

FUNCTIONAL TRAINING

Building the Ultimate
Superfunctional Body and Mind

and Beyond

FUNCTIONAL TRAINING

Building the Ultimate

Superfunctional Body and Mind

and Beyond

Adam Sinicki

CORAL GABLES

For permission requests, please contact the publisher at:

Mango Publishing Group
2850 Douglas Road, 2nd Floor
Coral Gables, FL 33134 USA
info@mango.bz

For special orders, quantity sales, course adoptions and corporate sales, please email the publisher at sales@mango.bz. For trade and wholesale sales, please contact Ingram Publisher Services at customer.service@ingramcontent.com or +1.800.509.4887.

Functional Training and Beyond: Building the Ultimate Superfunctional Body and Mind

ISBN: (p) 978-1-64250-503-0 (e) 978-1-64250-504-7

BISAC: SPO047000, SPORTS & RECREATION / Training

LCCN: Requested from the Library of Congress

Table of Contents

INTRODUCTION

Welcome to Functional Training and Beyond

To a lot of people, "fitness" simply means getting really strong, or perhaps being able to run long distances. Others equate fitness with yoga, losing weight, or looking good.

Some people just want to be able to move freely and without pain.

Whatever the case, when someone makes the determination to "get fit," they often start by choosing a training program and attempting to stick to it for a given duration. Invariably, this training program will revolve around a specific set of goals and will thus follow a predictable structure.

- If they want to build big muscles, they might try a bodybuilding "bro split."
- If they want to lose weight, they might start doing cardio or high intensity interval training (HIIT).
- If they want to get stronger, they might try weightlifting.
- If the aim is to improve mobility and pain-free movement, they might try yoga.

⚜ If they want to get fit and have fun doing it, they might choose football or dance.

After a few months, as the person starts to see changes, they declare this experiment a success: they are now fit! And as they grow more and more with their chosen sport or program, investing time in their chosen hobby and becoming a part of the community, they might well adopt a tribal mindset. They might covet their particular form of training at the expense of all others. This is the one true way to get fit.

> "The big three lifts are all you need!"

> "CrossFit is a way of life!"

> "Mixed martial arts (MMA) is real martial arts. Wing Chun is fake!"

In this book, I'm going to argue for a different approach. Limiting yourself to a single form of training is unnecessarily restrictive. Every system of training has something to offer. Likewise, there's no single style of training that can possibly cover the entire gamut of what constitutes "fitness."

There are arguments as to what is a more "functional" approach to training. Maybe it's calisthenics, maybe it's weightlifting. Maybe it's using the cable machine and medicine balls. But I believe that *true* functionality comes from versatility and variety. It comes from being able to thrive in any situation.

This demands a multidisciplinary approach.

If the aim of your training is to feel and perform better, why would you pick just one narrow aspect of your performance and focus purely on that? A person might dedicate years of training to being able to lift a few kilograms more in a particular movement pattern, despite being extremely weak in others.

This makes sense if you're a professional competitive weightlifter. But if you're simply training for self-betterment, it isn't the best strategy. There comes a point of diminishing returns: 5 kg more won't benefit you all that much outside of the gym. Especially when there are so many other aspects of fitness you may have overlooked.

Unfortunately, this has become the norm. Ask a personal trainer to write a general fitness program for a beginner and they will often prescribe a series of static lifts, with perhaps a little running on the side. It doesn't occur to most people that they can train *every aspect* of themselves. Or that these select few movement patterns do a poor job of emulating the variety of movement challenges we face in daily life.

This is even *truer* for athletic coaches. Relying on just three powerlifting moves to build every type of runner is an extremely limited approach, as we will see.

If you're just training for aesthetics, you may well be making yourself *less* functional and mobile in the long run, piling dysfunction on top of dysfunction.

What makes even less sense, is that 99.99 percent of programs completely neglect to train the brain. This is the form of training that would no doubt have the most direct and meaningful impact on your day-to-day lifestyle, after all. Brain training is *extremely* functional.

As we'll soon see, the brain can be trained just like our muscles. In fact, it may even be significantly *more* plastic! Using tools like meditation, brain-training exercises, breathing techniques, and more, we can actually develop specific brain areas and *sculpt* our brains the way we want them.

The human body is capable of moving and reacting in a hugely varied number of ways. It can adapt to truly remarkable circumstances. Anything can be trained.

I believe that a more modern approach to fitness should acknowledge this. I believe that a truly *comprehensive* training program should aim to bring every human trait up to a formidable level.

The move toward "functional training" is a step in the right direction. It reflects a desire, not just to look good, but to develop strength and skills with real-world applications, be it in sports or in life.

But I think we can go further.

Imagine what it would feel like to be stronger, faster, more mobile, more energetic, more creative, more patient, more agile, and more resilient *all at once*—to be SuperFunctional!

And the exciting thing is that all the methods we need to get there are already out there. You just have to know where to look.

Why does all this matter? Why does it matter if you can get into a comfortable resting squat? I would argue that it matters *no less* than being able to squat 200 kg. Moreover, when you choose to level-up every aspect of your brain and body, you increase the number of possibilities available to you. If you want to change your life for the better, you shouldn't ask what you need to *do* but rather who you need to *become*.

CHAPTER 1

Why We Need to Go Beyond Regular Training

Our bodies have nearly limitless ability to adapt and perform[1] but most people only ever tap into a fraction of that potential. What little training we use to push ourselves further is typically inherited from sports-specific strategies designed to build aesthetic muscle or max strength in just a few lifts. Either that, or it revolves purely around aesthetics and appearance. Thus, we go about our lives with permanent handicaps.

To go further, we need a new kind of training.

The largest proportion of people who actually "train," usually stick to workouts designed to improve their looks (no matter what this does to their ability to navigate the world). They build their "mirror muscles," such as pecs and abs, while ignoring the less sexy areas like obliques, serratus muscles, or erector spinae. They look good for a while, but eventually this leaves them stiff, hunched over, and in pain. Decidedly *not* sexy!

Others use exercise as a way to restore their health. Whether recovering from injury, or simply trying to fight the symptoms of aging, poor diet, or a sedentary lifestyle. Either way, this is exercise as rehabilitation. It is not

---

1   In cases like this, "body" refers to both the brain and the body.

"training." They are exercising to be well again, rather than training to be *better* than well. Should we be satisfied with being "good enough?"

The exception to this rule is the athlete. Athletes such as sprinters, MMA fighters, rock climbers, swimmers, and others, train to become the very best at their given sport. But even athletes will typically only train for specific skills and traits. This makes sense from a competitive standpoint, due to concepts such as specificity and the interference effect (more on this later). For the rest of us, it makes a lot less sense. Even most athletes could benefit from supplementing their specific training with more diversity.

Why is it then, that many of those people who aren't merely training for looks or basic health, will focus predominantly on a very limited number of lifts? Why is it that they train *specifically* like a powerlifter, marathon runner, or a triathlete? These are very specific methods with extremely focused goals and, therefore, results.

For most of us, it is better to be an all-rounder. To be highly capable in every physical and cognitive attribute in order to deal with unpredictable circumstances. If you are truly training to be better than you are now, doesn't it make sense to focus on every aspect of yourself?

I believe the average Joe and Josephine should train to improve every aspect of their physical and mental performance. Training to be faster, smarter, more mobile, more energetic, stronger, more focused, and more alert.

Being the best powerlifter isn't useful for the average person. Being *generally awesome* is!

In this book, I'll discuss training that takes those modest goals and goes even further beyond.[2] To do that, this book collects and explores concepts and ideas from a range of training disciplines, warrior cultures, and new research. We're going to discuss athletic training, movement training, old-time strongmen, gymnastic strength training, meditation, samurai training, yoga, calisthenics, bodybuilding, powerlifting, warrior monk training, martial arts, parkour (free running), military training, street workouts, Russian strength training systems, nootropics, flow states, sports psychology, and more. We'll look at what the science has to say about the best ways to build hypertrophy,[3] strength, mobility, and speed, as well as new research exploring the nature of intelligence, focus, and memory.

Then we're going to take the best stuff and attempt to combine it into a unique training system that will be awesome and fun. A workout that will take you far beyond well.[4]

Follow this strategy, and in an ideal world you'd be able to walk on your hands, bench press twice your bodyweight, stay focused like a laser and brim with energy when you wake up in the morning. And if you can't do all those things, you'll have a great time trying.

This is what I call "SuperFunctional Training."

---

2   Yes, that's a *Dragon Ball Z* reference.
3   Muscle growth.
4   "Well" will be a dot to you!

How Your Current Lifestyle Is Limiting Your Potential

The problem is that many of us are starting from *less than zero*. We are in negative territory.

Our modern lifestyles are crippling us. Our bodies are simply not evolved to cope with the demands we're placing on them. We are overstressed, overtired, tight, and in pain. It's no exaggeration to say that our daily routines actually shorten our life expectancies, while putting us at greater risk for all *kinds* of illnesses that wouldn't have troubled our ancestors.

Let's break down a typical day for the average person. Let's call him Hank. Hank is a middle-aged, five-foot-ten dude who works an office job. He loves reading and watching old episodes of *Frasier*. He has 2.5 beautiful children and a doting wife. He's also sporting quite the dad-bod, and his daily routine is slowly destroying his health.

It starts with an alarm that pulls him out of a deep sleep. That shock sends a surge of adrenaline and cortisol through his system, making him stressed and anxious before he's even begun his day. Chances are, he only got six hours of low-quality sleep. That, combined with the sudden awakening, means he will spend the next hour in a zombie-like state of "sleep inertia."[5]

---

5   That feeling of grogginess you get first thing in the morning.

To wake up, Hank drinks a big mug of coffee. Caffeine hits his system hard, blocking his adenosine receptors to mask feelings of tiredness, triggering a massive release of excitatory neurotransmitters. From a physiological perspective, it is stress in a cup![6]

After eating a breakfast that probably consists only of empty calories and simple carbs (meaning there is very little nutritional value and it's unlikely to keep him full for long), Hank heads to work. Did you know having people walk rapidly toward you is a universal fear that transcends cultures? Pushing his way down the busy high street is triggering even more stress. Hank is now wired, tired, and malnourished.

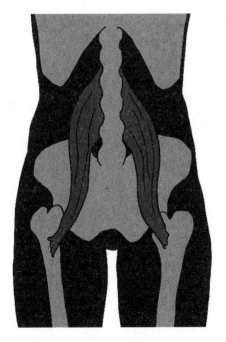

At work, Hank will sit still for eight hours. This *literally* shortens his lifespan, as the heart gets weaker due to lack of exertion.[7] It also causes all kinds of physical changes in his body. His hamstrings are short and tight from being in a constantly shortened position, and his glutes are weak. His hip flexors are likewise full of tension, including the psoas muscles. These muscles

---

6   I feel compelled at this point to tell you that I love coffee and almost certainly over-indulge. That doesn't mean I recommend it, though!

7   Rebecca Seguin, PhD, CSCS et al. (2013) "Sedentary Behavior and Mortality in Older Women." *American Journal of Preventative Medicine.* 46(2):122–135.

originate at the lumbar spine (lower back) and insert onto the femur (upper leg).

Thus, tightness here can tug on the lower back and create significant discomfort. Unbeknownst to Hank, this is why the first thing he does when he sits up in bed in the morning is to clasp his aching lower back. Sound familiar?

Because he constantly has to reach forward with his hands and arms, Hanks shoulders are hunched and rounded (this is called kyphosis) and his pecs are tight. He's also recently begun to notice his neck is often stiff and painful from looking at the computer screen at an awkward angle. Hank doesn't know this yet, but next year he'll need time off for a repetitive strain injury in his fingers and wrists.

Hank spends this working day feeling stressed. He has deadlines, awkward calls to make, and difficult colleagues. The stress response is therefore constantly running in the background, keeping him in a mild fight-or-flight state. This is intended to be an acute reaction to immediate physical danger and evolved to prepare us for combat or fleeing. Thus, it triggers a number of physiological changes:

- Heightened heart rate
- Thickened blood viscosity (to encourage rapid clotting in case of injury)
- Anxiety
- Increased sensitivity
- Muscle tension
- Tunnel vision

Blood is routed toward the muscles and the brain, shunted away from less immediately pressing functions such as digestion and immunity. This is perfectly fine and logical if you indeed *are* facing down a lion. However, there is no lion in Hank's office (nor yours, I imagine).[8] If this continues chronically for weeks and months because work is busy, then he is going to risk becoming ill and malnourished over time due to those permanently suppressed systems.

Work keeps Hank stressed then, but what it largely *fails* to do is challenge him in meaningful ways. Hank, you see, has been working in the same position at the same company for the last five years. "Same position" is an appropriate choice of words here.

> **The brain is really a learning machine.**

Thus begins the decline of Hank's mental health and intelligence. The brain is really a learning machine. That's what it's built to do, and that's what it *loves* doing. We enjoy games largely because they provide an opportunity for learning with a rewarding feedback loop. We'll talk more about this in a future chapter, but suffice to say that the brain can learn and adapt to stimuli thanks to something called "neuroplasticity." This term describes the brain's ability to grow and change shape in response to inputs and training, much like a muscle. This is mediated by the production of a number of hormones and neurotransmitters, such

---

8   If there is, you should let HR know.

as BDNF (brain derived neurotrophic factor), dopamine, and nerve growth factor. The more you learn, the more of these chemicals your brain produces. When you *stop* learning new things, those chemicals also stop, and you become significantly worse at picking up new information when the moment *does* arise.

So, when Hank travels the same route to work every day and does essentially the same tasks every day before watching the same rubbish on TV, it's no wonder that his brain doesn't have quite the *oomph* it once did. Since dopamine *also* help mediate attention and focus, this effect also bleeds over into general motivation, awareness, and brain function.

Eventually, a loss of learning opportunity may increase the likelihood of neurodegenerative conditions like Alzheimer's and dementia.[9] As Hank repeats the same day over and over, it's no surprise that he has lately been experiencing feelings of malaise and low motivation.

That evening spent on the couch is harmful to Hank in other ways too, by the way. Not only does it further encourage the atrophy of muscle and the loss of mobility, but the bright light from the TV screen confuses and upsets his body clock, leading to poorer sleep. Hank will spend the first hour in bed staring up at the ceiling.

Even the shoes Hank wears prevent him from using the muscles in his feet or receiving the correct proprioceptive feedback. Muscles are not just tools for exerting force; they're also *sensory organs*. They provide important feedback to our brains that help us to move and learn about the world around us.

---

9   Norton W. Milgram et al. (2006), "Neuroprotective effects of cognitive enrichment." *Ageing Research Reviews.* 5(3):354–369.

When you stop receiving that information, you eventually cull the relevant neural pathways. In other words, you lose the ability to receive that proprioceptive feedback even when it's available. This not only causes us to move incorrectly, it also reduces the amount of information coming into the brain. Loss of sensory information may even be linked with dementia: research shows a correlation between hearing loss and neurodegenerative disease—though it's not clear as yet whether the loss of hearing is a marker of the condition, or a causative factor.10 So Hank might also face dementia in older age.

During that entire day, Hank barely moved his body. He didn't climb, jump, crawl, or lift. And because we have designed everything to be at a convenient height for our bipedal lifestyles, he barely even had to stoop. Nor did he have any need to use his working memory or his creative problem solving.

Going to the gym for one hour, three times a week, won't undo that kind of damage. Especially not when the movements are one-dimensional and constrained. More on this in a moment.

I could go on: a lack of time outdoors reduces production of vitamin D and thereby hampers hormonal balance (and mood). Improper nutrition leaves us without the raw building blocks needed to build neurotransmitters and muscle tissue. Our tendency to eliminate all bacteria from our homes leaves us defenseless against harmful germs. Constantly flicking between content and screens wears out our dopamine systems and diminishes our ability to focus on tasks. A perpetual state of climate-controlled comfort

---

10   Frank R. Lin et al. (2010), "Hearing Loss and Incident Dementia." *JAMA Neurology.* 68(2):214–220.

means most of us can't bear being cold for more than five minutes.

The bottom line is that—like Hank—we have no energy, no strength, and no mental agility. At least comparatively. Unless you engage in some form of mobility training regularly, there is a high chance that you can't currently perform a full squat while keeping your heels on the ground. There's also a very good chance that you can't touch your toes or count the number of times you sit down in a day without forgetting about it (try it!).

Now compare this with the way were designed to use our bodies: running through the woods tracking prey, discovering new environments on a regular basis, fighting with animals and competitors, and eating meat, berries, and fiber.

The average modern human is to primitive man what an overfed poodle is to a wolf.[11]

So, when I say we are missing out on potential performance, I'm really not kidding!

As Yuval Noha Harari points out in his book *Sapiens*: we have been domesticated. Just as we domesticated poodles, we ourselves were domesticated by wheat, a plant that found it advantageous to have us living in one spot, caring for its needs twenty-four-seven.

But this isn't a book about paleo fitness. I'm not here to tell you that you should only eat things you can forage, or that you should go outside and throw rocks (though that would be pretty good for you). The point is that with all our modern advances, we should be *more* functional than we ever have been—not less!

---

11   This is not an attack on poodles—I love poodles!

The reason we're in this mess is because our bodies are so remarkably capable of adapting to our lifestyles and environments. Prehistoric man was brilliant at trail running and tree climbing, but likely didn't have much of a bench press. By understanding what makes the body tick, we can do better.

We have all this technology and scientific understanding, and yet we are the most out-of-shape we have ever been!

> We have all this technology and all this scientific understanding, and yet we are the most out-of-shape we have ever been!

Typical Training Programs Aren't Enough

You might think that you don't need to worry about these issues if you hit the gym. Unfortunately, most training programs don't offer enough of the right stimuli to make an impact. In fact, they often compound the problem!

A lot of training programs are predominantly based around aesthetics: building attractive muscle and stripping away fat. To that end, they focus on building the most well-known "mirror muscles" that are considered desirable:

- The pecs
- The abs
- The biceps

Notice something about these muscles? They're all on the front of our bodies. Thus, they all work to pull our bodies forward.

When you strengthen these muscles and forget external rotation, lats, erector spinae, traps, and others, you end up exaggerating the hunched forward look caused by all that office work.

Worse: when you train these muscles using purely isolation movements—movements that isolate and target just a single joint and muscle group such as bicep curls or lat pull downs—you create and exacerbate significant imbalances in muscle strength. You may also lose the ability to use the muscles in unison as they are designed to be used.

> **There is no real-world scenario where you would ever be required to perform a movement like the lat pull-down.**

There are few real-world scenarios where you will ever be required to perform a movement like the lat pull-down.

That's not to say this movement is wrong, or that resistance machines and single-joint movements don't have their place. They can be used in many ways to support other types of training. It's just that they're not enough on their own. Most people don't realize this.

But perhaps you're still feeling smug. Perhaps you have never been partial to isolation movements or bodybuilding-style training. Maybe you've always had a preference for the big compound lifts like squats, deadlifts, and bench presses. These do use the muscles together as a single unit, and they train many more areas like the core and the traps.

Unfortunately, the increasingly common belief that these lifts are all you need is also incorrect. Strength gains are specific to the muscles they target (on the whole). That's why a swimmer actually has poorer jumping ability compared with the average person according to studies: they have trained their legs in a specific manner.[12] Just like the swimmer, the person who squats heavy is training only a very specific type of strength, useful in a very narrow context.

Perhaps the most glaring issue is that you're only moving in a single plane of movement (the sagittal plane). That is to say, every movement is either straight up and down, or straight forward. At no point are you twisting your body or stepping out to the side (training in the transverse and frontal planes respectively). In an ideal world, you would be moving between these planes in fully three-dimensional movements, just like you do in real life.

The loss of rotational strength is particularly unfortunate. As Pat McNamara told Joe Rogan: "in the transverse plane lives life-saving and ass-kicking."

So, if someone were to push you from the side, you would still go down like a stack of cards! And in a wrestling match, you would lack the necessary strength to twist an opponent to the ground. That's in spite of your 150 kg. bench!

And you still aren't doing much for the external rotation of the shoulders or the traps, for that matter! Studies show that the traps grow more in response to direct training (moves like the shrug) as compared with deadlifts.[13] So you

---

12   Eloranta V. (2003) "Influence of sports background on leg muscle coordination in vertical jumps." *Electromyogr Clin Neurophysiol.* 43(3):141–56.
13   Conley MS. et al. (1997) "Specificity of resistance training responses in neck muscle size and strength." *Eu J Appl Occup Physiol.* 75(5):443–8.

could still end up with that hunched appearance, or even an injury down the line.

That heavy squat isn't even enough to develop complete strength within a squatting motion. Why? Because you will accelerate through certain parts of the movement. We tend to "explode" out of squats, which provides enough momentum and speed to help us fly past the most difficult angles.

> In most situations, it is far more useful to be able to exert some strength for a period of time, versus all your strength for ten seconds.

And if you only use the squat for a few extremely heavy reps, then you will only build max strength. What about strength endurance, the ability to exert strength for an extended period?

In most situations, it is far more useful to be able to exert some strength for a period of time, versus all your strength for ten seconds. In fact, very few of us will ever need to lift more than 70 percent of our one-rep maximum (1RM) during an average week.

When did you last have to lift 200 kg. off the floor? Maybe you can't remember. But what you probably can remember is the last time you had to lift 50 kg. multiple times. Or the last time you had to push a heavy piece of furniture at an awkward angle.

Chasing numbers is meaningless unless that's your passion or your job.

And all this is before we've even touched on training the ability to run full speed, jump higher, grip harder, sense the body in space, or focus the mind. That's the point at which you go beyond functional and become *SuperFunctional.*

Is All This Really Necessary?

Perhaps you train the big three lifts chiefly as a fun way to improve your general strength and see some measurable progress.

Maybe you *like* developing ripped abs, and you aren't too concerned about your loss of shoulder mobility.

That's fine of course. You don't need to train like Batman to be healthy!

After all, Batman is a fictional character who fights crime in the streets (and sometimes throws down with Superman). You, most likely, are not. You don't need to be able to jump fifty feet from standing, and you don't need to be able to punch through doors!

Fair enough.

Except that when you train to be better in every way, it affects every aspect of your lifestyle. Your current capabilities are what put a limit on your potential and the possibilities available to you. Or, as the saying goes, "Always do what you've always done, and you'll always get what you've always got."

So how can this type of training help you?

This book is concerned with training not only your body, but also your mind. It's concerned with helping you to improve your focus, to control your emotional responses, and to upgrade your memory. As we'll see, training the brain naturally goes hand-in-hand with training the body. Especially when you train in a more functional manner.

The benefit of brain training should be instantly apparent. When you are more focused, you can get more work done. I wouldn't be writing this book while running my online businesses and raising my daughter if I wasn't able to sit down and churn out 10,000-plus words in a single sitting. This has been a *huge* advantage for me, and it's something everyone can learn. It just comes down to focus.

Likewise, imagine how much better you could be at networking and dating if you didn't stumble over your words. What kind of impression could you make if you had easy confidence and a sharp wit?

What if you could dream up amazing ideas for new businesses and apps? Or simply come up with more creative ways to play with your kids?

I've really never understood why more people don't train their brains like their bodies. We know that the brain responds to training. We know just how important traits like focus, recall, problem solving, and emotional intelligence (EQ) are. So why do we do nothing to improve them?

Your general health will also impact on this performance. You can have the sharpest mind in the world, but if you have barely any energy, then you'll quickly burn out on tasks and struggle to stay motivated.

> Wouldn't having the youth and vigor of a young child be beneficial in every aspect of your life?

It is widely thought that one of the reasons young children have so much more energy than adults, is that they have a higher mitochondrial density. These are the tiny "energy factories" that live inside our cells and convert glucose into usable adenosine triphosphate (ATP). Think of it as the "energy currency" of life.

Wouldn't having the youth and vigor of a young child be beneficial in *every* aspect of your life?

Likewise, part of the reason many of us struggle to focus or perform our best is because movement is a chore. We're stiff and achy, and again, we have lost the range of movement that came so easily to us as children.[14]

Similarly, being able to breathe better will improve oxygen supply to the muscles and brain, making us instantly more alert, more focused, and more energetic. This is one amazing benefit of aerobic fitness, which even directly trains the lungs!

Steady state cardio is particularly good for increasing the size of the left ventricle of the heart. This helps to lower resting heart rate, lowers your risk of multiple diseases, and even helps you to feeler calmer and more relaxed.

Combining these elements, rather than sticking doggedly to one type of training, will net you all of these rewards and more!

Hormonal changes from training correctly also give us more energy, focus, and motivation. They help us to sleep better too. We all know that working out boosts our mood and memory.

---

14   My daughter Emmy will happily squat for minutes at a time while inspecting a toy on the floor (or handing me a piece of dirt that hasn't been vacuumed up). This, without any intensive training. Mostly because I am "not allowed to intensively train our daughter." Go figure.

Strength factors into this as well. Being able to quickly recruit motor units in the muscle means being able to quickly carry out actions efficiently and powerfully. As Bruce Lee put it: "when you want it, it's there."

Knowing that builds confidence like you wouldn't believe, and it gives you far greater ability to express yourself physically.

Being able to do muscle-ups is cool, but what's cooler is the kind of strength, explosiveness, and body control that the move represents. If you can muscle-up, then imagine what else you can do! And imagine how it feels to have constant access to that kind of stability and power.

Of course, if you ever engage in a physical competition or sport, then these skills become even more useful!

Then there is the fact that this kind of training helps to prevent injury and illness. We've seen how our modern lifestyles leave us tight, weak, vulnerable to illness and even mental health issues. It's only a matter of time before the wrong movement results in a strained muscle or torn tendon. Bending down to pick up socks shouldn't be a risky maneuver! But if you barely move in that manner, then it may become risky for you.

All these issues become worse as we age. Maybe poor insulin sensitivity gives way to full-blown diabetes. Or that "brain fog" develops into full-blown dementia.

Again, looking at examples of older civilizations, we see that the elder members were just as strong and physically active as their younger counterparts. It is possible to age without losing your physical and mental prowess. I'm not claiming that any program can guarantee you won't suffer from these problems, but it's certainly possible to at least improve your odds!

The obvious argument for training functional performance is that you might need it someday. You might one day find yourself being chased and need to leap over an obstacle. Or you might need to lift a fallen tree off of a friend. Maybe aliens invade someday (and wouldn't it be cool to be the person everyone turns to?).

I certainly agree with this argument. Having a body and mind that are ready for anything is a useful insurance policy. But my point is that even if you don't lie awake wondering what would happen in a zombie apocalypse, there are still *plenty* of reasons to train yourself this way.

Being faster, stronger, healthier, and more alert makes you better at everything you do.

For Athletes, Martial Artists, Coaches, and Others

If you are an athlete, a strength coach, or an MMA fighter, then there are many more reasons to train functionally.

In fact, this is something that the martial arts community is waking up to in particular. Case in point: Ido Portal's training of Connor McGregger (Ido being a movement coach and Connor being a high-profile MMA fighter).

If you're in a clinch and you move to knee someone in the stomach, having just a little extra hip mobility is going to mean the difference between reaching the target or not. If you're grappling, then rotational strength will mean the difference between throwing that person to the floor or not.

Training lungs can help you to last longer before tiring out, especially after taking a blow to the solar plexus!

Likewise, basketball players can benefit from training their foot muscles and single-leg strength to improve their vertical jump. Strength athletes can benefit from increasing their work capacity so that they can train with optimal performance, for longer durations.

A great athlete or athletic coach should have knowledge of all these different training methods and options, such that they can support and enhance their primary goals.

Of course, the "principle of specificity" comes into the conversation at this point, along with the "interference effect." This goes back to the swimmers with the poor jump height. The best way to become amazing at a specific skill is to practice that skill specifically. This is the "SAID principle":

- **S**pecific
- **A**daptations
- to **I**mposed
- **D**emands

The SAID Principle is something we'll come back to a lot in this book. To get better at something, the best type of training is to do that thing more!

While that's true, careful use of functional strengthening techniques can help to augment a well-rounded training program. The key is to select the exercises carefully, while keeping the focus squarely on practicing for the event itself.

But for everyone else? Being a jack of all trades makes sense. Maybe you'll never be an Olympic contender in every event. But you can be better than 99.9 percent of the population at pretty much everything.[15] Surely that's worth pursuing?

I like to think of this as the difference between traits and skills. You might never develop the skill to throw a perfect punch or an impressive shotput. But if you develop the right traits—ballistic rotational strength and hand-eye coordination—then you will do a better job than most people would on their first attempt.

And that will apply to everything else you do.

It's time to really ask yourself why you train in the first place. If it is literally only to look good, then you might be happy sticking with bodybuilding concepts and bro-splits (though it's worth mentioning that functional strength builds an incredible physique that is perfectly proportioned and detailed in ways a gym-bro is not). But if you actually want the physical aptitude to back that up, then you need to get more creative. If you want to open up a whole range of new opportunities and possibilities, then you need to be the best version of yourself.

If you want to be healthier, more confident, more energetic, more focused, stronger, and faster, SuperFunctional Training is for you.

---

15 That sounds like a bold claim, but remember: most people don't train at all. Advantage, us!

CHAPTER 2

What Is SuperFunctional Training?

In the last chapter, I explained why the training most of us use at the gym is insufficient to repair the decades of neglect we've shown our bodies. If that had you feeling a little pessimistic, I can only apologize.[16]

But that is where the rest of this book comes in. Herein, I propose a solution that I refer to as "SuperFunctional Training." But that in turn is built on the foundations of functional training—a buzzword as trendy as it is controversial and nebulous. In this chapter, I'm going to break down what all of this means.

Functional Training: An Awakening in the Way We Train

So, just what is functional training?

The most straightforward answer is that it is training *for* a function. In sports and athletics, that typically means

---

16   Sorry, not sorry.

training for the demands of a given event. This includes training that might supplement the practice of skills, but also "pre-habilitation" to avoid injury. This can be achieved by improving aspects such as proprioception, mobility, and stability. Indeed, these are core focuses of most functional coaches.

Functional training in this sense is often very specific to the sport in question, but it also incorporates a little more "generalized" training to provide the athlete with a stable foundation from which to develop their skills.[17]

A good functional coach must walk a fine line, providing enough training to support and enhance an athlete's skills without leaving them too fatigued to focus on that practice! They must therefore choose movements that will effectively translate to the movement patterns required by the athlete, with minimal "wasted" effort. This is also important to avoid unintentionally impeding the athlete's movement. Precisely how best to achieve this, is a widely debated topic.

The term functional training is increasingly being used outside of that context however and applied to general training. But this is where the confusion starts to come in: if you are not an athlete, what do you need specific functional training for?

Applying the same logic, functional training in this sense means training the functions required by everyday life.

More and more people are interested in functional training, because they no longer just want to look good. They want to restore and even enhance their human functionality.

_____

17   This is sometimes referred to as "GPP" or "General Physical Preparedness." This is often given its own mesocycle in training or used off-season to build more all-round performance in the athlete.

To regain the body's lost capabilities and to tap into those lesser explored.

The Basic Capabilities of Your Human Body

So, what should functional training look like for the average person?

One answer is presented by the "seven primal movements" as described by physiologist Paul Check. These are:

- Push
- Pull
- Squat
- Lunge
- Bend
- Twist
- Gait

The argument is that these are the natural movements we evolved to need, and that if we are strong and mobile in these patterns, we are functional. So those of us who can't squat, fail the test. Ditto for those that can't touch their toes. And likewise, if you never train your rotational strength, you're out!

This list is not arbitrary. Check has observed that they are hardwired into us from childhood and represent important developmental milestones.

However, the list is not comprehensive in describing human movement. The lunge could also include side lunge, otherwise there's nothing here for the frontal plane! Others have gone on to further divide "pushing" and "pulling" into their vertical and horizontal components.

Then there are all the variations and derivatives of these movements. How about rolling? Or independently moving limbs (kicking for instance)? There are countless ways we can break down human movement.

It's also key to understand the importance of being able to combine these movements or move freely between them, something addressed by hybrid exercises (more on this later) and practices like animal movement flows. What happens when you need to squat *and* twist?

Broadly speaking though, this is a useful illustration of the concept of functional strength and performance outside of sports.

We can also turn to Georges Hébert's Natural Method (or *la méthod naturelle*) for some useful structure. Hébert was a physical instructor for the French Marines in the early 1900s, who created a system of training based on the movements of indigenous people. Influenced by the writings of Jean-Jacques Rousseau, he felt that the training methods of the time fell short in teaching useful, harmonious strength and movement, and that the answer was to turn to nature.[18]

Georges wrote:

> *"The final goal of physical education is to make strong beings. In the purely physical sense, the Natural Method promotes the*

18   While Hébert is often credited as one of the early influences in movement training, others had written similar works before him—including Francisco Amorós, who wrote *Nouveau Manuel Complet d'Education Physique, Gymnastique et Morale* in 1847. This book sought to catalogue the full range of "practical movement aptitudes."

> qualities of organic resistance, muscularity
> and speed, toward being able to walk, run,
> jump, move on all fours, to climb, to keep
> balance, to throw, lift, defend yourself and
> to swim.
>
> "In the "virile" or energetic sense, the system
> consists in having sufficient energy, willpower,
> courage, coolness, and firmness.
>
> "In the moral sense, education, by elevating
> the emotions, directs or maintains the moral
> drive in a useful and beneficial way.
>
> "The true Natural Method, in its broadest
> sense, must be considered as the result of
> these three particular forces; it is a physical,
> virile and moral synthesis. It resides not only
> in the muscles and the breath, but above all
> in the "energy" which is used, the will which
> directs it and the feeling which guides it."

Another quote that he is known for is: "be strong to be useful."[19] While stationed as a first officer in the town of St. Pierre, Hébert was called upon to oversee the rescue of over seven hundred people from a volcanic eruption. This experience showed him that athletic skill combined with courage and altruism would be crucial in any kind of crisis.

While these notions may bear little resemblance to the most popular forms of training today, they have nevertheless had a lasting impact. For instance, Hébert was one of the first to suggest the value of assault courses for training, also known as "le parcours." Sound familiar? Many

---

19   Or *"Être fort pour être utile."* I also like the notion of being "strong enough to be gentle."

in the movement training field also credit his writing as one of their early inspirations. Hébert was also an early advocate for physical training for women!

There is little of the Natural Method to be found in the typical "bro-split" or powerlifting routine. However, this approach to training is gradually enjoying something of a renaissance. More and more, people are beginning to see the inherent value in training more than just their mirror muscles, or the three big lifts. Training systems, approaches, and schools such as kettlebell training, calisthenics, parkour (free running), XMA, Animal Flow, MovNat, gymnastic strength training, and more, all show a reverence for exploring the limits of human physicality. It's a veritable "movement movement."

Then there is functional training itself, which is the purposeful introduction of movements designed to strengthen human movement patterns. All these approaches of training have exploded in popularity, with handstands, kettlebell swings, and animal locomotion *all over* Instagram and YouTube.

Aiding this growth, is the fact that this kind of training is so visually appealing. There's something awesome about watching people carry kettlebells great distances, press bars over their heads with one hand, perform one-handed handstands, and skulk along the ground like lizards. It's way more interesting than repetitive curls and squats!

Great sites/channels/influencers like Pavel Tsatsouline, Vahva Fitness, Red Delta Project, FitnesFAQs, Gymnastic Bodies, Breaking Muscle, ThenX, Pat McNamara, Ido Portal, Simonster Strength, Mark's Daily Apple, Mark Wildman, Athlean X, and many others are gaining traction by exploring alternative forms of training that target more than just aesthetic muscle or numbers-based progress.[20] And might I humbly add my own channel, The Bioneer, to that list! For the past ten years, I've been developing my own training style to explore different aspects of human performance and sharing my research with others. With 163,000 subscribers and counting, it seems that many more people are starting to find this stuff interesting.

Meanwhile, athletic-style functional training practices are making their way into more and more gyms and onto more and more athletic programs. This training uses corrective exercises and strengthening movements to help plug the gaps in regular training, fix imbalances, and address poor range of motion. All this should be based on an understanding of human anatomy.

Functional workouts might include the use of movements like the wood chopper to train the obliques (twisting and pulling a cable as you might swing an axe), or the face pull (pulling cables toward your face using external rotation in the shoulders) to work the posterior deltoids. They might also include things like running to improve work capacity, or sandbags to build compound strength at a variety of angles. This simply develops a more well-rounded strength and endurance profile.

But while this movement movement is hugely positive in my eyes, we're also seeing a worrying number of people standing on BOSU balls on one leg while slowly curling light dumbbells. The marketable nature of functional fitness means that an increasing number of people are jumping on the bandwagon without really offering anything of value.

My approach to functional training is to combine different training modalities to build your body (and mind) in a far

---

20   The "Biohacking movement" is also tangential to this. But we'll get to that!

more comprehensive manner. By training in more than one discipline, we gain a broader spectrum of benefits. If we choose the right movement patterns to begin with, we don't need corrective exercise. All the necessary tools and movements are already out there, it's just a matter of finding them.

This also means recognizing just how much the body is capable of, and how much it yearns to move and learn.

Going Beyond Functional Training

Here's the thing: you are technically "functional" already. You are functional because you adapted to your current lifestyle. You can already do everything that you need to be able to do. Again, it's the SAID principle.

If you look at it this way, suddenly that loss of full range of motion (ROM) on the squat is not so bad. You can't squat because you don't *need* to squat. Your muscles have adapted to sitting because that's what you needed to do, and now you're pretty darn good at it! Your body is optimized for sitting. You are a sitting *machine*.

This is a *functional adaptation*.

If your main "function" is to sit in an office chair, then perhaps you don't need any additional training.

But as I've expressed here, I don't want train for the stuff I can already do. I want to train to be able to do stuff I cannot do currently. And in doing so, I want to create entirely new possibilities for what I can achieve. And I want to remove the constraints on my body that are both limiting and potentially harmful.

And moreover—like Hébert and Amorós before me—I want to integrate that physical training with mental training.

Functional training often means training as rehabilitation, simply restoring those lost basic movements. This is too modest a goal, in my view.

That's why what I'm recommending goes *beyond* functional training.

That's what SuperFunctional Training means to me.

If functional training means training for the functions required by life or by specific sports and activities, SuperFunctional means training to do *more* than is required of you.

Let's consider the handstand: this is a movement that you do not *need* to be able to perform. It is not functional; it is SuperFunctional.

And yet, it is a movement that I think can benefit a lot of people. Not only because it's awesome and an amazing party trick, but also because it develops shoulder mobility, proprioception, core strength, and more that can prepare you for the unexpected. Or even open up entirely new possibilities! The very act of learning this movement may help you to develop dormant brain regions and better navigate *other* unexpected orientations. It's also a beautiful act of self-expression.

Why stop at being "just good enough?" Why not aim to be *incredible*.

And why stop at just physical skills? Everything can be trained.

To put it another way, SuperFunctional Training is training like Batman.

Training Across Modalities: SuperFunctional Training

One of the biggest issues with the current approach to training is that it is so tribal. Each approach to training has its die-hard fans who will tell you that their way is superior above all others.

Powerlifters preach that you only need powerlifting. Some go as far as to claim that squatting and deadlifting will make you stronger in every movement, such that there is no need for specific training in the transverse plane.

MMA fighters will tell you that flashy kicks and Shaolin are phony martial arts.

Many people discover the kettlebell, fall in love, and never explore the potential benefits of swimming.

But if you only train in one modality, your body will become optimized for that activity and nothing else!

This is fine if you *are* a competitive athlete. But it doesn't take advantage of the body's full potential. Nor does it prepare you for the multifaceted and chaotic nature of the real world.

Kettlebell training for example involves swinging an oddly shaped weight around. This has the advantage of building ballistic strength. It can also be used for metabolic conditioning and works the body at unusual and unexpected angles. Performing a single arm kettlebell clean and press will develop muscles and movement patterns that a traditional squat just can't. The kettlebell swing is described by Pavel Tsatsouline as being "the closest thing to a fight."

But while these movements are awesome, there is simply no need to commit to only that type of training (as many do). For all their positive qualities, kettlebells almost never exceed 100 kg. (and even finding one that heavy is extremely rare). Therefore, you won't be able to build max strength in the sagittal plane as well as you could with a barbell.

> Just as the MMA fighter cherry picks the most useful movements from any and all martial arts, so too can we choose the best moves and strategies from disparate styles of physical training.

Likewise, calisthenics is brilliant for teaching proprioception, body control, straight arm strength, mobility, and more. If you ever achieve full planche, that will be an incredible display of total muscle control. But again, it's much harder to build max strength using calisthenics alone, especially in the lower body where you can really benefit from an external load.

So why be wed to just one option? Why not cherry pick the best from each and develop yourself more fully? There's no need to balance on a BOSU ball when a pistol squat is already an amazing option for building balance and single-leg strength!

To quote Bruce Lee again:

"Absorb what is useful, reject what is useless, add what is essentially your own."

And this is where things get extremely exciting. There is a veritable smorgasbord of training available to us, including concepts that are supremely effective and are rarely used in common workouts.

We can take ideas and concepts from neuroscience, brain training, martial arts, dance, old-time strongman training, biohacking, Shaolin warrior monks, athletics, parkour, and more. Why not take every awesome form of training and combine it into something that will build you up in every way?

Sound like an awful lot to try and juggle? With smart programming, this doesn't have to be any more "packed" than a regular training program, as we'll see.[21]

Traits vs Skills: The ATSP Hierarchy

Functional training is a term that is very misunderstood. This is because it is nebulous by nature and can have many different meanings depending on context.

Attempting to broaden the definition of functional training as SuperFunctional Training is equally rife with confusion!

Thus, I have developed a system to help better illustrate both these points. I believe this could be a useful tool for coaches and gym-goers when it comes to programming and exercise selection.

It also addresses one of the chief criticisms of functional training as a movement, that it ignores the law of specificity. Remember the SAID principle from last chapter?

---

21   For those of you protesting: "But...the interference effect!"; don't worry, I will be addressing this later!

Specific Adaptations to Imposed Demands. In other words, you become better at something by doing more of it.

The system is also part of a larger construct I call the "Ability Tree." This extends the usefulness of functional training beyond physical fitness and into the realm of personal development.

But first: the ATSP Hierarchy.

If the best way to get better at hitting a baseball is to *swing a baseball bat*, what value can functional training offer?

Wouldn't swinging something heavy, or swinging against resistance, forge competing neural maps?

Shouldn't you therefore simply train for general strength while *also* practicing your skills training?

The answer is yes—in a way. But you need to train for the right *kind* of strength. And the same goes for cardio and mobility. Squatting and bench pressing are not optimal here and will have minimal carry-over to the sport in question. So how do we select the best exercises for the intended goal?

That's where the ATSP Hierarchy comes in. This stands for:

- Specific physical **A**ttributes
- **T**raits
- **S**kills and techniques
- **P**roficiencies

The aim is to differentiate between traits and skills, as well as precise physical attributes and more general proficiencies.

Using baseball as the example, the "baseball swing" is the *skill*—the component relying on technique. But this skill is underpinned by some specific *traits*. These traits are what can differentiate two people with equally optimal technique.

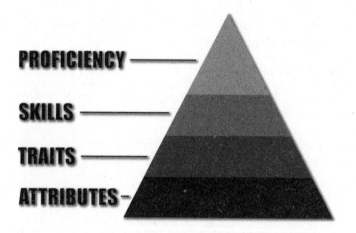

So which traits are relevant to the baseball swing? One answer is "explosive rotational strength." Other answers include "precise motor control" and "hand-eye coordination." We could also throw in some endurance for good measure!

You can develop these traits and still be awful at baseball. They are not enough on their own! But if you can already swing a bat, the right traits will only enhance your ability to swing it quickly, powerfully, and repeatedly.

Likewise, repeating the skill of swinging a bat will help you develop some of the traits that underpin it. Swing a baseball bat every day, and you'll gain explosive rotational strength that can also translate to a powerful roundhouse kick in martial arts.

This is a *two-way* relationship, then. But by isolating and specifically training the traits, we can increase the challenge and thereby trigger more profound adaptations.

Traits can best be described as "force multipliers." A force multiplier is anything that amplifies output from a consistent input, like a hammer. Try and hammer a nail with just your fist and you'll be there a long time! Use the same amount of force with a hammer though, and the output will be considerably greater.

By using the *same technique* with greater explosive strength, you can send the ball further.

But we can go deeper still. Supporting these traits are "specific physical attributes" pertaining to an individual's biology. For instance, someone who has explosive rotational power can also be said to have:

- A high density of fast-twitch fibers in the torso

- Specifically located in:

  - Obliques

  - Serratus anterior

  - Rhomboids

- A high level of inter and intramuscular coordination, meaning they can access this explosive strength

These specific physical attributes are properties belonging to parts of the body. They are also things we can target specifically with the right exercises. They expose the areas that we need to focus on, and therefore the exercises and programming that will provide the best results.

In this case, training the three muscles outlined in an explosive, coordinated manner, would provide the best results for developing the athlete. This core rotational power would then supplement the practice of the skill.

Any exercise that achieve this, such as the Pallof Press, will be ideally suited to a baseball player. Of course, that's only a small part of the specific traits and skills needed by that type of athlete.

This also helps make the argument for including brain training in a comprehensive functional training program. Traits such as focus and situational awareness can be crucial in sports and athletics. A baseball player needs impressive reflexes, great visual acuity, and emotional regulation to perform optimally. As we'll see, this is achieved as much through physical training, as it is through what we might consider to be "brain training."

We might identify the best supplementary training methods for any given sport or ability using the ATSP system by breaking it down into specific skills and techniques, then looking at the underlying physical attributes that can be developed.

Knowledge sits alongside physical attributes to support traits and skills, and it underpins everything from the perfect left hook, to the rules of a particular sport and the opportunities presented by those rules. This falls outside the jurisdiction of the functional coach, but it is useful for our "Ability Tree" that advises on personal development.

Likewise, physically training specific attributes is just one "input." Genetics also contribute physical attributes, while practice is the most important input for developing skills directly. However, it is the training of specific physical attributes that I believe to be the focus and value of functional training. Learning is a crucial input for developing knowledge.

This can extend beyond sports. What physical attributes help a knife thrower to perform their act? What physical attributes might enhance your productivity at work? Can they be trained?

To write this book, I needed to be able to write many pages in a short time frame. Therefore, I needed to work on my ability to focus—focus being the trait. How can that be further distilled into a physical trait?

Well, how about developing my brain's "executive control" and even more specifically, the anterior cingulate cortex. As it happens, we know that meditation can increase blood flow to that brain area[22] and so likely develop it through brain plasticity. All this will be explained later!

And here, knowledge becomes increasingly important. What knowledge will help you to perform better in your job?

The Ability Tree

We can take this idea even further by adding another letter to the acronym: A(k)TSP(g). Here the "g" stands for "Goals" and the K is knowledge. That's quite a mouthful though, which is why I just call this the Ability Tree.

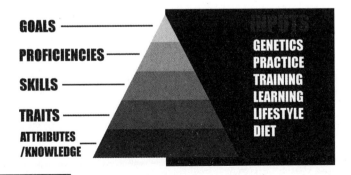

22   Yi-Yuan Tang et al. (2015) "Short-term meditation increases blood flow in anterior cingulate cortex and insula." *Frontiers in Psychology.* 6:212.

If you believe that you are responsible for "making your own luck," then it follows that you should facilitate any goal by looking at the skills and traits that will help you to get there.

Don't ask *what you need to do* to achieve your goals, but rather ask *who you need to become*.

Do you need to be kinder? More compassionate? More patient? This might help you raise the perfect child or become an amazing therapist.

Do you need to be stronger? More resilient in the face of challenge and disappointment? More stoic? More energetic?

What knowledge should you develop? What skills?

By choosing a goal first, you can then work backward to find the best forms of training to support those intentions.

The Ability Tree shows us other "inputs" that can be useful too, such as lifestyle factors, knowledge, genetics, and even diet!

But this relies on an assumption: that you have some kind of goal or proficiency to train for. This is what many people believe to be the sole benefit of functional training, and it is why people often raise their eyebrows at sandbags in the gym.

"But why do I *need* rotational strength if I'm not a baseball player?"

That's the common refrain of those protesting against functional methods.

I would argue that you need rotational strength every bit as much as you need squatting strength. Why?

Because traits *underpin* skills.

Even without *any* experience, you will have a better baseball swing if you have more rotational strength. You will be inferior to someone who actually plays baseball, but you will be better than your friend who has never trained that trait.

Likewise, you will have a better roundhouse kick and a better right hook. Again, you won't be anywhere near as effective as someone who has trained in martial arts, but you will be better than you would have been otherwise.

Rotational strength also lends itself to moving furniture, wrestling with friends, and opening heavy doors. It prevents you from putting your back out while pulling rubbish out of the rubbish bin.

And so it is for every other trait you might develop.

Great focus will help you at work, playing video games, enduring boredom, driving, and playing sports. Explosive leg strength will help you jump higher, run faster, and have a decent stab at sporting events like hurdles.

If you haven't chosen one discipline you want to master, it makes sense to be as good at as many things as you can be.

This is a far more "useful" method of training for the average person.

And of course, one could just as easily ask, why do you *need* to be able to squat 200 kg? Squatting is extremely useful and will develop many traits and attributes that likewise apply elsewhere. But there comes a point of diminishing returns. Is being able to squat 200 kg. that much more useful than being able to squat 180kg?

When is that *ever* necessary in daily life?

What about focusing on some *other* aspect of your performance at this point? Why am I the mad one for suggesting this!

This is the aim of SuperFunctional Training, and of this book. To employ training techniques to develop as many different *traits* as possible, such that you will be more competitive in any sport, more resilient against any injury, and more useful in daily life.

We will therefore gravitate toward exercises and training methodologies that have maximum benefits *across* the board. And we will likewise stay away from dogmatic adherence to a single training method that fails to provide a comprehensive solution for optimal performance. Likewise, we are not going to get addicted to numbers and progressive overload which can eventually become detrimental to our health.

We will go beyond simply training strength, and look equally at cognitive abilities, mobility, cardio endurance, and more.

We will train to be ready for anything. And to simply create *more options* as to what we want to do, and what we want to become.

Move freely; explore every dimension.

Move stronger; overcome any obstacle.

Move quicker; travel further.

Think bigger; see every possibility.

Train Awesome

In this chapter, I hope that I've outlined the value of functional and *Super*Functional Training. It prepares you for whatever life may throw at you, and it makes you a more well-rounded athlete and human.

But that's really not the point of why I personally train this way. Self-development is not the main "message" of *The Bioneer* YouTube channel, although most people interpret it that way.

Instead, I actually train this way for its own sake. Why? Because it's awesome!

I have always found it strange that so many people enjoy action films and computer games, only to then live rote and unadventurous lifestyles. I think we're all missing a little bit of Joseph Campbell's "Hero's Journey" in our lives. We could benefit a lot from a little more action and challenge.

When you train by climbing ropes, leaping over things, and performing handstands, you bring just a little bit of that excitement and adventure into your own life. Training becomes an action scene that tests your agility, strength, resolve, and mobility.

And researching ways to get stronger, faster, and smarter makes you feel like Tony Stark in his lab.

It's exciting, it's awesome, and it has the huge added bonus of fixing so many modern-day maladies.

The results are awesome too! I love it when someone I know is moving home and they ask me for help first because they know I'm pretty strong.[23] And I love the fact that performing handstands and muscle-ups can actually *draw a crowd*.

I train this way so that if I ever met Batman, we'd have something in common to talk about.

---

23   No, I won't help you move home.

CHAPTER 3

The Science of Movement and Strength

This book is all about combining a myriad of training styles to create something new and truly functional. Before we can get to that though, we first need to go back to basics: what do we know about the way we move our bodies and build muscle?

How are most people training right now? And what are the limitations of that training?

In the following section, you're going to learn how the brain and body work together to plan and execute movement. It gets pretty deep, and it's not strictly required reading. But if you're anything like me, you'll find it fascinating. I personally believe that *everyone* should know this stuff; simply knowing it can help you to move with greater awareness. Furthermore, it will illuminate everything that we discuss going forward. So please, bear with me while things get nerdy. It's not going to be the last time that happens.

How You Move

The human brain contains around eighty-six billion neurons,[24] and over a hundred *trillion* synapses, which are connections between those cells. Together, these form a "web" that somewhat resembles a mind-map, known as the

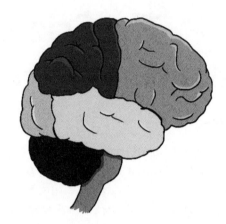

"connectome." It is due to this intricate structure, that the brain has earned its prestigious title as "the most complex known object in the universe."

You have one of those!

Each cell and network in that massive web represents an experience, a quale,[25] a sensation, a memory, a part of the body, or even a movement. These wait quietly and inert until they are activated by an electrical current called an "action potential." At this point, we experience the subjective sensation that is associated with that neuron. Action potentials then travel to nearby neurons across synapses, like a wave, until the signal fades.

---

24   Brain cells.
25   "Quale" is the singular form of "qualia," a word used by psychologists and philosophers to describe intangible units of inner human experience, like color!

> The human brain contains around eighty-six billion neurons.

Let's take the example of the bicep curl—one of the simpler exercises that can be performed in the gym—and consider how this neural activity translates to that movement.

When you decide to move your arm to curl a dumbbell, this begins as activity in the brain. That particular intention to move occurs in a region called the posterior parietal cortex. This same area has been linked with the very concept of free will.[26] (Just to freak you out for a moment, psychologists are currently unsure as to whether free will actually exists *at all*!)

From here, other brain regions such as the basal ganglia and cerebrum get involved.[27] The basal ganglia play a role in "action selection," helping you to commit to that intention. The cerebrum takes into account information from your senses: where you are in space, your orientation, and your balance. That information is then relayed to the premotor cortex, which refines the movement accordingly. The premotor cortex is also involved in our response to stimuli, such as our ability to block an incoming punch.[28]

Thanks to this process, you can make sure you're not standing too close to the wall during the curl!

Meanwhile, the cerebellum aids in providing balance and coordination during the movement, utilizing feedback from the muscles (proprioception). That includes tension

26   Michel Dsemurget et al. (2009) "Movement Intention After Parietal Cortex Stimulation in Humans." *Science.* 324(5928):811–813.

27   Stocco A. et al. (2010) "Conditional routing of information to the cortex: a model of the basal ganglia's role in cognitive coordination." *Psychol Rev.* 117(2):541–574.

28   Weinrich M. (1984) "A neurophysiological study of the premotor cortex in the rhesus monkey." *Brain.* 107(Pt 2):385–414.

in the core, which can be adjusted to keep us upright. This is important: in order to curl a dumbbell, you need to be standing in a stable position so as not to topple forward.

By addressing muscle length and tension in the bicep (using sensors in the muscles called muscle spindles and the golgi tendon organ), the body knows how heavy the dumbbell is and how much force to exert. We use this information to decide how strong the signal to our bicep needs to be. Without it, we might just overshoot, smack ourselves in the face, and knock our teeth out! (The cerebellum also plays a role in timing, which is an often-overlooked aspect of athletic performance.)

The supplementary motor cortex also chimes in to aid with more complex movements, especially those involving both hands. We also call on our procedural memory, the recall of thousands of previous bicep curls stored across these and other brain regions.

But the main action comes from the motor cortex itself, the literal "prime mover" if you will. This part of the brain has neurons (called motor neurons) that correspond to particular points of the body, like a tiny map. If you were to stimulate specific neurons within this region, you could trigger tiny muscle twitches in the body. This is not hypothetical. Studies have shown precisely that using patients undergoing open-skull brain surgery. By stimulating lots of motor neurons at once, you could even move them like a puppet.

The motor cortex is mapped in a manner that appears to be arranged in a similar way to the human body itself. In truth, it is simply the case that body parts that are usually used together have grown closer together in the brain (the fingers are next to the hand, and so on). The relative size of the different body parts is way off though—being dictated by the sensitivity and control of that region, rather than its physical size!

Multiple body parts are involved in the bicep curl. The bicep is a given, but we also need to involve the forearm, the fingers, and even the legs and core to keep us upright. During the movement, those areas of the motor cortex will "light up" as the action potentials pass through them.

These signals travel along the axons (tails) of their respective motor neurons to the spine. They then head down the spinal cord as nerve impulses to the relevant muscles. From there, they jump across the neuromuscular junction to act on the muscle cells themselves. In this case, the signal has now reached the bicep to begin the curl.

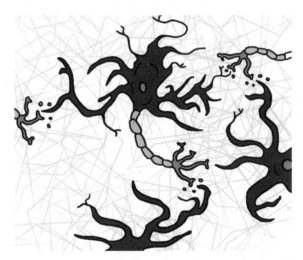

Neurons

Of course, all of this happens in a fraction of a second, and we are hardly aware of just how much is going on inside. The body is pretty incredible!

Note: Only conscious movement needs to go through this elaborate process. Reflexes over which you have no conscious control—such as your knee-jerk reflex—are known as "monosynaptic" reflexes. That means that they are controlled by a single connection, and the reflex is nothing more than an input/output response.

Contraction

Now that the signal has reached the muscle itself, it will act upon the muscle fibers.[29] Muscle fibers are individual muscle cells (myocytes), that have the ability to collapse on themselves like telescopic poles once they receive the necessary stimulus to contract.

Muscle cells are comprised of thousands of rod-like myofibrils, which are built from myosin filaments and actin filaments—the outer and inner tubes of the "telescopes." Via a chemical reaction, the myosin filaments get pulled inside the actin, shortening the length of the myofibrils. When this occurs on a large scale, it is enough to cause

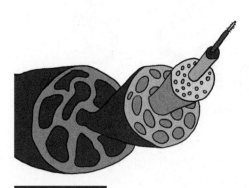

the entire muscle to contract and shorten. Bundles of myofibrils are called "sarcomeres."

Every muscle is made of hundreds of thousands of tiny muscle fibers, but

---

29   Klein CS. et al. (2003) "Muscle fiber number in the biceps brachii muscle of young and old men." *Muscle Nerve.* 28(1):62–68.

these are collected into groups called "motor units." Each motor unit is controlled (innervated) by a single nerve, which in turn is controlled by a single motor neuron in the motor cortex.

This means a nerve cannot cause a singular muscle cell to contract. Rather, it will control the entire group—the motor unit. This makes sense, given that it would be impractical for every single muscle fiber to be controlled by dedicated nerves!

Likewise, these signals are binary. That is to say, the motor unit either contracts or it does not. There is no gradation of force. You cannot contract half the muscle fibers in a motor unit, nor can you contract them "half-way." You can't even choose to "hold" a contraction as such, as it is over so briefly. What you *can* do, is to control just a portion of the motor units in a given muscle.

To that end, our motor neurons have an "excitation threshold." That means they will activate only when the incoming signal exceeds that minimum level. If one nearby neuron should stimulate another, this might not be enough to cause the signal to continue (depending on how sensitive it is). But if a nerve receives input from three different nerves, that can push it over the edge and cause it to discharge.

Thus, depending on the strength of the signal you send to your bicep (subjectively experienced as "effort"), you will recruit a greater or smaller proportion of your motor units to complete the curl. The bicep is estimated to contain around 774 motor units, represented by 774 motor neurons in the brain.[30]

---

30   Mary Kay Floeter (2010) "Disorders of Voluntary Muscle, Eighth Edition." *Cambridge University Press.* 10:1017.

A single contraction in a muscle cell is called a "twitch contraction" and lasts around a hundred milliseconds with a short latent period (ten ms.) prior to the contraction, and a cool-off period of around sixty ms.

But if you can only turn muscle cells on or off, and each contraction only lasts for fractions of a second, how it is possible for us to hold a dumbbell at 90 degrees with a continuous contraction? Wouldn't it just shoot up and then drop back down?

This continuous contraction is achieved through multiple twitch contractions occurring one after the other, throughout the muscle. What you perceive as continuous tension is actually a rapid pulsing sensation that never gives the dumbbell the *chance* to fall. Imagine firing a machine gun at a coin to keep it floating in the air. This is called a tetanic contraction. This also explains why you might notice your muscle vibrating slightly when you're trying to hold something heavy in place.

One exciting implication of all this, is that we actually tap into only a very small proportion of our latent strength at any given time. Even when attempting to lift your one-rep maximum, you won't be able to activate *every* motor unit at once. Doing so would leave you completely fatigued and would also limit the length of the contraction drastically.

Just how much strength can you tap into? For the average person, this is thought to be around 30 percent. Trained athletes might manage as much as 50 percent.

Later in this book, we will encounter rare situations that allow us to activate more of this latent potential. The most visceral example often given, is that of an electric shock. If you've ever seen a movie where someone gets electrocuted (think *Jurassic Park*), you'll know that they are always shown being blown backward several feet. This is not due to any kind of "explosion," but rather the result of every muscle fiber contracting simultaneously. The electric current serves to *activate* those muscles at once, causing the strongest possible contraction across the entire body simultaneously. The individual's own strength is what throws them that distance—demonstrating just how much power is hidden away in the muscles.

Muscle Fiber Types

Muscle fiber types can be loosely divided into three categories:

Type 1 a.k.a. slow twitch

Type 2a a.k.a. fast twitch

Type 2x a.k.a. superfast twitch

Type 1 muscle fiber is relatively slow and weak, but highly energy efficient. Type 2a is faster and stronger but fatigues more quickly. Type 2x is more powerful still, but even faster to fatigue. Or more specifically, fast-twitch fiber produces roughly five to six times more power than slow-twitch, whereas superfast twitch is around twenty times more powerful than slow-twitch.[31]

Whereas Type 1 fibers are oxidative and have a higher density of mitochondria, Type 2a and 2x are more anaerobic and thus contain fewer mitochondria. While the different muscle fiber types are often described neatly like this, the

---

31   R Bottinelli (1996). "Foce-velocity properties of human skeletal muscle fibers: myosin heavy chain isoform and temperature dependence." *J Physiol.* 495(Pt 2):573–586.

truth is more akin to a spectrum, with each fiber sitting more toward one end or the other and many "hybrids" found somewhere between the distinct type classifications.

Fast-twitch fiber is explosive, whereas slow-twitch fiber is endurant. Sprinting and lifting heavy weights require more Type 2a/2x muscle fiber, while walking and jogging require more Type 1 fiber. We can walk indefinitely, whereas we will fatigue after a short period when sprinting or lifting.

With training, we can convert Type 2a fibers into Type 2x,[32] which makes us stronger and more explosive. It is disputed among some whether Type 1 fiber can be converted into Type 2a or vice versa, though there is ample evidence for it,[33][34] only the extent remains uncertain.

Each of us has a genetic predisposition for more of one type of fiber, which is what makes some people better suited to endurance events or sprinting. Different muscles in the body also have varying proportions of slow and fast-twitch fibers, depending on how they are used. The biceps are slightly fast-twitch dominant, which is logical given that they are typically used for shorter bursts of explosive power (unlike the abs which keep us upright all day long and mustn't tire out).

---

32 Type 2x and type 2b are often used interchangeably, though this is not technically accurate.

33 Karp, J. R. (2001). "Muscle Fiber Types and Training." *Strength and Conditioning Journal.* 23(5):21.

34 Andersen, J. L. et al. (1994) "Myosin heavy chain isoforms in single fibers from m. vastus lateralis of sprinters: influence of training." *Acta. Physiol. Scand.* 151(2):135–142.

Motor units are typically comprised of just a single type of muscle fiber. Generally, those consisting of Type 2a and Type 2x fibers are also larger and contain a greater number of total cells. They also have a higher excitation threshold. That means that a weak signal will not only recruit fewer motor units but will recruit only those motor units comprised of slower twitch fibers. A very strong signal, conversely, will recruit all those smaller motor units and a bunch of larger ones.

This is called Henneman's Size Principle, which tells us that the body will recruit motor units in order of size and will only recruit as many as is necessary for that action.

Imagine you have a table with lots of ball bearings lying on it, and a fan pointed at them. Turn the fan up slightly and only the smaller, lighter bearings with roll away. Turn it up more, and you'll roll them all off the table. You cannot blow the big balls off the table without also blowing off the smaller balls.

This is important, because at lower levels of force, we actually have far more precise control over our movement. As we exert more force, the step change becomes larger.

Lifting a spoon to your mouth only requires a small number of the weaker motor units. Less electrical activity will be sent to the muscle based on your low effort, which means that only a few smaller motor units will be activated. Swap that spoon for a dumbbell though, and now you need a much stronger signal to achieve a similar motion against the resistance.

This contraction then pulls the bones together to close the elbow joint via the tendons, while constantly feeding back information to the brain about how much force is needed at any given point.

Hypertrophy and Strength Gainz

So that's how your muscles "work." Now the question is: how do you train them? How do you make muscles bigger and stronger? Or stronger without getting bigger?

The answer is that we don't really know.

Or at least, we don't have a 100 percent accurate picture of how muscle gets stronger in every circumstance. But we certainly do understand a number of different mechanisms through which growth occurs and how to increase its likelihood of happening.

We already know that we can make a muscle stronger by increasing the density of Type 2a/2x muscle fibers. To do this, we only need apply the SAID principle (Specific Adaptations to Imposed Demands, remember?). If we want more explosive muscle tissue, we need to train in an explosive manner.

Some of the best ways to do this are with plyometric training (such as clapping push-ups), ballistic training (such as kettlebell swings), and training with extremely heavy weights. What's key to recognize here, is that the body doesn't see a difference between acceleration and strength; it all just amounts to force. Either way, a strong signal is being sent to recruit lots of big motor units. So, you can either launch yourself in the air by performing clapping push-ups, or you can bench press 150 kg. Either way, you will increase the demand for Type 2x muscle fiber.

Keep in mind that we have an extremely limited supply of 2X muscle fiber, and most forms of training will increase the number of 2a and *not* 2x. The exception is training that involves extreme explosiveness (i.e. training with Olympic lifts moving 95 percent of your 1RM versus training with a heavy bench press for four reps).

However, because most plyometric movements only require a split second of maximum force production there is little time for "cross bridges" to form between the actin and myosin filaments. All this means is that the muscle doesn't spend long enough in an active state to send the optimum signals for growth. Thus, heavy weights are typically preferred for building max strength and size. This will convert more muscle fibers to Type 2 as the body calls on larger motor units, while also triggering hypertrophy (muscle growth) in numerous other ways.

There are three main stimuli that researchers *generally* agree are responsible for signaling hypertrophy. These are:

- Mechanical tension
- Muscle damage
- Metabolic stress

Mechanical Tension

Mechanical tension is literally tension sensed in the muscle by mechanoreceptors/mechanosensory neurons. When the muscle contracts strongly, this triggers the release of growth factors such as myokines.[35] These and hundreds of other secreted peptides also have effects on organs in other parts of the body, contributing to things such as fat oxidation![36] For this reason, muscle is actually described as a "secretory organ." Yeah, gross. This is an early indication of just how interconnected the body truly is.

This tells us that if there is a tension in the muscle, there should be some accompanying muscle growth. Thus, something as simple as contracting the muscles will help to encourage hypertrophy.

Muscle Damage

Muscle damage, meanwhile, occurs when the muscle fibers undergo microtrauma. Imagine pulling an elastic band until it starts to fray slightly. The body will then set about repairing the damaged tissue, and often this includes adding additional density in order to compensate and reduce the risk of *further* damage occurring. The greatest amount of muscle damage appears to occur during the lengthening phase of an exercise under resistance (the eccentric portion). That means that you will fray those muscle fibers when lowering the dumbbell during a curl or setting yourself back on the ground after a pull up. Slowing

---

35   Luana G. Leal et al. (2018) "Physical Exercise-Induced Myokines and Muscle-Adipose Tissue Crosstalk: A Review of Current Knowledge and the Implications for Health and Metabolic Diseases." *Frontiers in Physiology.* 9:1307.
36   Bente K. Pedersen (2012) "Muscles, exercise and obesity: skeletal muscle as a secretory organ." *Nature Reviews Endocrinology.* 8(8):457–465.

this portion of the movement down and adding more weight can therefore increase muscle size more rapidly.

Metabolic Stress

The final factor that stimulates muscle hypertrophy is metabolic stress. When you curl a dumbbell for twelve repetitions (reps), blood is sent to the muscle (due to changes in vasodilation/constriction) along with metabolites that stimulate growth. The contraction in the muscle has an occlusion effect, essentially trapping blood and allowing it to pool. This bathes the muscle in growth factors, which in turn increases growth via cell swelling (and possible other mechanisms).

At this point, it's worth noting that there are two different forms of hypertrophy. These are contractile and noncontractile hypertrophy, also known as myofibrillar and sarcoplasmic hypertrophy. While there is still some debate as to just how important these distinctions are, the general gist is that myofibrillar hypertrophy is the increase in myofibril volume, whereas sarcoplasmic hypertrophy is "muscle swelling." Here, the fluid and glycogen in the muscle cell increases, making the muscle appear larger without increasing the contractile strength. However, this may increase *strength endurance* by providing a greater supply of energy during continuous anaerobic activity (such as weightlifting for high reps or carrying your heavy shopping from the car).

Metabolic stress seems to be increased most by the concentric phase of an exercise; when the muscle is shortening under load. It is accomplished via the use of higher repetitions, which leads to a greater build-up of blood and metabolites.

What Happens Next

It's all good and well saying that the muscle is bathed in this hormone or that, but how does this result in it physically changing shape?

The body enacts these changes through altered gene expression (see below). This instructs the cells to incorporate more protein into myofibrils thus making them thicker, along with other adaptations. At some point, these myofibrils will split and multiply, thereby thickening the muscle cell further. This process contributes to the increased appearance of muscle size, along with greater contractile strength.

Note that Type 2 muscle fibers contribute more to muscle size than Type 1, which is one reason that more explosive forms of training are superior to steady state cardio for developing size.

How does the body go about rebuilding muscle to reflect these changes? That's possible thanks to something called "gene expression." Gene expression refers to the changeable nature of which *parts* of your DNA are active at any given time. If you think of your DNA as a gigantic alphabet, gene expression explains how parts of that alphabet can be "scribbled out" (tagged) in order to spell different words. This is how different cells in the body are able to behave so differently, despite having the exact same DNA.

It's also how a muscle cell can "remember" to repair itself at a new, bigger size. The "expression" part occurs via RNA (ribonucleic acid), the role of which is to convert information in DNA into the synthesis of new proteins which will be used for building and repairing tissue. Messenger RNA (mRNA) takes the blueprint from the DNA to its ribosomes, which are the machines that build the needed proteins.

There are countless alternative "versions" of you lying dormant within your cells. You reveal those alternate realities through training. This field is known as epigenetics.

The exciting thing is that changes that occur through epigenetics can actually be passed on to offspring. They also stick around seemingly indefinitely. If you have ever been really strong in the past, you'll find it much easier to regain that size and strength in the future![37]

Generally speaking, muscle hypertrophy does not occur due to an increase in the *number* of muscle fibers (a process called hyperplasia). In fact, whether this is even possible is a topic that is still debated.

One popular (but cruel) study demonstrated that muscle hyperplasia could occur under extreme conditions. In that study, birds were hung from their wings for days on end, resulting in an increased muscle fiber count in those muscles.[38] That said, a 1999 study has shown hyperplasia can occur in high-level, steroid-using powerlifters.[39] It's unclear whether this could also benefit the average Joe or Josephine; suffice to say we needn't make this a primary area of concern if we're trying to get stronger.

> There are countless alternative "versions" of you lying dormant within your cells.

37   Robert A. Seaborne et al. (2018) "Human Skeletal Muscle Possesses an Epigenetic Memory of Hypertrophy." *Scientific Reports* 8:1898.
38   Antonia K., & Gonyea WJ. (1993) "Progressive stretch overload of skeletal muscle results in hypertrophy before hyperplasia." *J Appl Physiol.* 75(3):1263–1271.
39   Kadi F. et. al. (1999) "Effects of anabolic steroids on the muscle cells of strength-trained athletes." *Med. Sci. Sports. Exerc.* 31(11):1528–1534.

Training also appears to increase the expression of androgen receptors in the muscles, making them more receptive to anabolic hormones like testosterone and growth hormone.[40]

With enough stimulation, satellite cells[41] are "donated" to the muscle cells. This further upregulates protein synthesis, increasing the muscle's potential for further growth.

This is important, seeing as muscle cells can contain more than one nucleus. Since nuclei[42] house the DNA, they are needed for growth to occur. However, myonuclei only have a limited "area of effect" or "myonuclei domain." The bigger the muscle cell, the more nuclei are needed to look after the area and provide the needed protein synthesis. Once a certain amount of hypertrophy has occurred, an increase in myonuclei will be necessary to prevent the muscle from topping out.

Like epigenetic adaptation, myonuclei remain even after we've stopped training. It isn't known precisely how long they last, but researchers have yet to find the point at which they disappear—suggesting that these changes may even be permanent. This is another reason that an ex-bodybuilder will find it easier to regain their lost muscle![43]

---

40   Marcas M. Bamman et al (2001) "Mechanical load increases muscle IGF-1 and androgen receptor mRNA concentrations in humans." *Endocrinology and Metabolism*. 280(3):383–390.

41   Precursors to muscle cells.

42   Which are known as myonuclei when they are located in the muscle, as myo = muscle.

43   This has also led to the somewhat controversial-though-logical-conclusion that using steroids for a single cycle could allow for greater muscle growth in athletes without long-term side effects. However, there are still health issues surrounding this idea, and it certainly isn't a strategy that I would recommend. Apart from the legal issues, even one-time steroid use has the potential for side effects that wold leave you very much NOT SuperFunctional!

Finally, training with heavy weight can also cause neural adaptations. We have already discussed how the body recruits motor units during exercise, and this is something that can be optimized with training.

Through neural adaptations (such as improved rate coding,[44] and increases in acetylcholine receptors[45]) we may be able to increase strength with no accompanying changes in muscle size. But of course, the aim is to accomplish both.

The Biphasic Nature of Muscle Growth

All of this is to say, that in order to trigger muscle growth, your time in the gym should be spent placing the muscles under tension, creating tiny microtraumas, and ensuring a build-up of metabolites. You also need to exert a lot of physical and mental effort.

But it is not in the gym that muscle actually grows. Growth happens at home during rest, at which point protein synthesis (the creation of new proteins) will be upregulated. This is the crucial one-two punch needed for hypertrophy: training provides the stimulus, but recovery is when the actual growth happens.

> Training provides the stimulus, but recovery is when the actual growth happens.

If you spent every day training for hours at a time without giving your muscles any chance to recover, you would simply break them down more and more. You'd lose a lot of strength and even size in the process.

---

44 The speed at which the nerve impulses fire.
45 Which play an important role in the communication between nerves and muscles.

Thus, at some point, we need to promote "anabolism." This is when the body produces maximum amounts of testosterone, growth hormone, IGF1, and other growth-stimulating hormones. During this window of opportunity, as long as you have eaten enough protein, this can be broken down into its constituent amino acids and used to repair and grow muscle tissue.

Anabolism lies in contrast to "catabolism," which is when the body is aroused and focused on exertion and the breakdown of tissue. Think of these states as yin and yang—both are necessary for optimum performance and progress.

But these states are not binary. Rather, we are constantly hovering somewhere between catabolism and anabolism, and countless factors throughout the day will impact just how anabolic we are. This even links to the time of day and our thoughts! We'll discuss this more in a future chapter.

Suffice to say that we are most anabolic immediately following training, immediately after eating, and while relaxing and sleeping. We are conversely most catabolic during training, when stressed, when hungry, and first thing in the morning.

In a fed, or "postprandial," state, a protein called Mammalian Target of Rapamycin (mTOR) is upregulated. This in turn increases hormones like IGF-1, which regulate the growth and proliferation of cells.

Eating and sleeping are critical to growth and recovery then, which will again be covered in a future chapter. And the more muscle damage and neurological fatigue you have caused during training, the longer this period of recovery needs to be.

Whew, that was a lot of information!

While your head might be spinning, this should give you enough of a background to understand how and why different approaches to training result in different adaptations.

So, knowing all this, how do the current, most popular forms of strength training work? How do bodybuilders build massive physiques? And how do strength athletes add big numbers to their squats and deadlifts?

Wouldn't you know it, that is what we shall be exploring in the next chapter!

CHAPTER 4

The Current State of Training

By this point, I've already mentioned that our current training methods are incomplete for maximizing our potential. Partly, that's because the vast majority of us aren't doing *any* training whatsoever.

But it's also because the training that the rest of us are doing is based almost exclusively on concepts from bodybuilding and powerlifting. Most training programs you find online will either recommend performing the three big lifts or using bro-science to develop bigger biceps.

This is not wrong. We can learn a lot from how these programs work, and a complete training program should definitely incorporate these ideas. But it is also insufficient.

You know how teachers say that a set curriculum can actually limit what children learn in a classroom, because they aren't free to follow their own interests or explore broader topics? It's kind of like that. Except it's worse, because you're training for an exam you will *never take*, unless you happen to enter yourself into a powerlifting competition or bodybuilding pose-down!

And the training you'll be doing will be very limited compared with what your body is capable of. You'll never explore just how explosive, how mobile, or how dynamic you can be.

In this chapter, we'll take an in-depth look at the training styles that are currently reigning supreme. We'll explore how they work in light of the physiology we learned about in Chapter 3, and what we can take from that.

And then we'll see what's missing.

How to Get Bigger Muscles: Bodybuilding-Style Training

In modern bodybuilding, athletes will typically select exercises that focus the effort precisely on a single muscle or one range of motion. These include many exercises that are described as "single-joint," meaning only one joint will be involved in the movement.

Examples include:

- Bicep curls
- Tricep push downs
- Pullovers
- Pec flies

Each of these movements involves keeping the body rigid, while moving one or two joints against resistance. They can even be performed sitting down in many cases and using resistance machines designed to guide the joint through a precise arc.

This type of training focuses all the effort onto one muscle, allowing the bodybuilder to take it to the point of complete fatigue, while also allowing for the maximum build-up of metabolites within the muscle. During a bicep curl for example, only the elbow joint closes, which makes the bicep predominantly responsible for the effort.

This will be combined with a relatively light weight (often around 60 to 70 percent of the athlete's one-rep maximum)[46] taken to a high number of total repetitions (ten to fifteen), often with "continuous time under tension." Continuous time under tension means that the joint is never locked out, such that the muscle is kept under some amount of pressure for the entire set of exercises. All this builds muscle "pump."

By the time the bodybuilder has reached the twelfth set of their dumbbell curls, they will have fatigued the majority of their muscle fibers, forcing the larger motor units to take over. There will also be a large simultaneous build-up of metabolites (as the blood hasn't had a chance to escape from the muscle), resulting in a huge temporary swelling of the muscle, and subsequent sarcoplasmic hypertrophy.

Bodybuilders rely on this type of training in conjunction with some more complex "compound" (meaning multi-joint) exercises, such as squats and bench presses, in order to build general strength.

Why doesn't the bodybuilder use the bench press and squat as a primary means of building muscle? That's due to the compound nature of those movements. Squats require multiple muscles working in unison. If you take a squat to

---

46   One rep maximum-or 1RM-is the most weight that an athlete can lift a single time during a specific movement. 70 percent of the 1RM, therefore, is 70 percent of this total.

total failure, not only is this dangerous (you should only ever go to "technical failure" with a compound movement like this)[47] but it also fails to guarantee that you have maximally exerted any single muscle group. Squatting involves the quads, hamstrings, glutes, erector spinae, abs, and more muscles, all working together in unison. If your hamstrings become somewhat fatigued (let's say 60 percent) and your quads become somewhat fatigued (let's say 50 percent), then you may no longer be able to perform any more reps. The collective strength in your body is not enough to perform a squat with reliable technique.

But at the same time, no single muscle group has been taken 100 percent to failure. Therefore, you have left *gainz* on the table. Moreover, the fact that you lock out at the top of the movement and multiple muscle groups are working together to begin with, means that the blood and metabolites never pool in just one area to the same extent and metabolic stress is not maximized.

Intensity Techniques

To enhance muscle growth further, bodybuilders use a selection of interesting methods called "intensity techniques."

These were famously collected by media mogul and cofounder of the IFBB (International Federation of BodyBuilders), Joe Weider, who codified them as the "Joe Weider Training Principles." He did this after observing the bodybuilding stars of his time, such as Frank Zane, Sergio Oliva, Franco Columbu, and, of course, Arnold

---

47   This is the point at which your form breaks down and it is no longer a beautifully clean squat (or clean clean).

Schwarzenegger. This was during what is often referred to as the "Golden Age of Bodybuilding," between the 1950s and 1970s. At this time, bodybuilding was enjoying a huge surge in popularity (due predominantly to Weider's own efforts), but had not yet to succumbed to the extensive overuse of drugs seen today (though more moderate use of anabolic steroids had begun to creep in by this time).

Intensity techniques include the likes of:

- Drop Sets
- Burns
- Flush Sets
- Negatives
- Supersets
- Assisted Reps
- Partial Reps
- Cheats
- Pre-Exhaust

These are used in most cases to help the bodybuilder go beyond their maximum capacity (beyond failure) and thereby to stimulate even more growth with sufficient rest.

Drop Sets

I won't go into each of these methods in detail—that information is easy to find. But I will describe how drop sets work, as I feel they perfectly illustrate the general approach, and are a fantastic tool that we can utilize in other ways.

The aim of a drop set is to take a set to failure, at which point you reduce the amount of weight as quickly as possible, before continuing to perform more sets.

This strategy allows you to maintain tension in the muscle even when you can perform no more reps at the starting weight. You can now do a set of thirty repetitions or more, while still starting with enough weight to ensure mechanical tension and sufficient muscle damage.

You can drop the weight as many times as you like as well. "Running the rack" means performing dumbbell curls starting at one end of the dumbbell rack with 25 kg., for example, and moving all the way down to 10 or even 5 kg. At this point, your muscle is so fatigued, you can barely lift 10 kg. for more than a few reps.

The Bro Split

Remember what I said about recovery? The more intense the training, the more time you need to dedicate to rest and recovery.

Well, surprise, surprise. These so-called "intensity techniques" lead to some rather intensive training sessions!

Thus, bodybuilder-style training requires lengthy periods of recovery between workouts for each muscle group. Hence, the "bro split."

A classic bodybuilding training split involves targeting a single muscle group (or two or three) during each workout. This way, you can increase your training volume per workout (meaning lots of stimulus), while also maximizing recovery time between workouts for a given muscle.

A classic bodybuilding split might look like so:

Monday	Pecs, shoulders
Tuesday	Abs
Wednesday	Back
Thursday	Rest
Friday	Triceps, biceps
Saturday	Legs
Sunday	Rest

A good bodybuilding split should aim to keep similar muscle groups as far apart as possible. For example, the pecs and triceps are used in many of the same exercises, so it is advisable to keep at least a day between them.

Some professional bodybuilders might take this even further: training twice a day in order to target their forearms and serratus muscles with dedicated training days, or to hit certain muscle groups twice during the week.

Arnold Schwarzenegger is, in many ways, responsible for the health and fitness industry as we know it today. It was through films like *Pumping Iron* and *Terminator*, as well as the muscle mags of the '50s, '60s, and '70s, that he popularized the very notion of strength training for an entire generation.

"Skipping leg day" has become a meme!

Thus, a lot of the training concepts we still use today actually come from the golden-era bodybuilding that forged Arnie's physique. This has given rise to the image of the "gym-bro" who uses bodybuilder-like techniques with little regard for function or scientific accuracy. Think Johnny Bravo.

The problem is, a lot of less experienced gym rats will take the concept of training in isolation to the extreme. Likewise, they focus too much on aesthetics, without paying respect to the emphasis a true bodybuilder places on balance and detail. The average gym-bro may well ignore or downplay their triceps and lats (they're hardly sexy), while focusing almost exclusively on their pecs, biceps, and abs. "Skipping leg day" has become a meme!

This is what leads to so many physically active individuals developing dysfunctional and imbalanced physiques. As we discussed in Chapter 1, training the muscles on the front of the body at the expense of those less visible muscles actually compounds many of the issues created by long periods of sitting.

Moreover, an increasing number of studies now suggest that hitting muscles once a week is only suboptimal for growth.[48] Total volume of training per week/month may in fact be one of the single most important factors contributing to hypertrophy.

One alternative option that is currently very popular however, is to use a split called Push Pull Legs or PPL. This groups together all pushing exercises, pulling exercises, and leg exercises. That is a logical combination, seeing as these are the muscles that are most often used simultaneously in any movement. For instance, the bench press uses the pecs, shoulders, and triceps, while the military press uses the shoulders, pecs, and triceps.

PPL can be performed twice a week, allowing you to hit each muscle group twice also. This might look like so:

---

48   Schoenfeld BJ. et. al. (2016) "Effects of Resistance Training Frequency on Measures of Muscle Hypertrophy: A Systematic Review and Meta-Analysis." Sports Med. 46(11):1689–1697.

Monday	Push
Tuesday	Pull
Wednesday	Legs
Thursday	Push
Friday	Pull
Saturday	Legs
Sunday	Rest

Note: a week "block" of training like this is referred to by strength coaches as a "microcycle." This is the smallest "unit" of a training program (barring individual workouts).

Non-Functional Muscle?

Many people view bodybuilding as being antithetical to functional training. In fact, there is a recent trend of bashing bodybuilding as both a sport and a training method.

The issue here, is that training muscles in isolation does not build *intermuscular* coordination and strength. Thus, many people believe it to be the *least* functional form of training. In real life, we very rarely use a single muscle in isolation. Even when opening a door, we brace our body while moving at both the elbow and the shoulder (possibly throwing in a bit of hip rotation). That's in contrast to a curl where we are sitting down and hinging at the elbow *only*.

Further, training with lighter weights means that the athlete won't be developing their neural drive or Type 2x muscle fiber enough to optimally increase maximum strength. At least not in the explosive manner necessary to tap into all that strength immediately at the start of a lift.

Then there's the rife use of anabolic steroids within the sport of bodybuilding. Anabolic steroids work by simulating or augmenting the effects of anabolic hormones like testosterone and growth hormone. This enhances recovery, resulting in much greater muscle growth at the expense of general health. Combined with pump training and large amounts of protein, this allows bodybuilders to build monstrous physiques that appear almost inhuman. Unfortunately, by continuing to reward competitors who value muscle size over other qualities—and by failing to properly test athletes for illegal substances—organizations such as the IFBB have done little to discourage this trend.

(This is very much a modern problem. Bodybuilders from the golden era are still considered to have the most desirable physiques by many, having found the perfect balance between size and definition.)

Taking advice from bodybuilders has been called into a question for this same reason. Sure, high intensity training with a week-long break works well when your system is flooded with steroids, but that doesn't guarantee it will work for the average Joe or Josephine.[49]

The image of the bodybuilder has been severely tarnished. The narrative is that bodybuilders build huge and non-functional physiques using vast quantities of drugs. The muscle they have built is likewise branded as pure "swelling" that doesn't translate into real strength or performance. Many people question the motivations that drive bodybuilders to pursue such ideals.

There is certainly some truth to these accusations. But I'd also like to take a moment to defend bodybuilding.

---

49   In my personal experience, this style of training works very well for building an aesthetic physique when you are younger (especially during puberty when testosterone is through the roof). However, it is a young person's game and as life become more stressful, the opportunity for the required amount of recovery is severely diminished—increasing the likelihood of injury and setbacks.

(Perhaps I'm a little biased. I trained this way predominantly for years before moving onto more functional styles and always found it to be fun and rewarding.)

Firstly, I take issue with the insinuation that building noncontractile muscle through sarcoplasmic hypertrophy is in some way inferior. I've heard bodybuilding muscle described as "fake muscle" or "cheat muscle," that is purely aesthetic.

Bodybuilders are still extremely strong. Franco Columbu (Arnie's old, best friend, who trained using this style) was known as one of the strongest men alive during his heyday. His feats included inflating hot water bottles until they exploded and lifting the back two tires of his dad's car off the ground. Bronze and silver era bodybuilders demonstrated even more amazing feats of strength and athleticism, as we will touch on in the next chapter.

When you go to failure on any given exercise, you actually exhaust your smaller and intermediate motor units, meaning that the body has no choice but to recruit the largest and strongest ones to complete the set. This means that rep ten of your 70 percent 1RM is in some ways very similar to rep 1 of your 100 percent 1RM! This *does* build strength.

Training for pump and volume will also increase your strength *endurance*. By adding to the glycogen stores in the muscle cells (along with other adaptations, such as an increase in capillaries fueling the muscles with blood), you improve your ability to exert strength *over time*. Again, this is the SAID principle. By lifting weight for longer durations, you become *better at lifting weights for longer durations*!

Which is more useful on a day-to-day basis: lifting something extremely heavy just once or lifting something moderately heavy multiple times? I'd argue the latter, any day of the week.

Finally, using spot training to strengthen specific muscles, is a useful strategy for *any* athlete, so long as it is used in conjunction with other methods. Training with the leg curl machine can help improve your sprint speed for example, while the leg press can build strength for the squat. In fact, the very best bodybuilders understand more than anyone the importance of building a truly balanced physique that leaves no muscle underdeveloped.

Bodybuilding certainly is not perfect, nor even optimal for all-round performance (it's a different story if you are training to become a physique athlete). But we shouldn't throw the baby out with the bathwater. As we will see throughout this book, *every* style of training has something valuable to offer. Bodybuilding is certainly no different.

How to Get Stronger: Powerlifter-Style Training

Bodybuilding has its merits, but powerlifting is superior if your interest is in developing *max strength*. Maximum strength describes the total amount of power you're able to put into a single movement, which in the case of powerlifting means one of the following:

- Bench press
- Squat
- Deadlift

To perform a bench press, you will lie flat on a bench with a barbell suspended above and behind you on a rack. You then lift the bar off, lower it to your sternum, and then press it back upward until the arms are locked for a single repetition. This trains the pecs, triceps, shoulders, and core.

A squat requires you to rest the barbell across your shoulders, then squat directly downward (as though sitting into an invisible chair) with your heels flat on the floor and feet shoulder-width apart. You should continue until your buttocks are as low as they can comfortably go (charmingly referred to as "ass-to-grass," or ATG). You'll then drive through the heels, leading with the head, until you are standing completely straight again. That's one rep. The back must remain neutral, and you should look forward the entire time.

Finally, to perform a deadlift, you will start by laying a barbell on the ground just in front of you. Bent down by pivoting at the hip, while bending the knees slightly. Grip onto the bar using an overhand grip.[50] The aim is to stand up fully while holding the bar so that it

hangs in front of you, with your arms straight. The spine must remain neutral (no rounding to avoid injury), and you should keep looking forward. You will then reverse the movement to place it back down. This trains the lower back, the traps, the grip, the legs, and the core.

---

50   Or mixed grip, which means one hand is supinated and one hand is pronated.

These three movements use a large number of muscles in unison, so they are considered compound lifts. This makes them more functional, as they mimic movements we might actually have to perform in real life: squatting, pressing, and bending (three of the primal movements, for those who remember Chapter 1). This teaches us to use the body as a single, functional unit. And by combining the strength of multiple muscles, the three big lifts allow us to exert significantly more force and lift more weight.

If the aim is to build strength, lifting more weight is the key!

It follows then, that we should also increase the amount we lift on each repetition. Instead of lifting 70 percent of your 1RM for eight to fifteen reps per set, you're now going to be using 80 to 90 percent of your 1RM for one to four reps. We can't really go above this number of repetitions, because that's all it will take for the body to become fatigued and unable to lift anymore.

In fact, we can calculate the optimum number of repetitions for a given weight by using tables such as Prilepin's chart:[51]

Percent	Reps/sets	Optimal # reps	Range
55–65	3–6 REPS	24 REPS	18–30 REPS
70–80	3–6 REPS	18 REPS	12–24 REPS
80–90	2–4 REPS	15 REPS	10–20 REPS
90+	1–2 REPS	4 REPS	10 REPS

There are other protocols and guides you can refer to if you prefer, but in every case, more weight = fewer reps.

Lifting at 90 percent of your one-rep max will develop neural drive by forcing maximum muscle fiber recruitment,

---

51   Created for Olympic weightlifters by A.S. Prilepin, a Soviet era sports scientist.

FUNCTIONAL TRAINING AND BEYOND

it will encourage the creation of more Type 2x muscle fiber, and it will generate a lot of muscle damage and mechanical tension. In short, this may be optimum for building max strength and explosive starting strength.[52]

Of course, you can also build strength by training with your maximum strength (i.e. 100 percent). Performing your one-rep max will require maximum effort and motor unit recruitment, though the tempo will become slower, which may be less effective for developing explosiveness.

This style of training is also extremely intensive and creates a large amount of nervous-system fatigue. This requires a lot of recovery time and increases the chance of injury, ultimately handicapping the athlete's progress. For that reason, many trainers will recommend that their athletes stick to around 75 to 85 percent of their one-rep max most of the time, with a corresponding marginal increase in sets and reps. Many coaches recommend that athletes only try to attempt a personal best very rarely during training. As ever, though, lots of opinions abound!

Powerlifters will also typically take longer rest periods between sets in order to fully recover before attempting to lift the weight again. Whereas a bodybuilder might rest thirty to ninety seconds, a powerlifter will rest for two to five minutes, or even more!

Programming for Big Lifts

Powerlifting has become increasingly popular among the general gym-going public, as bodybuilding has fallen somewhat out of favor (depending on your chosen corner of the internet). Many people getting into strength training

---

52   Starting strength is the strength you can access initially for an explosive force production. This is also called "rate of force development."

for the first time will now gravitate toward programs such as StrongLifts 5x5. This involves training the entire body three times a week, using these compound movements for five reps and five sets.

Most of these programs will also incorporate complimentary lifts to target specific muscle groups, or to train slightly different angles.

An example program from StrongLifts 5x5 looks like so:

Monday	Squats 5x5, Overhead Press 5x5, Deadlift 5x5
Wednesday	Squat 5x5, Bench Press 5x5, Barbell Row 1x5
Friday	Squat 5x5, Overhead Press 5x5, Deadlift 1x5

Note: Some form of warm-up will also be incorporated. Often this will involve "warm-up sets," sets performed at a very light weight (possibly just the bar) in order to practice the movement, light up the neural pathways, and get some blood flowing to the muscles.

Dynamic Effort & Heavy Partials

There are other ways to build strength in the big lifts besides sticking to 80 to 90 percent of a 1RM. These involve interesting mechanisms, that we can learn from and borrow for our own training.

Dynamic Effort Method

One example is the "dynamic effort method," used by the Westside Barbell Method.[53] The objective of this style of training, is to increase rate of force production by replacing heavy resistance with acceleration.

Remember, as far as your nervous system is concerned, there is no difference between explosive speed and explosive strength. What difference there is, is more to do with stress placed on the bones and connective tissue, along with the strength curve. As far as motor unit recruitment is concerned, lifting 50 to 70 percent of your one-rep maximum[54] as quickly as you possibly can, is like lifting 80 to 90 percent at a regular speed. This "compensatory acceleration" therefore allows us to replace the need for using extremely heavy weights.

Many clubs and coaches use a combination of dynamic effort with max effort to achieve the best results.

Heavy Partials

Another strategy is to use something called a heavy partial. Here, you will be lifting a weight that is heavier than your 1RM, but only through a small portion of the range of motion. A great example is the rack pull. Here, you start with the barbell elevated to around knee height, by resting it on the pins in a power cage. You will then "deadlift" that weight using a much shorter movement; sometimes as little as a few inches. By doing this in the strongest portion

---

53   Also referred to as the Conjugate Method, developed by Louie Simmons, and popular among many powerlifters. Westside Barbell is a gym that has produced over 140 world records. That said, the gym and the method also have their detractors within the sport.

54   As recommended by the book *Supertraining*.

of the movement, you can train with heavier weights than you would normally be able to use.

This is a method used by many notable advocates, including YouTuber Alpha Destiny, with impressive results.

Heavy partials work extremely well, because they allow you to increase strength in your grip, along with stabilizing muscles. They also build confidence without putting you in danger. In short, you can train your body to get used to moving that kind of weight, thus making it far less daunting when you go for it for real.

There is even a theory that this kind of training could help you to override muscle "shut-off" mechanisms that rely on feedback from the Golgi tendon organ to prevent over-exertion and injury. This theory is controversial however, with no concrete evidence to support it.

Similar methods use resistance bands and even chains that dangle from barbells in order to alter the amount of resistance at different points in the strength curve. For example, were you to perform squats with chains dangling from either side of the bar, the chains would only touch the ground (thus lightening the load) when you were in the bottom of the movement. This is known as "accommodating resistance."

As we will see in the next chapter, similar methods were also used by the old-time strongmen that predate modern powerlifting.

Progressive Overload

While these strategies are cool and fun, they are advanced methods that are primarily applicable to high-level lifters.

The rest of us would do better to focus on progressive overload. This is a central concept for any kind of strength training. This is the part where you actually *get stronger*.

Progressive overload simply means increasing the challenge over time as your body adapts. If you consistently squat 120 kg. for four reps, you will eventually get to the point where this is easy. Perhaps your 1RM on the squat has gone from 150 kg. to 160 kg. You can now increase the amount of weight on the bar by 10 kg. and continue.

Alternatively, if you would prefer to work on your strength endurance, you might simply increase the number of reps per set by one (going from four reps per set to five reps per set, for example). After doing that for a while, you might could drop down to just four reps but with 130 kg.

> **Milo was said to have held onto a pomegranate while challengers attempted to pry it from his hands.**

The most famous illustration of progressive overload comes from the legend of Milo of Croton. Milo was a sixth century BC wrestler from the Grecian city of Croton. Milo was a six-time Olympic champion who was known to consume raw bull meat in front of adversaries to intimidate opponents. Among his many legendary demonstrations of strength, Milo was said to have held onto a pomegranate while challengers attempted to pry it from his hands. Not only did he maintain his grip on the fruit, but he did so without damaging it.

The legend goes that Milo developed his incredible strength by carrying a calf on his back every single day.

Over time, that calf grew into a full-sized bull. As the bull grew, so too did Milo's physique, providing him with the progressive overload he needed to develop incredible strength!

Overcoming Plateaus

For new lifters, this kind of gradual increase in strength will likely continue in a predictable and reliable manner (noob gains). Eventually though, you'll reach a plateau, at which point you'll find you can no longer increase strength in a consistent and reliable manner.

It appears that strength adaptation works best when we approach it in a cyclical manner. That means we need to gradually increase strength, only to then back off for a period. You can then resume progressive overload with the hopes of reaching a higher peak before plateauing once again.[55] This is a form of cycling, and many strength training programs are built around the concept. Often, the aim of a "macrocycle" (a strength training cycle consisting of smaller mesocycles and microcycles) is to reach maximum peak right before the competition. This is called periodization when writing training programs.[56]

We don't know precisely why strength gains must be built in this nonlinear manner, but I speculate it may have to do with the way neural adaptations occur. I observed this when I watched my daughter learn to crawl; she would get closer and closer to achieving the skill, only to then get "stuck" at a certain point and not make any progress

---

55   Check out Pavel Tsatsouline's interview with Joe Rogan for an excellent explanation of this.

56   Mesocycles can also be used in other ways; to develop other aspects of an athlete's performance for example. A sports coach might include an "endurance" cycle, and a "power" cycle.

for weeks. Extremely frustrating when you are an overly invested parent!

> **Plateaus are a normal and necessary part of the learning process.**

According to the excellent book *The Brain That Changes Itself* by Norman Doidge, when learning any new skill there is normally a period of consolidation before the next breakthrough. Here, plateaus are described as a normal and necessary part of the learning process. When my daughter learned to raise herself on all fours, it took a significant period for her to cement those new neural networks through myelination and other processes. But it was essential that this should occur *prior* to her learning to lift one arm from that position.

Along with cycling, other techniques can be used to beat plateaus. One can spend longer at a set weight (even when it is easy) but take a bigger jump in weight, once ready. The aim here is to "cement" the gains before moving on.

A lifter might also take time to address weaknesses and issues in their form. Perhaps there's a particular sticking point in the movement where they are struggling? Or perhaps they aren't breathing properly through the movement?[57] In this case, specific training strategies can be used to address those issues.

Still Not Perfect

Many people swear by the three big lifts and believe that this is all they need for a complete training program. But as you will already know from reading Chapter 1, that is not a stance I can get behind!

The clue was when I mentioned that the three big lifts mimicked *three of the seven primal movements*. What about the other four?

The issue lies with the tribal nature of much of the fitness industry. Many advocates of each training modality are so eager to promote their style that they downplay or flat-out-deny any limitations. The loyal followers of that method will often fall into the same trap. Those who have dedicated their life to training in a certain manner are loathe to admit they could have spent their time more wisely. There are many advocates of power lifting who claim it will literally make you stronger in *any* movement, which simply isn't true.

Training the big three lifts will indeed make you stronger in many ways. But will it carry over to rotational strength? No, it won't.

Ask a powerlifter to perform a one-armed push-up and most won't be able to do it. That's not because this is a

---

57   Another interesting technique is "microplating." Here, you will increase the amount of weight by just 0.25 kg. or even lighter each workout. The idea is that the body can barely recognize the difference and will have a much better chance of adapting to such a small shift. Over time though, this gradual increase will result in greater overall performance. This also brings to mind another legend: of the ninja who would plant a bamboo shoot and then jump over it every single day. The height would increase by a fraction of a millimeter each time, but eventually the ninja would be leaping meters in the air!

"skill" they haven't learned. And it's not because they're too heavy (if they can overhead press 150 kg., they should be able to lift a portion of their bodyweight with one hand). Rather, it's because they haven't trained their obliques and they're not used to having to depress their shoulders during lifts. Likewise, they can't brace their core from that position. In short, they're not strong enough.

The same goes for straight arm strength, external rotation of the shoulders, thoracic strength, and more. None of this is addressed in a pure powerlifting program.

And that's before we even address other factors like proprioception, mobility, strength endurance, balance, relative strength, etc. I have known both powerlifters and bodybuilders who got out of breath climbing the stairs!

Many people hail the squat as the king of movements, or as one of the most functional movements, but it's not clear how it earns this title. Sure, the movement patterns itself as a fundamental feature of human mobility. But under extreme load? That's certainly not a *natural* requirement. Without a squat rack, it's not even clear how you would get that much weight onto your shoulders, so it's hardly likely to have been a key concern for our ancestors. Nor is squatting fully something we typically do during sports.

Even if our ancestors had squatted with a load across their shoulders, it certainly wouldn't have been a perfectly balanced weight like a barbell.

Jumping from one leg, on the other hand, is a far more common activity for athletes, for hunter-gatherers, and for modern humans. So is quickly changing direction, or even dropping quickly into a crouch.

This isn't to say that the squat isn't a useful movement or that building strength in these lifts isn't a worthy pursuit.

Just keep in mind that these are lifts that were specifically selected for a competition. They aren't a magic formula for maximizing all aspects of human performance, or even strength—as many gym rats now seem to believe.

I don't believe that building maximum strength in just three lifts is of any more value to the average non-strength athlete than any of the other aspects of performance that I just described. Far from it, in fact.

There are lessons to be learned here. This is one piece of the puzzle. But for all-round development, we need to go further than bodybuilding and powerlifting.

And it starts by taking a journey back in time.

CHAPTER 5

The Forgotten History and Techniques of Physical Culture

Bodybuilding and powerlifting are both aspects of what is broadly known as "physical culture." This is a movement to develop the body physically as an end in itself, rather than merely a means to improve athletic performance or military might.

These two approaches are the only aspects of physical culture that many people are exposed to. However, the movement has a rich history that dates back to at least the nineteenth century in Germany, the UK, and the USA. We took many stops along the way getting to where we are now, and there are many other training techniques approaches that have been forgotten with time.

Gradually, there is increasing interest in bringing these methods *back*.

It is my belief, that many of the unusual lifts and strategies employed by old-time strongmen, bronze and silver era bodybuilders, and even classic martial artists, have much to offer. In fact, they go a long way toward plugging the "gaps" seen in modern training strategies.

They represent true functional training.

Training Lost to Time

Humanity has been training since time immemorial.

The "original" strength training of course was not intentional, but rather came from the physically demanding nature of early humans' lifestyles. We would run, climb, and fight, and this would form muscle and endurance. We'll come to why this kind of training still has many unique merits in a future chapter.

Perhaps the earliest roots of bodybuilding and strength training though can be traced back to Ancient Greece and the likes of Milo of Croton, who we met in the last chapter. During the Classical Period, the Greeks would aspire to the "Grecian Ideal" of the superhero-esque physique depicted in statues.

This is also where we see the oldest-known gyms pop up. "Gymnasium," means "naked place."[58]

Training was still *predominantly* a means to an end at this time, with the goal being to improve performance in a range of sports and, of course, the Olympics. That said, looking after one's health was also considered generally important.

Even Socrates said:

"No man has the right to be an amateur in the matter of physical training. It is a shame for a man to grow old without seeing the beauty and strength of which his body is capable."[59]

---

58   Tell that to your trainer the next time you're told to put your shirt back on!
59   Unconfirmed whether Socrates could perform full planche

To that end, we could mark this as the start of what we now refer to as physical culture.

Old-Time Strongmen

Allow me to jump forward a little to the period most associated with the rise of physical culture, the era of the old-time strongman.

The title "old-time strongman" typically refers to travelling strongmen during the early 1900s, who would perform feats of incredible physicality for audiences. Classic examples include the likes of Arthur Saxon, Joe Greenstein (a.k.a. The Mighty Atom), and Maxick among many others. This was a time before powerlifting and Olympic lifting. It was a time before bodybuilding and muscle mags. It was also a time before steroids and other performance enhancing drugs.

> These were superhumans walking among their contemporaries.

Physical training was not a common pastime among the general public as it is today, so the amazing feats performed these characters seemed all the more extraordinary. These were superhumans walking among their contemporaries. And in some cases, their demonstrations of power are still unmatched today.

Many of those unmatched feats remain so because they simply aren't trained today. Old-time strongmen were partial to lifting things over their heads with one hand, or even lifting weights with a complete absence of strict technique.

Indeed, early Olympic lifting competitions included "freestyle rounds," dumbbell pushes, and one-armed lifts. It wasn't until the 1920s that these began to be standardized. By 1928 there were just three lifts: the military press, clean and jerk, and snatch. One-handed movements were dropped altogether. This would remain the status quo until 1972,[60] when the clean and press was also removed.

Because these lifts were dropped from competitive weightlifting, it seems they were also dropped from most gym programs. But why should they no longer have merit for the average person?

The "two hands anyhow" is a lift that permitted the athlete to lift as much weight as they possible can over their heads with *any* technique using two separate weights. The move is no longer simply a matter of using the perfect form to move weight through a set motion; now it's a creative challenge!

Very often this would incorporate a move such as the bent press, which allows the athlete to apply leverage to work *themselves* under the bar. This would be performed in one hand, while a kettlebell could be lifted with the free arm.

Such a movement targets the obliques to a large extent to brace the core. The obliques sit on either side of our torso and provide strength wen rotating or bending laterally. These muscles have little involvement in conventional powerlifting other than to help stabilize the trunk, and some bodybuilders *actively* avoid training them as thicker obliques can lead to a thicker waist.

---

60   Dave Randolph (2015) *Ultimate Olympic Weightlifting: A Complete Guide to Barbell Lifts—from Beginner to Gold Medal*. Ulysses Press.

It's no surprise then that the record for this lift is *still* held by Arthur Saxon, who lifted a 336-pound barbell and 112-pound kettlebell simultaneously in the early 1900s. That's a total of 448 pounds or 221.35 kg. Saxon likewise still holds the record for the bent press at 371 pounds (168 kg). Lifting that kind of weight overhead with one arm—even using such a technique—is simply bonkers.

The bent press involves keeping the weight steady in one hand as you shift to position your body underneath.

Now, this is not to undermine the accomplishments of modern-day strongmen. Modern strongmen are considerably stronger in the vast majority of lifts.

The point is that this is a *different* type of strength that few people today are trying to replicate. This is a strength that has been lost to time.

Modern competitions focus on two-handed lifts like the clean and jerk in Olympic powerlifting or the log press in strongman because they allow athletes to lift *more total weight*. This is a competition that is measured in pure numbers, and max strength is easy to quantify. It's also good for business.

The big difference is that old-time strongmen were showmen, not sportsmen. That's an important distinction, because it placed the focus firmly on the kind of physicality that is impressive to an audience of laypersons. Lifting a weight with one hand and keeping it balanced above your head is inherently amazing to behold.

But while this may be showmanship, I don't believe it is impractical. In real life, being able to generate power from one hand while stabilizing the entire body is just as useful— if not more so—than being able to deliver maximum strength from both hands. Very rarely are we required to lift something that is perfectly flat and straight with two hands, using perfect form. More often, we are required to unfold a pram with one hand while holding a baby in another.

A one-handed movement, or movement with different weights loaded on each side, is considered an "offset exercises." Such movements require that you engage the obliques on the opposite side of the body to prevent it from bending under the load.

This kind of strength is *directly* relevant to real life. Ever needed to carry a heavy suitcase around an airport or carry your kid over one shoulder? This kind of stability also translates particularly well to a wide range of different athletic pursuits. For example, wrestlers become significantly harder to push over once they're able to brace against force applied to one side of their body! Much of wrestling amounts to trying to twist an opponent to the ground.

In fact, it is generally agreed that a stiffer core translates to faster and more forceful movement of the limbs. As Stuart McGill says:

"Proximal stiffness enhances distal athleticism."

This type of movement is called "anti-lateral flexion," meaning that you are resisting gravity's attempt to bend you sideways in the lumbar spine. This is now a popular concept among functional trainers who might employ far less impressive training methods such as side bends (hold a dumbbell in one hand and then bend sideways). Turns out that old-time strongmen were *way* ahead of the curve in that respect! Core stability is a *big* topic in functional training, and we'll be addressing that more in coming chapters.

While moves like the bent press and two hands anyhow have fallen by the wayside, two competition lifts are still practiced today by Olympic weightlifters: the snatch and the clean and jerk. These are two movements that allow an athlete to move the greatest amount of weight the greatest distance, thus making them perfect for competition. What's really interesting about these moves is that they are almost plyometric in nature (like a clapping push-up) as they rely on a sudden burst of strength from a stretched position. Olympic lifting will likely develop more Type 2X muscle fiber as compared with the slower lifts seen in powerlifting, and incorporates some of the most explosive, full-body movements imaginable. Amazing though these moves are, however, they are still entirely constrained to the sagittal plane with very little variety.

How to Catch a Cannonball

The bent press is just one example of the kind of strength developed by old-time strongmen that is largely forgotten today but still extremely valuable. Another focus of this training was grip strength.

Many old-time strongmen were also savvy entrepreneurs and made a lot of money selling pamphlets and books explaining the methods they used (or claimed to use) to develop their strength. Many of these touted the importance and benefits of developing a super-strong grip,[61] and would recommend exercises such as scrunching newspapers or lifting heavy books with the fingers. Others suggested developing the forearms by raising heavy items placed on the end of a broom, then holding it at the other end (creating more resistance via leverage).

Grip strength was also *key* to the success of the shows. Reportedly, old-time strongmen would enjoy challenging members of the audience to come up on stage and attempt the same feats of strength.

Of course, they would always fail.

But to ensure this was always the case, the strongmen would rig the game in their favor. After all, it would be terrible for their career if an average person were able to lift even close to the amounts they did.

To ensure that this never happened, these showmen would use thicker bars on their barbells and dumbbells. This meant that even if the challenger had the strength to perform a heavy bent press or military press, they still

---

61 Thomas Inch (1930) *Developing the Grip and Forearm*; Mike Brown (1974) *Iron Claws: Grip Development and Bench Press Course*; Edward Aston (1946) *How to Develop a Powerful Grip*; George F. Jowett *Molding a Might Grip*.

wouldn't be able to get the weight off the ground in the first place.

But it was Strongman Thomas Inch who took this concept to its logical conclusion, developing the "Unliftable Challenge Dumbbell." This was an almost Arthurian dumbbell that many professional strongmen today are still unable to move from the ground. The dumbbell weighed 172 pounds and had a handle with a six cm. diameter!

The Powerful Little Fingers of Samurai Warriors

Grip strength was also a priority in other parts of the world and other points in history. Take the samurai for instance, who knew better than anyone the importance of grip strength and more specifically, little finger strength.

In fact, one of the worst punishments for a samurai warrior, was to cut off their little finger. The reason? By losing a pinky, they would become significantly less dangerous with a sword (katana). That's because the ulnar digits (the two smaller fingers) are actually responsible for 34 to 67 percent of our total grip strength. Without those fingers, it would be relatively easy to knock a sword out of an opponent's hands.

This might come as a surprise, but it makes sense when you recognize that the hand is designed to work as a single functional unit. The reason we call it an "opposing thumb" is because it opposes the little finger. And that's rather important: when you clasp the thumb over your fist, you create a closed loop.

This also means that by simply altering the position of your grip, you can significantly alter the strength of your grip. In particular, by making the conscious effort to wrap your thumb back over your fingers when clasping onto a bar you can generate a stronger hold.

This can also alter the activation of distant muscles during a repetition. For example, when you place the knuckle of the pinky finger on top of the bar during a pull up (rather than hanging from the fingers), this increases lat activation. When holding a barbell or dumbbell by your side, bringing the pinky finger further under the handle will increase flexion in the wrist and result in superior training for the grip.

Another occasion where grip and finger strength took center stage was in the case of John Holtum, the Cannonball King.

Born in 1845, Holtum was best known for catching cannonballs fired from a canon using his bare hands and chest. During one unsuccessful attempt, John actually lost three fingers! Yet this did not prevent him from repeating the trick successfully in future shows.

> Holtum was best known for catching cannonballs fired from a cannon using his bare hands and chest.

Another extremely popular old-time strongman trick that is still practiced by many performing strongmen today is nail bending: contorting and reshaping nails using nothing but pure finger strength and grit.

Horseshoes, frying pans, and countless other metal objects are similarly considered fair game.

While these stunts are undoubtedly impressive, they are not only good for wowing audiences. It turns out that grip strength truly is as valuable as the old-time strongmen suggested, even if you have nothing against nails. Apart from anything else, grip strength actually correlates with life expectancy and quality of life in old age.[62]

Whether you are an athlete or a casual gym-goer, if you spend time developing your biceps, then you should *absolutely* spend time developing your grip too. Grip strength is what gives you your connection to the ground or the thing you are trying to move. If you don't develop your grip, this will *always* be a limiting factor in your performance. In fact, taking time to strengthen your grip will likely improve your numbers across every other lift.

If your brain senses that you don't have a tight grip on something, it won't *let* you exert your maximum force.

And again, grip strength comes into play *constantly* during our daily lives. The things we lift out there in the real world are rarely barbell shaped. More often, they are awkward pieces of furniture, wriggling children, or the karate gis of opponents. In the wild, we would have needed to lift rocks and climb up thick, tough, branches.

---

62   Christina Musalek et al. (2017) "Grip Strength as an Indicator of Health-Related Quality of Life in Old Age—A Pilot Study." *Int J Environ Res Public Health*. 14(12):1447.

The Mind-Muscle Connection

But while grip strength and offset exercises are important, I believe it's another old-time strongman technique that has the most to offer. That is to develop the "mind-muscle connection."

Old-time strongmen did this in at least two ways: by consciously controlling the muscle, and by using overcoming isometrics.

We'll start with overcoming isometrics, as it is a little easier to understand.

First, an isometric contraction is any contraction of the muscle that doesn't result in movement. If you were to lift a weight and then hold it at arm's length, you would be maintaining isometric contractions in several muscle groups to accomplish this. The lengths of the muscles involved are not changing. This is in contrast to a concentric contraction (shortening of the muscle) or eccentric contraction (lengthening of the muscle).

Holding a weight out in this manner is what you would call a "yielding isometric exercise." That means you are consciously holding a joint in place against resistance.

Another type of isometric contraction is an "overcoming isometric." Here, the objective is to try to push or pull an immovable force. In other words, you contract the muscle with the *intent* to move, but you rig the game to ensure you cannot. You are trying to shorten or lengthen the muscle to no avail.

For example, if you were to lie under a bench press, load up the weight to 300 kg., and then try to lift the bar off the rack with all your might, that would be an overcoming isometric. Likewise, attempting to bend an iron bar and failing would be considered an overcoming isometric. This is how modern strongmen still often incorporate this type of training.

Or we can take a cue from the legendary Indian wrestler, "The Great Gama," who would reportedly attempt to push down trees!

As it happens, this type of isometric contraction is able to develop impressive strength by increasing the "neural drive." This term describes the ability to activate muscle fiber in a given muscle. The more you use overcoming isometrics, the more you will learn to tap into the full extent of your latent strength and power.

What causes this effect?

Effectively, an overcoming isometric is like trying to lift 110 percent of your 1RM. As in max lift, you are required to recruit 100 percent of your strength. The difference is that because there is no strength curve, you're able to maintain this maximum output for longer.

Consider an Olympic lift like a clean and snatch. This is an undoubtedly impressive demonstration of incredible strength.

However, it is only during the initial part of the lift where you are required to exert maximum strength. After that, momentum and technique will play a large role.

Even in a 100 percent 1RM bench press, the relative load on each muscle group will alter throughout the movement, and there will be points in the range of motion where you are stronger. Even if this were not the case, the entire movement will still only take a couple of seconds.

You're only generating maximum strength from any given muscle group for a few seconds at best.

In an overcoming isometric hold however, you are *maintaining* that maximum power output for a continuous period of time (six to ten seconds is generally recommended for each "rep"). You can likewise target the movement to focus on a single muscle, just like a bodybuilder would in order to encourage hypertrophy. The SAID principle comes into play again, and this can lead to improved motor unit recruitment.

If you perform a "ballistic isometric" meanwhile, you will add an explosive component by adding an explosive intent to the movement. Try to press the wall or the tree forcefully and suddenly, as though exploding into it. You can still then either hold that maximum contraction, or even create multiple explosive efforts.

Among the many old-time strongmen to use this kind of training, Alexander Zass is perhaps the most compelling. Zass served in the Russian Army during World War I and was placed in a prisoner of war camp after being captured. Amazingly, the story goes that he was able to escape from that camp *four times*. The final time he did this, he used his incredible strength to break free from shackles and then literally bend the iron bars to climb out of his jail window.

In short, he attempted to bend the bars until his body adapted, and he did.

Zass, who also went by the name "The Amazing Samson," went on to use this amazing strength to perform as a strongman, breaking chains on stage and carrying extremely heavy objects. He also worked as a wrestler, putting his immense power to further good use.

But key to his "Samson System" was the combination of isometric training, and heavy focus on the grip and wrists.

Some of Samson's other feats reportedly include carrying a grand piano, pianist, and dancer on his shoulders simultaneously, catching a woman fired from a cannon, and pounding five-inch spikes through thick planks of wood using the palm of his hand. It's also said that he carried his injured horse to safety on his shoulders during wartime.

Almost a century later, modern-day strongman Dennis Rogers would appear on *Stan Lee's Superhumans*. Dennis looks unremarkable but is considered by many to be one of the strongest men in the world pound for pound. He regularly performs feats such as rolling up frying pans and bending horseshoes and sells bending programs that rely heavily on isometric training. On *Superhumans*, researchers determined that Dennis was indeed able to recruit a larger percentage of his motor units, accounting for the amazing strength that seemingly defies his smaller frame.

Of course, isometric training in this manner is not perfect. Apart from anything else, it appears to have a limited effect, only resulting in strength gains within 30 degrees of the joint angle. In other words, if you wanted to build strength through the full range of motion in a bicep curl, you would need to exert effort in at least three separate joint angles to get the full effect.

Quasi-Isometric

Quasi-isometrics do not come from old-time strongmen, but rather from Russia—and much more recently. This method is used by Russian martial artists practicing a style (or a collection of styles) called Systema and involves moving the body extremely slowly through the full range of motion in an exercise. Generally, this will use a bodyweight movement such as a pull up or push-up, in which case a single repetition can take thirty to sixty seconds.

Quasi-isometrics are a wonderful evolution of the yielding isometric, and they provide amazing benefits for developing the mind-muscle connection. Unlike an overcoming isometric which focuses on maximum power, the aim here is to use a more precise and controlled amount of force, engaging just the right number of motor units in order to adjust your position by a fraction. Whereas overcoming isometrics build brute power, quasi-isometrics develop finesse.

This type of training forces you to take your time through every portion of the range of motion. There is no way you can use momentum to skip past a sticking point where you are weakest. You need to be strong in every position. When performing a quasi-isometric squat for instance, you will find the hardest part is slowly emerging from the bottom of the squat.

Moving slowly through a repetition also teaches perfect technique. During the squat you'll be able to ensure that your back is straight the entire way, while also feeling which muscles are engaged. You can make sure you are driving through the heels, and you learn how placing your feet slightly wider or closer together affects the way the movement feels.

This is also an opportunity to practice controlled, shallow breathing, while keeping your core tight.

And you can develop even greater control by using a "passive quasi-isometric." This means that you will attempt to relax as much of the body as you can, while exerting *only* the necessary force in the specific muscle groups needed in order to continue the movement. This helps make your movement significantly more efficient. Passive quasi-isometric reps are in contrast to active quasi-isometrics, which involve contracting the entire body to maintain maximum tension throughout the movement.

The benefits of slow movement aren't limited to resistance training. If you have issues with your golf swing or your jab, try slowing the movement down to find where those issues are and to reinforce the correct patterns.

Note that quasi-isometrics are *not* suited to all types of training. This won't work with a kettlebell swing for instance and shouldn't be practiced with very heavy weights for obvious reasons.

Mind Over Muscle

The second method of developing a stronger mind-muscle connection is simply to practice activating muscles at will.

This was best demonstrated by Max Sick,[63] a German strongman born in 1882. The story goes that Max was extremely sickly as a child[64] but managed to build up an incredible physique using only light weights and "muscle control exercises." Max developed his strength to the point that he could reportedly lift a man forty pounds heavier than himself over his head sixteen times!

In his book *Muscle Control*, Max details how he learned to individually contract and relax different muscles in his body.

---

63   He later rebranded as Maxick, seeing as having "sick" in your name is apparently not good for business as a strongman and fitness author!

64   This is—rather suspiciously—the backstory of a *lot* of old-time strongmen!

He could make individual forearm flexors pop out of his arm without contracting the surrounding area, or contract one half of his rectus abdominis while leaving the other half fully relaxed. He also demonstrated amazing scapular control (moving his shoulder blades).

Max believed that the secret to his amazing strength lay not only in his ability to call upon strength in a given muscle, but also his ability to fully *relax* the antagonist muscle.

Usually, when you attempt to perform a bicep curl, the tricep will contract slightly creating additional resistance. That makes the bicep the agonist and the tricep the antagonist. By learning to control the impulse to contract the tricep, the idea is that you can exert even greater strength.

Most of us know how to contract our biceps and make them pop without moving our arms. But now try to do the same thing with your forearm muscles. Can you make your forearm "pop?" Can you make your forearm wider without causing any movement elsewhere?

If you find this tricky, try altering the *intent* in your movement. Hold your hand open as though gripping an orange and then imagine crushing it: but don't allow your fingers to move. See how your forearms contract now?

With training and the right cues, you can gain this kind of precise control over many muscles throughout your body. Maxick branded this method as "Maxalding," along with fellow performer and early bodybuilder Frank Saldo.

Depending on how much you use any given muscle group, your control over that area will vary. For example, when you see Terry Crews perform his "pec dance," he is able to do so because he has developed that much control over his pecs.

Now consider that you have fifty-three motor units in your biceps. Here, it is not a matter of being able to move the muscle or not, but rather the *amount* of the bicep you are able to control.

Ever been told you have a "good side" in photographs? Some people believe that is because you have slightly greater control over the muscles in that side of your face (usually the same side as your dominant hand) which therefore increases your range of expression, your charisma, and your attractiveness!

One person who may have benefited from muscle control techniques is none other than Harry Houdini. Born Erik Weisz in Budapest in 1874, Harry would become famous for his performances as a magician and escape artist. Other tricks involved taking blows to the stomach, holding his breath underwater (for a then impressive three to five minutes), and swallowing locked padlocks and keys only to regurgitate them again having opened the lock!

Many of these tricks relied on the mind-muscle connection. Reportedly, Houdini was able to flex individual muscles in his forearm to make his wrists physically larger prior to being placed in shackles. He could then relax those muscles to easily escape once the countdown began. Likewise, taking blows to the stomach and even regurgitating items requires an increased awareness and control over stomach muscles. Speculation suggests that Houdini learned how to take blows to the stomach from The Mighty Atom (Joseph Greenstein) and that he may have learned muscle control from Maxick. It's through a similar method of developing muscle control that Houdini was able to perform incredible feats of regurgitation![65]

I find it incredible to think that simply by gaining supreme control over the human body, we can perform in a way that appears *superhuman* to onlookers. Even magical!

More Uses for the Mind-Muscle Connection

While Maxick's technique is interesting, it's not something that we often see employed today. This suggests a somewhat limited utility as compared with other forms of training—but, interestingly, the concept is not completely missing from modern training. Moreover, it actually has plenty of uses outside of the gym and stage.

Bodybuilders, for instance, often speak about the "mind-muscle connection." To them, the utility of this is to ensure that the correct muscles are most involved during a movement. If you are trying to train the pecs during dips, this requires the body to be angled forward slightly; otherwise, the triceps will handle a lot of the work. Likewise, the tricep push down aims to target the triceps specifically, which requires the torso to remain static. If it does not, then the movement essentially becomes a crunch.

Only by feeling the tension in the muscles and actively engaging them during movements, can bodybuilders be sure they are maximizing mechanical tension and growing the target area.[66] Arnold Schwarzenegger describes how he

---

65   They would swallow items attached to string and then practice bringing those items back up, feeling the muscles of the stomach working and learning to perform those movements at will! Awesome and gross.

66   Old-time strongmen would similarly aim to contract and squeeze a target muscle at the apex of a movement, reportedly increasing strength AND size. In fact, they sometimes used dumbbells with built in springs for this very purpose!

FUNCTIONAL TRAINING AND BEYOND

would focus hard on the biceps during a curl and imagine them swelling to fill the whole room.

In functional training, this mind-muscle connection is likewise used to ensure proper technique during a movement. Cues such as "drive your heels through the floor" during a squat can ensure that the hamstrings and glutes are properly engaged in the movement, and that the quads aren't taking over.

Likewise, if you're trying to perform a move such as the freestanding handstand (much more on this soon) and you keep falling over, you might not be fully concentrating on tightening the core to keep the upper body rigid. Understanding this can be the difference between success and failure.

Changing the "intent" of a movement can likewise alter its nature and benefits. During a bench press, trainers might give their clients cues such as, "imagine you want to launch the bar through the ceiling!" This change of mindset can be enough to introduce more explosiveness, and thereby build more power.

A simple change in intent and awareness can transform the activation of muscles, improve outcomes for sports, and prevent injury. Listening to your body is actually one of the most important strategies any athlete can use to perform better.

Why Old-Time Strongmen Still Matter

While there are some specific concepts and tricks we can learn from old-time strongmen, I also think we need to learn something from their general approach to training and physical culture.

One thing that sets the strongmen of this era apart, is that they were also all-around athletes. Old-time strongmen were not only capable of lifting extremely heavy weights, they would also perform feats of gymnastics (flips, handbalancing), and even bodybuilding routines. They would rollerblade down the street on their hands, and they would hammer nails into wooden boards with their fingers. This wasn't just strength training, but training in every aspect of physical culture.

In fact, old-time strongman Eugene Sandow is widely hailed as the "Father of Modern Bodybuilding." Sandow was one of the first individuals to incorporate pure physique demonstrations as part of his routine. This experimentation, and admiration for the human body, is what ultimately led to our appreciation of the athletic form today. Without Sandow, we may not have had *Men's Health* cover models, for better or worse!

These icons built themselves up as physical specimens and found new ways to push the limits of human performance: to push forward physical culture. They were creative with what the body was capable of, and they inspired others to push their own limits as a result. They made training exciting, varied, and compelling to watch.

So why should we be content with dumbbell curls and squats?

> *"What a piece of work is a man! How noble in reason, how infinite in faculty! In form and moving how express and admirable! In action how like an angel, in apprehension how like a god! The beauty of the world. The paragon of animals."*
>
> **—Shakespeare**

CHAPTER 6

Kettlebells: A Secret Weapon for Functional Power

Just as we have learned from strongmen of the past, they also borrowed lessons from those that came before them. Old-time strongmen were extremely partial to kettlebells, iron clubs, and sandbags, long before their recent surge in popularity as functional training tools.

But what a surge in popularity these tools have enjoyed. The kettlebell in particular now finds itself all over Instagram and YouTube. Such is the versatility and inherent appeal of this strange-looking weight.

Far from being a fad, kettlebells actually deliver on the promise of being a more functional and effective form of training. Their potential application also goes far deeper than most people recognize, especially when combined with other tools like the clubbell. The same is true for the sandbag, the medicine ball, and countless other seemingly obscure tools. With correct application of these tools, it is possible to develop aspects of strength and physicality that would otherwise be overlooked. This is yet another way we can access some of our untapped potential.

Introducing the Kettlebell

Kettlebells are heavy iron cannonballs with flat bottoms and a handle on top. The unusual shape means the weight is slightly offset from the handle; the point of contact is not the center of gravity. This can be used to create a lever or to allow the weight to hang slightly below the arm. The position of the handle in relation to the center of mass *also* means that the weight can be swung, wherein lies much of the potential.

Swinging a kettlebell means introducing momentum, torque, and constantly changing angles of resistance. This creates a far more active and dynamic form of training and opens up a plethora of alternative moves.

Kettlebells are traditionally measured in "pood." A single pood is 16.38 kg. or 36.11 pounds. Typically, athletes will work with kettlebells weighing 1, 1.5, or two pood—though they can go significantly higher. That said, if you're buying a kettlebell online, it's normally easier just to go with kilograms or pounds.

For those new to training, a kettlebell that is around 15 percent of your bodyweight will be a safe starting point. If you're a little more experienced, something around the 30 percent mark will serve you well. That said, as with a dumbbell, it very much depends on what you intend to do with the kettlebell.

A Brief History of Kettlebell Training

Some historians have suggested that the origin of kettlebell training dates all the way back to classical Greece. The ancient Greeks trained using weights called *halteres*. These looked quite different from kettlebells and could also be considered prototypical dumbbells. The similarity though, lies in the swingable nature of halteres and the way they were used.

The kettlebell as we know is more often traced back to eighteenth-century Russia. Farmers used the weights (called *girya*) as a counterbalance when weighing crops. Russian strongmen took to these implements as a method for building strength and, with time, they would be manufactured explicitly for this purpose.

In the West however, old-time strongmen were really the first to popularize these tools for weight training. More recently, author, fitness instructor, and all-round badass Pavel Tsatsouline is largely credited with the modern kettlebell renaissance and its subsequent takeover of social media.

Like many old-time strongman tools, the kettlebell allows an athlete to target lesser-trained aspects of their physique and performance. Whereas dumbbells and barbells are predominantly used for training in a straight line, using constrained and predictable movement patterns, kettlebells are constantly changing and shifting position.

This forces you to adapt to those sudden changes in force by bracing at the core. You must exhibit mobility AND stability in the shoulders and be strong at unpredictable angles. Again, this is considered "functional" insofar as it mirrors how we use our bodies in daily life and in sporting events.

Kettlebell training is particularly popular with martial artists. Swinging a kettlebell is similar to wrestling an opponent in that it requires you to not only generate power and stability in the core and hips, but also be able to adapt to sudden changes to the angle and amount of force being applied.

Kettlebell Swings, Getups, and Walks, Oh My!

Consider the kettlebell swing, for instance, often called the "king" of kettlebell movements.

This movement pattern primarily trains the hip hinge but also builds explosive and functional strength in the entire posterior chain. To begin the swing, you will stand with feet shoulder-width apart and the kettlebell firmly on the ground. Bend at the knees slightly and hinge at the hips to deadlift the weight off the ground with both hands. Keep the back straight.

As you bring the weight up, you're going to thrust the hips forward to straighten your torso. In so doing, you will naturally drive the kettlebell up and forward, keeping your arms locked the entire time. If you've done this correctly, the weight should follow an arc trajectory and then "hang" around shoulder height before gravity takes hold again. Note that there should be minimal activation in the shoulders and arms—it is the hip drive that propels the weight and not the arms.

As the weight comes back down you will pivot again at the hips and bend slightly in the knees to allow it to pass between your legs and behind you (this part can be scary the first time). Your arms will rest against your leg which will slow the momentum of the weight. Once you reach the end of the movement it will naturally begin to swing back like a pendulum. Go with this by repeating the movement and driving the weight upward once again.

Due to the role of gravity and the design of the kettlebell, no two repetitions will be exactly the same. It is the job of your core and legs to stabilize your body and to avoid being pulled forward or backward as the kettlebell moves around you. It is almost like you are *fighting* against the weight, and this provides a far more dynamic and challenging workout than deadlifts would with the same weight (just as well, seeing as kettlebells are generally significantly lighter).

The kettlebell swing is ballistic in nature. Because you are moving as explosively as possible,[67] this utilizes a lot of fast-twitch fiber, even despite the low weight. Using the glutes to explode out of this movement is very much

The kettlebell swing

67   This depends a little bit on the style of swing employed. Some competition swings are less explosive and rely more on momentum to swing the weight.

using them in the way in which they were designed. These are the largest muscles in the body, and they are intended for *propulsion*. It's no surprise that kettlebell swings translate to better deadlifts, squats, sprints, *and* vertical jumps for many people.

> [The glutes] are the largest muscles in the body, and they are intended for propulsion.

The ability of the kettlebell swing to improve performance in countless, seemingly unrelated activities is so widely recognized, that it has been affectionately dubbed the "what the hell effect."

And because this movement is continuous and cyclical, it actually lends itself perfectly to long rep ranges that will build strength endurance and work capacity. This can even be used as a form of resistance cardio (cardiovascular training that also challenges the muscle), meaning that it can contribute to weight loss.

In fact, this is a big reason for the sudden popularity of kettlebell training. Many people now use large sets of kettlebell swings in order to burn fat while also developing toned cores and buttocks. Kettlebell HIIT routines are commonplace and highly effective.

Another kettlebell movement that is extremely efficient is the Turkish Getup. This move involves lying flat on the ground, holding a single kettlebell above one shoulder with a locked-out arm, and then using your remaining three limbs to stand back up.

This involves a specific technique which I won't detail here, but suffice to say that it requires amazing shoulder stability to keep the weight steady, along with core strength to stabilize the body as you stand up. It also means working muscles arranged diagonally across the body, which we will discuss more in a moment.

Pavel Tsatsouline has this to say about the Turkish Getup:

> The get-up is an old-time strongman stunt that is the king of 'functional training.' While everyone pays functional training lip service, the get-up delivers. When done with sufficient weight, it teaches the body many movement lessons that cannot be learned through exercises using balls, bands, and Ken and Barbie dumbbells. Once you have conquered the get-up, you will be the master of your body, not its guest.

> "The get-up does magic for one's shoulders, making them remarkably resilient against Brazilian jiu-jitsu shoulder locks and heavy bench presses. The get-up is also one of the best ab exercises.

Another common strategy for training with kettlebells is to hold one in each hand and *walk*. This is known as a "loaded carry." The most commonly known carry is the "farmers' walk," as farmers would regularly need to walk long distances with heavy loads. The same move is also possible with other tools (such as the trap bar) but is particularly well-suited to the kettlebell thanks to the position of the handle.

In some ways, this is the most "functional" exercise there is, something we actually still need to do on a daily basis (such as when walking home from the grocers with bags of shopping). This is particularly useful as it trains walking (gait) under load, helping to strengthen the hips, the core, and balance. After walking a few meters, you'll begin to feel the challenge in your grip, as well as the traps. You should aim to maintain slight activation in the traps, meaning that you don't want the shoulders completely depressed but rather ever-so-slightly raised.

Like the kettlebell swing, loaded carries are actually a fantastic tool for burning fat, as you can increase the difficulty by aiming for more distance, time, or speed, rather than simply adding more weight.

You can make this type of training even more challenging by only loading up on one side. This then involves the obliques in just the same way as other offset exercises discussed in the previous chapter. You are now fighting gravity to prevent lateral flexion in your body.

The unique properties of the kettlebell make it infinitely adaptable. Halos, figure eights, and other movements help to challenge the core and shoulders in a myriad of ways that simply aren't available with conventional barbell and dumbbell moves.

> **The club as a symbol of strength dates back to the legend of Hercules.**

If you're interested in learning more about any of these moves, YouTube is your friend.

Heavy Clubs

While kettlebells are now commonplace on Instagram and YouTube, heavy club training remains a little more niche. Like the kettlebell though, the heavy club is an immensely useful and unique tool that is also thought to be among the oldest forms of training.

The club as a symbol of strength dates back to the legend of Hercules and even "The Epic of Gilgamesh"—an epic poem from ancient Mesopotamia that is thought by some to be the oldest surviving great work of literature.

Club swinging as we think of it today originated in the Indian subcontinent and Persia. Persian Pehlwani wrestlers (or *Phlwans*) would swing large war clubs to develop their strength. A blunt mace called a *gada* was used by Indian soldiers in the 1800s as a means to develop strength, mobility, and agility.[68] In the nineteenth century, British soldiers stationed in India would recognize the merits of this kind of training and bring the tools back the Europe, where they were once again adopted into the physical culture craze that was sweeping the nation at the time.

Today there are a few different types of heavy club, each one bringing something slightly different to the table. The British-style Indian club is usually wooden, slightly lighter, and is often wielded with one in each hand. The heavy

---

68 Mauryan and Gupta era coins from fifth to seventh century CE also depict kings swinging what appear to be Gada, suggesting that its use throughout the Indian subcontinent goes way back too!

club or steel club is much heavier and is typically used more like a kettlebell. Mace training is also still a thing, placing the weight even further away from the hands at the end of a long pole.

The heavy club is in some ways like a kettlebell on steroids. As with the kettlebell, the steel club features an uneven weight distribution that places the heaviest part a significant distance from the grip. This creates a lever, which in turn increases the amount of relative resistance for you to overcome. This of course can change as you maneuver the club into different positions, thereby creating a dynamically changing resistance. You can also choke your hands up and down in order to shorten or increase the lever.

The amount of force you generate simply by swinging a heavy club is very significant owing to this unique design. In fact, simply gripping onto a heavy club when it is in motion is a significant challenge in itself, making this an effective method for developing grip strength too. Just make sure your gym partner takes a few steps back before you try this for the first time!

If the kettlebell swing is the "king exercise" of the kettlebells, the gama cast is the king of the clubs. This movement is similar to kettlebell halos, the aim being to drive the club around your head while keeping your torso straight. To do so, you'll start with a single clubbell held out in front of you in two hands, pointing directly upward. You'll then drive the club over one shoulder, leading with the tip, before bringing your arms around over your head to pull it around the other side.

This targets the scapulohumeral girdle, training the muscles that provide shoulder stability. At the same time, the slight pressure exerted during the apex of this movement is enough to actually increase mobility in this position, helping overcome some of that forward slouch caused by endless sitting and typing. If you can't lift your arms straight over your head, then the gama cast is a great option for rehab (starting with a suitable weight of course).

Other popular club movements include windmills, barbarian squats, the push press, and the hammer. The hammer is my favorite as it involves simply swinging the clubbell around in front of you in a huge circle like a fan. You look like a lunatic![69] It's also possible to swing the clubbell just like a kettlebell, though you'll need a little more ground clearance.

Many of these movements involve bracing the core against bombarding forces to prevent rotation and flexion, and to develop rotational strength. Clubbells (and kettlebells to a lesser extent) are also fairly unique in their ability

---

69   An *awesome* lunatic!

to create tractional force in the joints rather than compressive. In other words, the force is pulling the joints apart rather than crushing them together (as is the case with 99 percent of movements in the gym). This not only contributes to improved range of motion, but also helps to protect against joint issues in the long-term.

There are countless other exercises you can perform with kettlebells or clubs, and even moves that are regularly performed with dumbbells will take on a more dynamic and functional character when they're involved.

For example, you can perform a kettlebell clean and press by pulling one or two kettlebells off the ground into rack position and then pressing them overhead. Rack position is simply the position that is most comfortable to hold kettlebells for a long time. The elbow is bent, and the cannonball is resting on the outside of the arm around shoulder height, making sure to keep wrists straight and not in extension (called the "broken wrist" position).

From this position, you can also perform squats, lunges, and other movements that challenge the legs. Alternatively, you can grasp a single kettlebell in front of you to perform goblet squats. In both cases, the front-loaded nature of the movement will create more activation in the quads than a regular back squat and become an anti-flexion movement—meaning it is now your job to keep your spine straight even as the weight is trying to pull it forward. This can be great for preventing injuries caused by poor lifting techniques.

You can likewise use kettlebells to perform explosive movements like the clean and jerk, or the snatch. The jerk involves thrusting the weight up overhead by generating power from the feet rather than the arms. In fact, kettlebell training offers a great way to experiment with the kind of power generation used in the Olympic lifts in a safer environment.

Hardstyle Kettlebell Training

Swinging a cannonball around your head is, in my humble opinion, inherently cool. But believe it or not, there is a lot more nuance and craft to kettlebell training than may at first be obvious. Choosing to train with a kettlebell opens up a whole world of branching techniques and methodologies, each with their own unique benefits.

In hardstyle kettlebell training for instance, additional focus is given to the amount of tension in the muscles at different points in the movements. This form of training was developed in Russia to support the *goju ryu* karate-oriented combat training used by Soviet Union spec ops in the 1980s.

Here, a distinction is made between allowing the body to become fast and loose, versus hard and rigid. It is easy to see the *goju ryu* influences here; where fighters (called "karateka") are encouraged to stay loose and whip-like as they throw a punch, only to contract and become hard as a rock at the moment of impact.[70] Some have described

---

70   Kris Wilder (2007), *The Way of Sanchin Kata: The Application of Power.*

hardstyle kettlebell training as being more akin to a "weighted martial art."[71]

> Some have described hardstyle kettlebell training as being more akin to a "weighted martial art!"

The hardstyle kettlebell swing looks just like any other kettlebell swing to the casual observer, but places emphasis on this transition between hard and soft. During much of the swing you will be relaxed, before exerting maximum tension in order to propel the weight upward. Even breathing is key. The exhalation is timed with the contraction to help exert additional force and power and add spinal stability. Again, this is very similar to performing a karate kata, which includes a spirit shout or "kiai" upon impact.[72]

Compare this to the competition kettlebell swing, which aims to guide the kettlebell through a pendulum-like motion and create a more fluid repetition that can be sustained for longer. This is ideal for developing cardio fitness or competing for time, but less-so for generating maximum power. Neither is superior to the other; they each have their place.

Again, practicing awareness—the mind-muscle connection—allows for different results and the

---

71   In fact, the term "hard style" is primarily used to refer to a particular category of martial art that focuses on tension and force development, such as shotokan karate. This is in contrast to "soft styles," such as Tai Chi, that focus on keeping the body loose to facilitate greater speed and impact. Okinawan martial arts styles such as goju ryu karate and—to a lesser extent—wado ryu karate (which I practiced) attempt to combine both approaches.

72   This being the "hiyaa!!" that you see martial artists shout in movies.

development of tremendous muscle control and power. You can perform the *precise* same movement, but by ever-so-slightly altering your intent and focus, you can completely transform the impact it has on the body.

A Little Bit About CrossFit

There does already exist a style of training that incorporates several of these concepts into a single methodology, and that is CrossFit. Perhaps you've heard of it.

How does CrossFit fit into the modern physical culture landscape?

Created by Greg Glassman, CrossFit was formally founded in 2000. The aim of CrossFit is to combine multiple different lifts and movements, largely performed for volume (the highest number of reps possible).

Exercises preferred by CrossFitters include deadlifts, medicine ball cleans, air squats, push jerks, "kipping pull ups" (pull ups performed using a lot of momentum), even runs, rope climbs, and handwalking. Those wishing to take part can attend a CrossFit "box" (their name for a gym) or follow the WOD (Workout of the Day) published on the website.[73] At the time of writing, today's WOD reads as follows:

24-21-18-15-12-9-6-3 reps for time of:
Med-ball cleans
Push-ups
♀ Fourteen-pound ball ♂ twenty-pound ball

73   www.CrossFit.com.

If at home, modify with a jug or other heavy object. Share your at-home modifications and time in comments.

An alternative WOD could be going for a mile run, then performing high reps of deadlifts (perhaps fifty), followed by fifty sit ups, and then fifty step-ups. These are varied functional movements, performed for volume and time, and often combined in unusual ways.

Each year, the most successful devotees will have the opportunity to enter the CrossFit games. This competition consists of a series of varied events aimed to challenge every aspect of fitness. Events may include foot races, rope climbs, handstand walking for distance, weightlifting events, swims, and more. The winner is then crowned the "Fittest on Earth."

This kind of training has advantages and disadvantages. Detractors point out that performing technical lifts like the deadlift to failure—especially when already fatigued by a long run, as is commonplace—can lead to injury.

Likewise, movements such as the "kipping push-up" intentionally sacrifice form at the altar of volume, thereby minimizing potential crossover to other movements requiring full-body strength. Not helping matters was the old mentality of pushing oneself to total exhaustion,[74] the seemingly arbitrary nature of WODs, and the

---

74   This was played up in the early days of the sport, presumably for marketing purposes.

minimal amount of tutelage required to become a CrossFit instructor.

But putting all that aside, there are also some solid arguments in favor of this style of training. In real life, you may not have the luxury of stopping when you're fatigued. Batman wouldn't only need to lift that heavy crate once. He'd need to chase an opponent across a rooftop, fight with them in the alley down below, and then smash the crate across their heads.

In short, to be truly functional, you should be able to perform well when fatigued. There's an admirable mental aspect to this kind of training, too.

Moreover, training for high repetitions can create numerous favorable adaptations. This will increase capillary density and sarcoplasmic hypertrophy, while simultaneously challenging the cardiovascular system, and minimizing body fat. A lot of people also really enjoy the full-body challenge that an intense CrossFit workout represents. Oh, and it builds pretty amazing physiques, too. Many CrossFit athletes look like bodybuilders but with more functional performance layered on top.

Although there are some shady CrossFit instructors out there, the same could be said of any category of personal trainers or coaches. There are also some extremely knowledgeable coaches running CrossFit gyms, who simply fell in love with the sport.

That said, the way you train should be different from the way you perform if you are going to encourage longevity. There are ways to achieve similar goals that don't involve lifting extremely heavy weights while fatigued (simple calisthenics exercises lend themselves better to high repetitions of compound movements, for example). Likewise, staying away from advanced calisthenics or demonstrations of max pushing/pulling strength, is a big limitation of the sport. There is minimal attention paid to mobility or other features. CrossFit appears to pick and choose the aspects of fitness that appeal, which is fine so long as those are the areas you're interested in. CrossFit is ultimately a sport, meaning that there is a set prescription of movements that must be trained.

So, even when performed carefully, CrossFit still pulls from a limited pool of exercises with the focus being very much on volume and time. The focus on all-round fitness is to be applauded, but CrossFit still only represents one piece of that puzzle.

Kettlebell Flows and Juggling

Then you have kettlebell "flows" which combine multiple exercises into a single seamless movement. The same concept can apply to a number of other tools, such as sandbags (see next chapter).

A flow challenges stability and functional strength even more by challenging the body during transitions between one movement to the next. A one-armed kneeling kettlebell press is hard enough, but if you need to get into that position to perform it from a one-armed kettlebell swing, you're going to be introducing all kinds of new variables.

Flows are a form of "hybrid exercise." Hybrid exercises are likewise movements that combine two or more other movements into a single rep. A flow simply takes this concept a little further by including three steps or more.

Man-makers are among the best-known hybrid exercises. These are push-ups performed while holding dumbbells against the ground in each hand. You then row each dumbbell by bringing it up to your side pulling from the lats, then bring your feet up in a jumping motion (like a burpee) to finish with a squat rep holding the dumbbells in racked position.

A more advanced kettlebell flow could involve rowing the weight, performing a clean and press, dropping to one knee with the kettlebell still extended, then getting into position for a goblet squat, standing up, and setting the weight down before repeating on the other side.

> Kettlebell flows and hybrid exercises are truly functional methods of training, as they get us outside of constrained, repetitive movement patterns.

Kettlebell flows and hybrid exercises are truly functional methods of training, as they get us outside of constrained, repetitive movement patterns. In daily life, you are rarely required to move through a set, a predictable constrained range of motion for reps. Far more often, you'll be challenged to move from one posture to another.

When my daughter Emmy was first born, I would often find myself supporting her weight in one hand while opening the trunk with my spare hand, pulling out the pram, and attempting to assemble it at the same time. That challenges numerous stabilizing muscles, while also requiring me to move seamlessly between positions.

This type of movement challenges the body in ways you can't expect or predict, which are typically the ways in which you are weak.

As flows are highly complex and compound movement patterns though, it is important to avoid training with heavy resistance past the point where the form begins to break down. For beginners, this should be done under the watchful eye of an experienced coach.

Kettlebell flows have become extremely popular in recent years and take their cues from yoga—where transitioning between static poses and dynamic moves is common. This is where we begin to see the internet work as this fantastic melting pot between training approaches and styles, yielding countless, fascinating permutations and combinations.

Farmer Strength

The effectiveness of kettlebell flows and hybrid movements comes from the fact that you are combining multiple movements into a single flow. At this point, your training may start to look less like a workout and more like manual labor. This is a good thing.

We hear legends of samurai warriors and

Spartans all the time, but rumors have likewise circulated about another exceptionally strong group throughout history—farmers.

They might not look mean or tough, but "farmer strength" is the stuff of legend, and it refers to manual workers of all kinds. People with farm-strength aren't necessarily bulky or ripped, but through endless repetitions of laborious movements, they have developed incredible grip strength, strength endurance, mental grit, tendon strength, bone strength, stability, and resilience to injury. Think about digging a hole. It involves hundreds of repetitions of a movement that is fairly similar though never identical. A single rep involves leveraging a heavy load of earth out of the ground, twisting the body while holding it, releasing it, and then driving the shovel forcefully back into the ground. The hole will get deeper with time, altering the position of the laborer, and often requiring them to stoop while placing the weight more on one side. All the while, the farmer is drinking up plenty of sun and fresh air, and intermittently shifting wheelbarrows full of dirt across large distances.

There is no movement quite like this in the gym, even taking into account the many different functional tools available to us. Moreover, no form of programming is going to involve the same kind of "all-day reps."

But perhaps by combining multiple movements with unpredictable weights to create "flows," we can achieve something at least somewhat similar.

KB flows can even be performed with a partner. Kettlebell partner passing involves actually throwing or handing a kettlebell to another person, combining ballistic strength, timing, and play. Along with some other forms of kettlebell training, this also provides "deceleration training" as you're forced to absorb and control an incoming force.

Kettlebell juggling is generally a solitary activity that likewise involves letting the kettlebell go at the apex of various swings in order to swap hands, or even let the handle flip or spin around before catching it again.

Of course, with all these things, there is a very important element of "risk versus reward." It's crucial to work up to the fancy movements you see on Instagram, and not dive straight into the deep end. Otherwise we're not looking at injury *prevention* so much as injury invitation.

Hopefully, this chapter has sold you on the promise of kettlebell training. These tools deserve all the attention they're getting, as extremely powerful additions to any training program. If you're looking for a way to make your workouts more functional, simply adding some of the chaotic and unpredictable kettlebell moves listed in this chapter will do that for you. Everyone can benefit from the increased grip strength, stability, and dynamic control that kettlebells build.

But that's just scratching the surface of the myriad training tools favored by functional athletes and coaches. In the next chapter, we're going to explore why medicine balls and sandbags also deserve a place in your routine.

CHAPTER 7

Unusual Tools for Unusual Strength

Thanks to their popularity when it comes to building real-world strength and performance, kettlebells have sprung up in gyms around the world, and are a favorite tool among functional trainers looking to prepare their athletes for competition.

Of course, those aren't the *only* alternative tools that you'll find at your local gym these days. In fact, when you hear the phrase "functional training," you probably think of alternative tools like sandbags, medicine balls, and even tires. These tools are likewise appearing in gyms and on social media at an increasing rate. But do they have a place in your training? Just what can a sandbag offer that a dumbbell can't?

More Gym Curiosities

In this chapter, we are discussing what many people traditionally think of as "functional training." That means using less commonly used tools to develop stabilizing muscles and dynamic strength in ways that supplement athletic training or a regular lifestyle.

This is also where some controversy starts to seep in. Throwing a medicine ball is eye-catching, therefore it can be exploited when it comes to marketing for gyms or coaches. The danger is that we end up throwing balls and standing on one leg for the sake of it. Which is a little silly.

This practice has unfortunately given functional training a bad name in some circles, particularly among those that don't fully understand what this broad topic can and should encompass. When it comes to tools like tires and sandbags, the key is understanding the unique benefits of each item and the core exercises.

To use that classic Bruce Lee quote again, we're going to:

"Absorb was is useful, reject what is useless, add what is essentially [our] own."

Tires

One of the most visually striking functional training tools is the tire. Typically, this will be a hulking-great tractor tire that the athlete must then attempt to flip or press.[75]

Tire flipping has the unique benefit of being a *concentric only* movement. What this means, is that the biceps will shorten as you flip the tire, but never be required to lengthen under load. Once the tire has been flipped, it simply drops to the ground.

In his book *The World's Fitness Book*, author, adventurer, and fitness coach Ross Edgley explains how he used tire flipping as a way to train biceps for gigantic volume (every single day) without overtraining or incurring injury. He did

75   Heck, if Samson can lift a piano and a dancer, lifting a tire shouldn't seem all that strange!

this in preparation for an incredible stunt that saw him climb enough rope in twenty-four hours to cumulatively reach the height of Mount Everest! By training his biceps every single day, he could massively increase his work capacity and endurance in that area (it also gave him *gigantic* arms).

The eccentric lengthening portion of the movement is the part that causes the most microtears and muscle damage. However, the concentric portion of the movement alone still provides the other two stimuli for muscle growth: mechanical tension and metabolic stress. This way, Ross could build incredible strength and performance without worrying about causing damage to his arms that would derail his goals.[76]

Other uses for the tire include:

- The "push over"—Tipping the tire to a partner or against a wall

- The front squat—Squatting while supporting one side of the tire

- The leg press—Lying on your back and pushing the tire up and away

You can even add weight to a tire by having a partner sit on it or lean against it. Or, if you're feeling like releasing some pent-up aggression, you can try swinging and hurling the tire across a field.

Another option is to repeatedly smack the tire with a hammer. This sledgehammer training actually has a host of

---

76   Ross would go on to become the first person to swim all 1,780 miles around Great Britain. An inspiring example of a modern-day athlete pushing human potential in new and exciting ways, combining physical culture with the spirit of adventure!

unique benefits as a brilliant form of ballistic training that works a huge number of muscles together. Sledgehammer training is also fantastic for burning calories quickly. It's highly cathartic but it also has a relatively high risk of injury that must be weighed against the positives.

Sandbags

Sandbags are heavy canvas bags of sand that can be hauled around a gym. These take some of the concepts of kettlebell and club training even further, by providing a tool that has a *changing* center of gravity. When you perform a sandbag snatch, a sandbag shovel (moving it off the ground from one side of your body to the other), or a reverse lunge (swinging the bag to one side while lunging), the sand will move *inside* the bag.

If you've ever tried lifting your partner or perhaps a sibling over your head,[77] you'll know that this is harder than it should be. That's because, unlike a barbell, a real person is going to shift their weight and squirm around.[78] A sandbag is a similarly "uncooperative weight" meaning that no two lifts are ever exactly the same.

The shape of the sandbag also forces you to hold it in a less convenient fashion. During a front squat for instance (squat with the weight held out in front like the goblet squat from Chapter 6), the large circumference of the bag moves the weight further from the trunk. This is achieved to a greater extent than could be managed with a zercher

---

77   No, just me?

78   Then there's the small matter of certain areas being inappropriate to grab hold of!

squat for instance, where the barbell is held in the crook of the elbows.

The position of a sandbag front squat therefore forces the athlete to brace the spine more to prevent flexion (forward bending) and accompanying rounding of the back that may lead to injury. Purposefully challenging the spine in this way may sound dangerous, but in fact it is just the opposite. By developing this kind of strength consciously, you become better at preventing accidental rounding of the spine during a deadlift, squat, or house move.

The key is to make sure that you are performing these movements correctly and with a suitable weight for your fitness level.

The sandbag is also soft and malleable. That means you can afford to make mistakes with it that might be extremely dangerous with other tools. It also means that the sandbag can conform to your body. You can drape it over your shoulders or even place it on your lap or back while keeping your hands free. This is a convenient way to add weight to a push-up, or to a tricep dip.

While the amount of weight you can put in a sandbag is limited, it lends itself perfectly to unpredictable and dynamic training. And for these more complex and unpredictable moves, you actually don't want to create *too* much resistance.

Sandbag training also supports plenty of movements that work outside the sagittal plane,[79] and that can only be a good thing. The woodchop for instance involves swinging the bag diagonally from above one shoulder down to the

---

79   The sagittal plane is the forward plane of motion that we move in almost exclusively when using traditional vertical and horizontal movements in the gym.

opposite lower-side of the body. This develops rotational strength, engaging the obliques to create torque.

And lest you think that the sandbag is just some new "fad" like so many others making their way into gyms, it actually has a long and rich history. Sandbags have been used by athletes—particularly wrestlers—for hundreds or even thousands of years. Sandbags were another favorite of old-time strongmen but may even have been used by soldiers in ancient Egypt.

Medicine Balls

Medicine balls also have a long history, with some ancient drawings depicting their use by Persian wrestlers over three thousand years ago. Apparently, Hippocrates stuffed animal skins and instructed patients to throw them for medicinal benefits. Roman gladiators are also reported to have used something similar.

A medicine ball is a heavy ball, often with two handles (though not always). In some cases, it will have a slight bounce, while other times it will be designed to absorb impact. Either way, it is intended to be thrown ballistically against a wall or into the ground, which provides the perfect way for athletes to train their acceleration. This is very similar to the compensatory acceleration that we saw in Chapter 4, in that it focuses on the rate of force development. How quickly and how forcefully can you sling the ball?

Taking the medicine ball overhead and them slamming it into the ground is known as a medicine ball slam and is an another amazing full-body, explosive movement. Rotational throws and shot-put throws once again incorporate movement in the transverse plane (meaning the body is twisting). This kind of training is fun, cathartic, excellent for building power, and well-suited to metabolic conditioning circuits designed to burn calories.

Medicine balls have many other purposes too. They can be used as an unstable surface during a push-up for instance or can offer light resistance during a sit-up or crunch. They can also be swung from side-to-side in a manner similar to a sandbag. Medicine balls don't get all that heavy however, so there are better tools for encouraging hypertrophy and building max strength.

Balance Boards and Stability Balls

Finally, many coaches now use stability balls and balance balls to help their athletes develop increased core stability and proprioception. This is known as "Unstable Surface Training" or UST.

A stability ball is simply a large blow up ball that an athlete can use as a support. For example, they might rest their hands on a ball while performing tricep dips, or they might rest their legs on one while performing decline push-ups.

Unlike performing these same movements on a bench however, the stability ball is inherently unstable (making the name something of a misnomer). This means the athlete must stabilize themselves in order to maintain balance, engaging core muscles and stabilizers in the shoulders, hips, and wrists.

The same thing happens when you stand on a balance board. This is a plank of some sort with a round base. The BOSU ball looks like half of a stability ball but can be used upside down as a balance board as well. You can even place a plank of wood on top of a ball or a can of Coke.

But this is where things get controversial. After all, balancing on an unstable surface while curling a dumbbell is potentially dangerous. The individual need only slip to find themselves out of action for weeks or months.

This makes unstable surfaces extremely unsuitable for training with heavy weights. In fact, the body won't *be able* to engage significant strength from such an unstable position. That means that the amount of challenge will almost always remain low, reducing the potential for adaptation and rendering any benefits minimal.

With limited time in the gym, is curling a light dumbbell on a balance ball really the best choice?

The other issue is that this type of movement does not mimic a situation we are likely to find ourselves in in real life. In sports and in day-to-day existence, there are few scenarios where the *ground* is unstable. Uneven maybe, but not generally unstable. Exceptions include skateboarding or hopping from rock-to-rock when crossing a stream. But these are relatively uncommon.

That said, if we're interested in *SuperFunctional* Training, then we're aiming to go *beyond* what is practical. The argument could likewise be made that neither prehistoric nor modern humans often find themselves lifting 100 kg. The aim is to challenge ourselves beyond common function, in order to develop *uncommon* ability.

The other argument is that balance training could be a useful means for training proprioception. Could we gain super balance, by practicing complex movements on unstable surfaces?

Proprioception Training: Move Like Spider-Man

Proprioception refers to your body's ability to sense where it is in space. It achieves this by receiving feedback from the muscles regarding stretch and contraction.

Proprioceptors of the body include:

- Muscle spindles: These are stretch receptors that detect when muscles change length. By knowing the length of each muscle in the body, the brain can create a mental image of the body. Which limbs are outstretched? What angle is your arm currently at?

- Golgi tendon organs: These are found in the tendons and tell us about alterations in muscle tension. We briefly encountered these already when discussing strength training. Golgi tendon organs can help us avoid injury but are also used when gauging the weight of an object so as to know how much force is needed. It's thanks to our golgi tendon organs that we aren't constantly ripping handles off of doors. They also allow for precise movements during balancing exercises.

❧ Pacinian Corpuscles: These are located in the skin and detect pressure changes. These tell us about texture and temperature but can also help us know how much weight is placed on one foot versus the other, for example.

Proprioceptors work in tandem with information from the senses in order to help us balance and move. For example, if your eyes and vestibular system show you that the world is currently tilted 30 degrees, you then need additional information from the muscles in your neck and core to understand that this is because you are *leaning* to one side. Otherwise, the body will think it is falling and take action to right itself.

Proprioception plays a key role in the mind-muscle connection. In order to better control the muscle, you first need to be able to feel it.

Many coaches will recommend this type of training for rehabilitation, especially among the elderly population who may struggle with balance issues (often the result of a lifetime of disuse). Balance boards can also be useful for regaining lost ankle stability following an injury such as a lateral sprain—caused when the ankle "twists" to one side. In both cases, UST may help to restore proprioception in the tendons surrounding the ankle, thereby improving stability and preventing further injury. This is a legitimate and helpful application of this form of training.

It's from here that this type of training has crossed over into the mainstream. Because balancing on a board *looks* cool, it was only a matter of time before it would be prescribed for more people.

The problem is that the research does not support balance boards as applied to a wider population. That is to say that the use UST has not been shown to prevent injuries in trained athletes.[80]

Standing on a balance board will primarily challenge the muscles of the shin that control inversion and eversion of the foot. But it seems that most of us have ample control over these muscles to begin with, reducing the usefulness of training in this way.[81]

Note: A similar effect can be achieved by using suspension straps such as TRX. These straps attach to a fixed point overhead and can then be used to support the hands or feet during a push-up or bodyweight row. They're very popular in gyms trying to cater to a functional audience.

I do not recommend the use of suspension straps, however. In the next chapter, we will touch on gymnastic rings— which are infinitely superior thanks to their ability to support your full bodyweight during ring dips and similar movements. The big difference is that TRX will set you back a hundred dollars as a branded fitness tool, whereas gymnastic rings will cost about thirty dollars on eBay. Don't be fooled by fads!

How to Improve Balance— Neck Training?

If UST is not a useful protocol for improving proprioception and balance, then what is? We

---

80   EM Cressey (2007), "The Effects of Ten Weeks of Lower-Body Unstable Surface Training on Markers of Athletic Performance." *Journal of Strength and Conditioning Research.* 21(2):561–567.

81   Don't throw out your balance board just yet though: we'll see in an upcoming chapter that there may yet be other cognitive benefits it can offer.

will address some answers to this question in the next chapter using calisthenics and particularly unilateral leg exercises. Likewise, we have already seen how to improve stability in the core by using heavy offset exercises.

But what can also be very useful is, surprisingly, neck training. Why is this important? First, it turns out that strengthening the neck can actually improve the transmission of signals through your central nervous system. All information from your brain needs to pass through this data superhighway to reach the rest of your body (and vice versa).

At the same time, the muscles in the neck are crucial for understanding where the body is in space—as we have already seen. Your brain needs to marry information from the senses with information from the neck in order to calculate its orientation relative to the rest of the body.

Keeping the head steady is of course preferable for balance and performance in general. The neck and head have a self-stabilizing mechanism to try and keep vision steady (also helped by small muscles in the eye). When you land from a jump for instance, the head is naturally pitched forward and will roll and yaw. Likewise, a strong neck allows you to counteract forces created by running, preventing it from being left behind while the trunk accelerates.

For these reasons, it should come as no big surprise to learn that the neck is among the areas with the highest density of muscle spindles.

This falls under the topic of "eye-head coupling." Another example is the way the neck works in tandem with the vision in order to track objects and aspects of the environment. In fact, this is so hardwired into your system, that you can demonstrate it with a fun little experiment:

Keep your head upright and look forward. Now place one hand on the back of your neck, and while keeping the head still, dart your eyes from left to right. You can actually feel the muscles in the back of the neck move. These are the splenius capitis, and they are contracting in anticipation of the head movement that is likely to follow.

As coach and neck-training advocate Mike Gittleson puts it, "where the head goes, the body follows."

Training the neck has many other benefits too. Really, it is the "missing piece" of your core training, and it can even be used to generate torque during gymnastic movements. Athletes prioritize neck training to help absorb impacts and prevent concussions. And male celebrities like building thick necks because it helps them to look significantly more masculine and bulkier.

So rather than standing on balance balls, your time may be better spent training the neck. To that end, you can employ a different tool: a head harness. This lets you dangle a weight from your head on a chain or attach it to a cable. This is a less obvious "functional" tool that nevertheless deserves a place in your workouts.

This can be paired with isometric contractions using your own hand to offer resistance, or light neck curls using a weight plate held gently against the relevant part of the head. Many coaches focus on neck flexion, lateral neck flexion, and neck extension, but don't forget neck protrusion, retraction, and rotation. Start light, and build-up.

More Options: Bands, Ropes... and Chairs?

Functional training also commonly incorporates other alternative tools. Resistance bands can be used to develop mobility, while also providing gentle resistance for movements in less stable positions. A unique property of resistance band training is that the band offers more resistance the further it is stretched—thereby altering the strength curve as compared with a dumbbell or kettlebell.

Cables and pulleys are stationary machines that allow athletes to pull and push handles in order to move variable amounts of weight. These can be used for a number of typical bodybuilding moves as a means to isolate specific muscle groups, but they can also be used to move through more dynamic ranges of motion. For instance, the high-to-low woodchop is a move similar to the sandbag woodchop or even sledgehammer training with a tire. Take the cable from a fixed position above shoulder height in two hands, and then chop diagonally downward with both hands, twisting through the core and hips.

Unlike sledgehammer training or similar moves with sandbags or clubbells, the angle of resistance when using cables is coming from *behind* the athlete. You are pulling the weight down and forward against the resistance provided by the pulley. Conversely, if you were to swing the clubbell in the same fashion, the angle of resistance would be straight down—provided by gravity—meaning that it would target the wrong muscles. Cables and bands are *extremely* useful because they can be fixed at different points, thereby altering the angle of resistance to suit the specific aims of a given exercise. Using cables to perform wood chops means that the obliques, hips, and core are all engaged during the movement.

These unique properties also mean cables can be used to fix imbalances that may otherwise cause pain and loss of mobility. For instance, face pulls offer a form of external rotation for the shoulders that is sorely lacking in our day-to-day lives. This is a perfect antidote to our regularly hunched-over posture and preference for pressing movements in the gym. To perform a face pull, you simply draw the cables toward you at face height, pivoting specifically at the shoulder rather than pulling from the lats.[82]

---

82 Even "simply" performing a cable press from a standing position is extremely beneficial. This becomes an anti-rotational movement as well as a press, which is how you push things in real life! When was the last time you needed to push something while lying down? If you can't coordinate strength in the core with strength in the pecs and shoulders, it won't be highly transferrable to the real world. This also teaches you to use your proprioception to "sense" how much force you can apply without toppling over. This forms your "perceptual motor landscape." Uncoupling strength from perception rarely makes sense in the real world. Fail to use these in coordination regularly and you can eventually lose the ability altogether. You may become "movement blind."

> Any item can become an effective functional training tool.

At the other end of the spectrum is perhaps the oldest training tool of all: the massive rock. These days, rocks used for training are often perfectly spherical and referred to as Atlas stones. While they're hard to come by, Atlas stones are fantastic for training the posterior chain as well as grip. Lifting the Atlas stone requires rounding of the spine but since your upper body is wrapped around the stone, the risk of injury is minimized.

Still used in strongman competitions today, Atlas stones are brilliant for developing real-world strength and lifting weights and objects with no convenient handles or bars. Moves like lapping—where the weight is placed onto the athlete's lap—can come in genuinely useful when trying to lift other awkward objects.

The list goes on: the Bulgarian bag is a heavy bag that you hold from a handle on either side and swing almost like a kettlebell. It looks like a strange sandbag, but in terms of the benefits it is more like a kettlebell crossed with a medicine ball. It's also possible to attach a rope to a medicine ball, which is awesome for flinging them across fields.

Hopefully, this chapter and those preceding it have given you enough knowledge of rotational strength, ballistic training, and other related concepts, so that you can assess any given tool and see how it might fit into a program (or not).

Anything Can be a Functional Tool

While sandbags and medicine balls each have their own benefits, it is not the tool that maketh the workout! That is to say that any item can become an effective functional training tool when used in the right way.

A while ago on my YouTube channel, I made a video about training with a chair. You can grab a chair with a leg in each hand and then swing it over your head just as you might perform a medicine ball slam (stopping short of hitting the ground). Alternative, you can hold it in one hand and attempt to point the chair out in front of you to create as long a lever as possible for forearm training. There are countless other things you can do with a chair, or with a small table for that matter. Or a with a lamp. A bag of compost or cement can be a great alternative to a sandbag. Any piece of old furniture can be manipulated too.

In short, don't fall into the trap of "boxed-in thinking" and don't assume you need to spend a fortune on exotic tools.

The Right Tools for the Job

Some of these options provide new and powerful benefits over more common forms of training, which is ironic considering most of them have been around for thousands of years.

Thus, we are able to train aspects of strength and performance that are neglected by more conventional methods. Developing these traits come with huge benefits for athletes, but also Joe public.

Only today, I was required to collect fence panels from a delivery truck, along with some posts, and bags of heavy cement. To carry the cement bags, I used a sandbag clean technique, then held them in a zercher position and walked with them.

This required me to brace my core to keep it from rounding and causing injury, and to maintain that position even as I began to fatigue over the distance to the house.

Lifting the fence panels required me to hoist them up on one side of my body, using the serratus muscles on the other side to stabilize. Again, I then had to walk with them, while also ducking beneath branches and squeezing through narrow gaps. It required significant grip strength maneuvering them into position, too.

> You know you can cope with whatever life throws at you!

An interest in functional training prepared me for this very real example of an everyday strength challenge where squats and bicep curls would not have. Knowing I had this ability meant that I didn't have to be a diva and demand that the delivery man carry my fence panels further than would be reasonable. It also meant I didn't need to feel anxious, leaving them outside for a potential (very strong) thief.

This is an example of how functional strength can directly impact on your day-to-day life. Not only by preventing injury, but also by creating new opportunities for how you use your body. Being more physically capable and *adaptable* has the potential to eliminate issues that cause you stress.

You know you can cope with whatever life throws at you.

Such training can benefit everyone. I have likewise programmed offset farmers walks for an older client who was falling over a lot. This strengthened the stabilizing muscles in the hips and core to minimize future accidents, where squatting alone would not have.

The Serape Effect

For athletes, many of these moves are even more valuable. Consider how a movement like the sandbag woodchop or shotput throw with a medicine ball mimics an action such as pitching a baseball or serving in tennis. Such movements rely on something known as the "serape effect."[83]

Moves that involve the serape effect require rotating the trunk, first by moving the shoulder back and opposite hip forward. This position stretches multiple muscles across the entire torso ready to exert maximum power. To see this effect for yourself, go to throw a ball with your right arm and you'll find you naturally

---

83   Logan & McKinney (1970), *Kinesiology.* W. C. Brown Co.

twist to move that shoulder back and your left hip forward.

There's an anatomical basis for this. The rhomboids, serratus anterior, and internal and external obliques combine to form an X-shape across the body (resembling the Mexican "serape" that gives the effect its name). These muscles are aligned diagonally, demonstrating the significance of rotational movement in the human body.

"Contralateral movement" is found in countless sports and activities, walking being the most notable example. During our natural gait, we move the supporting foot back and automatically swing the opposite shoulder forward.

Similarly, when opening a door or when throwing a stone, we will use very similar movement patterns. Even our neural wiring is set-up to support this kind of movement, as we will see in a future chapter.

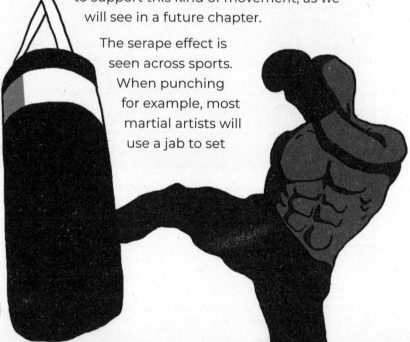

The serape effect is seen across sports. When punching for example, most martial artists will use a jab to set themselves up for a more powerful cross. As a result, a fighter can bring the dominant shoulder back while rotating the opposite hip forward, again loading themselves up for the following punch. Chaining movements together like this is what is known as "kinetic linking."

By tapping into this function of the human body, a trained martial artist or boxer is able to throw a punch that delivers up to five thousand Newtons of force! That's more than the pressure that half a ton would exert on the ground. A powerful kick that also places the martial artist's mass behind the movement can generate up to nine thousand Newtons![84] The serape effect also explains how a baseball pitcher can throw a ball at over one hundred miles per hour. The human body is truly capable of incredible power.

This serves as an example as to the value that can be attained by training with alternative tools and smart programing.

But the danger is in assuming that "different is always better." Or that training less common positions and movement patterns is somehow superior to lifting heavier weights. Indeed, many of the same benefits can be achieved using conventional methods, even if tools like kettlebells are slightly better suited. It is not the tool that makes a movement worthwhile, but the intent and the focus.

---

84   These figures were collected by Cindy Bir et al. from the Wayne State University in Detroit.

Choosing a tire over a trap bar for a deadlift will make little difference. In fact, by significantly reducing the amount of weight and placing the grip much higher off the ground, this choice will actually undermine some of the benefits of that move. Of course, as a way to add variety and interest to workouts, this still has some value. Some people just enjoy lifting tires!

> It is not the tool that makes a movement worthwhile, but the intent and the focus.

The challenge is recognizing where the genuine benefits in each form of training lie, and to make sure to implement them for the right reasons. Adding rotational movements with the sandbag, ballistic movements with medicine balls and kettlebells, and heavy loaded carries can be extremely beneficial to overall performance.

When you recognize the gaps in each type of training and borrow concepts from other areas to plug them, you can start to become a true all-rounder. You can start to use your body as it was meant to be used—not neglecting a single aspect of its performance. Moreover, you'll be developing a training style that is unique to *you*.

That's why I love the idea of kettlebell flows, or even "clubbell yoga" which combines yoga and clubbells (championed by Summer Huntington). These ideas take aspects of two training styles and then combine them for even more functional results.

Think outside the box! Get creative! And draw on the myriad influences and tools available to you.

But perhaps the best tool of all? That would be your *own body*. In the next couple of chapters, we're going to learn how you can master your own bodyweight to develop incredible power, mobility, and agility.

CHAPTER 8

Mastering Your Body

By now we've discussed everything from juggling kettlebells to striking tires with sledgehammers. You'd think we'd have just about covered everything! In fact, we have yet to address one of the biggest and most valuable categories of training: calisthenics.

Calisthenics, also known as bodyweight training, covers any exercise that utilizes bodyweight to provide resistance.

As far as the nervous system is concerned, there is no difference between a dumbbell, a kettlebell, or your own arm. Resistance is resistance. Force is force. Therefore, you can provide yourself with a perfectly great workout using only your own body and a little gravity.

But calisthenics is *much* more than simply a convenient way to train without weights. Rather, calisthenics helps you to develop complete *mastery* over your own body. Because you are using your own bodyweight, any increase in strength will improve your *relative* strength. As you become stronger while remaining a similar weight, you gain agility, explosiveness, speed, and more.

And by using so little resistance, calisthenics allows you to train in more vulnerable positions, and with more complex movement patterns. With enough practice the result is a fluidity and beauty in motion that borders on superhuman.

Push-Ups, Pull Ups, and Squats

While bodyweight training *can* incorporate advanced calisthenics moves, the basics also have an important place in your physical development.

The most common bodyweight movements are:

- Push-ups
- Sit ups
- Pull ups/Chin ups
- Squats

These are universally recognized, and employed by PE teachers, military drills, and sports coaches the world over. On top of these, we can also incorporate a number of slightly less obvious movements to hit lesser-worked areas of the body:

- Indian squats—squats performed on the toes to target the quads
- Calf raises—raising the body up with just the calves
- Pike push-ups—push-ups with a more downward angle to work the shoulders
- Tricep dips—a movement that targets the triceps by placing the hands on an elevated surface to raise and lower the upper body[85]

---

85 Avoid a pronated hand position to reduce internal rotation on the shoulders.

- Leg raises—raising the legs either while lying on the ground or suspended in some way

- Supermans—lying face-down and then raising the head and legs to train spinal extension (provided by the erector spinae)

The list goes on and on.

Together, these work a wide number of different muscle groups and movement patterns. And because they are simple and low risk for the most part, they are well-suited to metabolic conditioning circuits for burning fat. They also work well for those that want to improve fitness and muscle tone without building bulk, and they are ideally suited to beginners.

The issue of course, is that these moves can only ever provide a limited amount of resistance. A push-up will only require you to lift around 60 percent of your bodyweight, whereas a strength athlete might be able to lift two times their bodyweight or more during a bench press. In short, this does not develop the full potential of our strength.

So, what is the solution?

There are actually several options:

- Perform extremely high-rep ranges

- Switch to unilateral (one-sided) movements

- ⚜ Extend the lever arm

- ⚜ Train explosively

The simplest of these is training with high volume.

These movements are largely closed-chain, meaning that the limbs are fixed to the ground and not free to move around. Despite involving multiple muscle groups, they remain relatively safe with low risk of injury. This also helps target specific muscle groups with a degree of isolation.

Thus, the staple bodyweight exercises are perfect for building strength endurance and even some hypertrophy. By training to failure, these types of movements can also stimulate the precise same kind of sarcoplasmic hypertrophy that is possible with bodybuilding intensity techniques. You'll increase blood flow to the target muscles, you'll recruit larger motor units once the smaller muscles fatigue, and you'll trap plenty of blood and metabolites in the muscle to trigger sarcoplasmic hypertrophy.

Legend has it that the Indian Wrestler Gama (who we have already encountered in this book), would train using ridiculously huge sets of bodyweight moves—five thousand Hindu squats and three thousand Hindu push-ups, to be precise!

We also associate extremely high-rep ranges with "prison workouts." Prisoner-style workouts typically refer to extremely high-volume bodyweight movements, popularized by celebrities such as Charles Bronson. In his book *Solitary Fitness*, Bronson claims he would do two thousand push-ups daily.[86]

---

86   Some inmates would also reportedly use each other as weight! This is a technique my buddy Goof and I attempted to replicate for one video. "The Two Man Workout" was definitely one of the more ridiculous entries on my channel!

Extreme high volume was also a trick used by golden-era bodybuilder Tom Platz. Platz was renowned in bodybuilding circles for having the best legs in the business. To get there, he reportedly would train one hundred rep leg presses, increasing the amount of weight over time. By the end, he was reportedly able to perform multiple sets of a hundred reps using 225 pounds. Of course, this isn't an example of bodyweight training, but the precise same rules would apply here. The leg press is a similar closed-chain movement that can be used with a relatively light load. Bodyweight squats should work just the same.

Mike Tyson reportedly used a similar method to develop huge legs while in jail, squatting down to pick up individual cards from the floor. This helped create a more concrete challenge he could engage with that would provide a form of external focus to encourage commitment and effort. Gamifying training like this is a great strategy for anyone.

In my experience, performing hundreds of push-ups in a single workout has helped me to develop large pecs and significant strength with carry-over to the bench press[87] and even handbalancing pressing movements. This is precisely how I began training in my bedroom when I was thirteen and had no idea what I was doing. I believe it provided me with the foundation that I was able to build on as I got older.

The only issue with this type of training? It's extremely dull! That, and it does not develop complete performance on its own, which is the limitation we've run into for every individual form of training thus far. While these movements

---

87   Similarly, golden-era bodybuilder Tom Platz is said to have used extremely high reps of light squats to develop what were widely considered to be the best legs in the business. He was eventually able to perform over a hundred reps squatting with 225 pounds!

are compound and multi-joint, they are also very constrained and safely within the sagittal plane.

At some point, we must find ways to make the individual movements themselves more challenging and varied. And this is where the true power of bodyweight training makes itself known.

Because when you work with lower resistance, you are capable of far more intricate and complex movements, some of which seemingly defy the laws of physics.

Training Core Stability with Calisthenics

We have already met a menagerie of colorful characters by this point in the book. From Indian wrestlers and old-time strongmen, to ancient philosophers and prisoners of war.

But few people come to mind as readily as Bruce Lee when discussing feats of incredible physical prowess. Bruce Lee is famous for bringing Chinese martial arts to Western audiences through his filmography, as well as for developing the fighting style of Jeet Kune Do, the underlying philosophies of which would go on to inspire MMA.

Bruce's philosophy and charisma played a large part in helping him to grab the world's attention, but just as important was his sheer physicality and the way he expressed himself through his body. Bruce had a physique that looked like an anatomy diagram, with estimates putting his body fat percentage at somewhere between 6 to 8 percent.

> **Bruce had a physique that looked like an anatomy diagram.**

Most amazing of all though, was the way that Bruce delivered his kicks and punches with incredible power and speed. Countless urban myths circulate about him. He is said to have been able to punch his finger through steel cans of unopened soda and swap a coin in your hand for another one before you could close it. Some reports describe him holding seventy-pound barbells at arm's length for extended periods of time.

Whether any of this true is the subject of vicious debate on countless internet forums. But the fact is that Bruce moved with such power as to inspire those kinds of tales.

Where did this power come from? I believe the answer may lie with a few of his most famous physical feats, *especially* the two-finger push-up.

The Two-Finger Push-Up: A Perfect Unilateral Movement

The two-finger push-up is just as it sounds. Bruce would perform a push-up resting all of his weight on just a thumb and index finger on one side of his body.

This of course required extraordinary finger strength. But more than this, it also required excellent core stability.

We've touched on stability as it pertains to functional fitness already. Stability is often misunderstood, a term that refers to the ability to keep a body part rigid and set in place. If you were to hold your arm out to one side and keep it there while someone else tried to push it down, you would be relying on your shoulder stability to resist those forces.

In the case of the two-finger push-up, Bruce Lee needed to engage his obliques in order to resist the rotational force caused by the uneven base of support.

With his left arm off the ground, gravity would try to twist his body back down on the other side. Only by bracing his upper body could Bruce Lee perform the movement as perfectly as he did, keeping his torso parallel to the floor. This is core stability.

In the last chapter, we saw how movements like the wood chopper could develop rotational force and the serape effect. Here, we see how to use those same muscle groups to *prevent* movement using only our own bodies to apply the necessary stimulus.

We call such a movement an anti-rotational movement.

The one-handed farmer's walk that we discussed early is likewise a tool that builds exceptional core stability. In that case, you are preventing the body from bending sideways, which is anti-lateral flexion.

We've also encountered anti-flexion already, the ability to hold the spine upright against forces trying to pull it down and forward, as in the goblet squat. Anti-extension is the opposite, preventing the spine from bending *backward*.

The two-finger push demonstrates one option for making bodyweight moves more demanding by using only one side of the body (making the movement "unilateral"). As well as the stability component, switching to a unilateral movement means that a single arm is now holding that 60 percent of the bodyweight, effectively doubling the amount that each side is training with and encouraging more growth.

The single-legged squat achieves something similar, as does a one-armed chin up.

Anti-Extension Movements

Another of Bruce's showstoppers was the dragon flag, which is a classic anti-extension movement. This exercise involves holding your upper body steady using some kind of anchor (a bar behind the head in most cases or the end of a bench you are lying on) then raising and lowering the lower torso with the legs outstretched. You start with the feet pointed at the ceiling and only the shoulders touching the ground. You end with the feet raised just above the floor, the back still perfectly rigid. Here, you must do all you can to resist letting the back bend under the weight of the feet and the leverage created by the body.

So, what does all this have to do with Bruce's lightning punches and kicks? Why might you choose to incorporate bodyweight moves that offer anti-extension in this manner into your training?

Watch Bruce Lee, and you'll notice that his upper body appears almost rigid much of the time, while his limbs fire out forcefully.

The ability to keep your core rigid is *crucial* for delivering any kind of powerful strike. The easiest way to visualize why this is to imagine hitting someone with a nail attached to the end of a plank of wood. It would hurt right?

But now imagine hitting someone with a nail attached to a bendy tree branch. It would hurt less. That's because the branch has some give, meaning some of the force is spent bending the branch rather than being transmitted to the target.

What's more, the trajectory of the nail will have been slower and less efficient when travelling to its target.

And it actually goes farther than this, because when muscles contract, they exert force on both ends, the insertion and the origin. Thus, energy is wasted in moving the core rather than being transmitted to the limb.

The capacity for rigidity is fundamental to the operation of the body, which consists of numerous kinematic chains. A kinematic chain is any system comprised of rigid bodies and mobile joints (called junctions), allowing for the translation of force. Think of a crane, which is a series of long metal masts attached by pivoting joints. If any part of the crane were "floppy," then it would not be able to move any weight.

Our aim then, is to ensure that no part of us is floppy.[88]

Although that isn't quite true. When I discussed a similar topic on my YouTube channel, a lot of the commentators pointed out that being permanently rigid would not be desirable. Martial artists are taught to "whip" their punches and stay lose and fluid in the process. Athletes need to extend their torsos in order to load their muscles like a bow and take full advantage of the serape effect discussed in the previous chapter.

---

88   Phrasing.

Some went as far as to ask whether training for core stability would make them less agile or mobile!

But training core stability doesn't mean you are permanently rigid. It simply means you have the *ability* to become rigid as necessary. If we consider the full instruction given to a martial artist delivering a punch, it is to be fast and lose until the moment of impact, at which point they should contract the body to become rigid and hard. This is where the force generated must be transferred to the target. If that sounds familiar, it's the same concept of controlling rigidity that we encountered discussing "hardstyle" kettlebell training.

And this is how Bruce was able to demonstrate a third crowd-pleasing demonstration, his one-inch punch. This technique allowed Bruce to send a hapless volunteer flying backward from a punch delivered from only a few inches away.[89] He did this by perfectly generating power through hip rotation and transferring that into his fist.

And the secret to that trick was all in his core stability built, at least partially, with these perfect bodyweight moves. Moves such as the one-handed push-up and the dragon flag are a perfect fit for developing core stability. They allow you to train using your own bodyweight (improving proprioception and muscle control) and the lack of weight means you're less likely to cause injury. Bending the spine *under load* is not advisable under most circumstances.[90]

---

89   It was in fact never just a single inch, but roughly the length of his fingers.

90   There are some exceptions, such as the Jefferson curl recommended by coach Chris Sommers of Gymnastic Bodies.

The LaLanne Push-Up and Other Anti-Extension Moves

An alternative anti-extension movement comes from another legendary icon of fitness: Jack LaLanne. Born in 1914, Jack LaLanne was a fitness guru and early advocate for the widespread benefits of physical training. He opened one of the earliest gyms and invented a number of popular exercise machines including the Smith machine, cable pulley machine, and leg extension.

However, he is perhaps best known for some of his incredible feats, such as swimming the length of the Golden Gate with over 64 kg. of weight strapped to his body at the age of forty. At forty-one, he swam from Alcatraz Island to Fisherman's Wharf, handcuffed. He went on to top this at the age of sixty, performing the same stunt, but this time while also towing a thousand-pound boat behind him.

The move in question is the LaLanne push-up, which requires the individual to get into a push-up position with their arms outstretched in front of them. Only the fingers should be in contact with the floor, and from there you will perform push-ups using the full range of motion available to you. This challenge requires not only significant shoulder and finger strength, but also a strong core that must prevent sagging at the waist. If you want to demonstrate even crazier mastery over your body, try a one-handed LaLanne push-up.

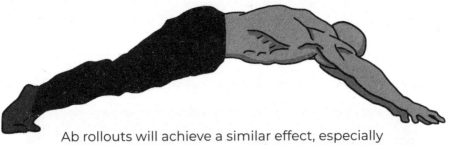

Ab rollouts will achieve a similar effect, especially when performed from standing. I've loved this move ever since I saw Jackie Chan execute perfect reps in the film *Gorgeous*.

Perhaps the best anti-extension move, used commonly by gymnasts, is the hollow body. To perform the hollow body, you lie flat on your back and contract your core to raise your shoulders and feet off the ground. The lower back will be the only point in contact with the floor. You can keep your hands by your side or point them over your head if you want to add challenge.

This movement teaches you to create a rigid core that will make many other advanced calisthenics movements possible. It also trains the transverse abdominis, which wraps around the mid-section and helps produce flat abs and greater spinal stabilization.[91]

Lest you think that this kind of core stability is only useful for martial artists, you'll use anti-rotation every time you need to open a door. The farmer we encountered in Chapter 6 would likewise need to resist rotational forces when digging. And of course, any athlete can similarly benefit from being able to generate more power from the hips or speed in their upper limbs.

---

91   To train the transverse abdominis specifically, you can try using ab-vacuums. These involve trying to suck the belly-button in toward the spine. This was a favorite among golden-era bodybuilders looking to develop flatter abs. This can be done while on all-fours which is charmingly referred to as the "cat vomit" exercise in Tim Ferriss' *The 4 Hour Body*.

Since training core stability with calisthenics, I have noticed my own performance in nearly every movement improve significantly. This is particularly apparent when performing clapping push-ups. Before, these moves would involve a significant sag in my waist and an almost whiplash effect when I landed. This prevented me from generating all the power from my arms and legs (which is the aim), and made the movement look significantly uglier and less "crisp."

Now I can keep my core rigid during the same movement, and that makes me look and feel far stronger, explosive, and more athletic.

Advanced Calisthenics

Incredible though Bruce Lee's feats of athleticism were, I believe that even he would be forced to take his hat off to some of the superhuman demonstrations of relative strength and bodyweight mastery that are to be found on Instagram.

These are people who can perform a slow handstand push-up, then lower their body to become perfectly parallel to the ground (called a planche). They may then push-ups from that position without their feet ever touching the ground, perhaps launching into the air and clapping behind their back for good measure. There is no shortage of videos like this on Instagram.

Such movements appear to completely defy gravity and logic and come extremely close to appearing truly superhuman.

Let's examine a few of these moves in a little more detail, to see what secrets they hold.

The Freestanding Handstand

We'll start with a recognizable movement: the freestanding handstand and its variations (handstand push-ups, one-handed handstands, etc.).

There are two ways to perform a handstand: the straight-line handstand and the banana handstand. The latter is easier and is the default for most people trying a handstand for the first time.

Here, the spine is in extension so that the feet "hang" forward over the head. From a side-on perspective, you will be the shape of a banana with a concave spine. This is an easier position to balance but is also less effective at training the shoulders and core. It also limits available progressions. You can't easily perform a one-handed handstand using a banana position, for example.

In a straight-line handstand, you will have all your joints stacked on top of each other to create a pencil-straight line. Your wrists are directly under your shoulders, which are directly under your hips. To achieve this, you need good shoulder mobility *and* core stability.

In fact, this is where anti-extension and flexion moves start to pay off. Upside down, you'll find it difficult to get your bearing and feel where your legs are in relation to the rest of your body. The moment you allow yourself to go into extension though, you will end up in a banana position. Knowing how to keep tight and strong on the ground, helps you to do the same thing while upside down.

This makes the handstand one of the best movements I can think of for developing true proprioception. It is *significantly* more effective to that end than training on a balance board. You'll be using your body in a way you likely aren't familiar with, and only by truly focusing on your position will you be able to balance. Upper body proprioception is something that is focused on far less frequently.

> **Knowing how to keep tight and strong on the ground, helps you to do the same thing while upside down.**

(If you really want to enhance the effect this kind of training has on proprioception, try performing hand balancing movements with your eyes closed. This forces you to rely 100 percent on your vestibular system and proprioception to stay in position. Of course, you also need to practice caution by ensuring you have a safe landing should you fall!)

Hand balancing will likewise improve wrist mobility, build shoulder strength, and open up a host of future movements you can use to train. That's one of the best things about advanced calisthenics. The more strength and control you develop, the more training options you unlock.

The Planche

I keep teasing that we're going to cover "superhuman" looking movements. Behold! The Planche!

There are few positions that the human body is capable of that are more spectacular to behold.

In full planche, a calisthenics athlete will essentially be in the top push-up position without their feet touching the

ground. In other words, your entire body weight is on both hands, while your body appears to hover out behind you, parallel to the ground. It looks truly gravity-defying.

> **The more strength and control you develop,**
> **the more ways to train you unlock!**

The key to this movement is an aspect of strength that no other modality we've covered thus far explores: straight arm strength, or scapula control.

A bent arm planche is a real movement, but it is considerably easier. In a *true* planche position, the arms are completely straight so that the elbows are locked out. In order to avoid instantly collapsing, you must therefore be leaning slightly forward, which places great strain on the biceps as stabilizer muscles, not to mention challenging the anterior deltoids (front of the shoulders), and requiring scapular control to avoid retraction. Meanwhile, your core needs to remain completely rigid so that your feet don't lower and touch the ground and your waist doesn't sag in the middle. This is where repetitious use of the hollow body and front squats can become extremely useful.

Straight arm strength requires you to not only lock out the elbows against resistance, but also move the arm from the scapula, engaging the scapular protractors. This type of strength has huge benefits across sports, letting martial artists add extra power to their punches and "pre-habilitating" the biceps against injury. This can help a powerlifter to avoid common deadlifting injuries, for example.

I consider learning planche to be a kind of masterclass in fitness and physiology. You simply cannot dive into this movement and force your way to success. It requires caution, deliberate patience, amazing proprioception, and an understanding of biomechanics. The lessons you learn here will be invaluable when applied to other movements.[92]

Attempt planche too early without first strengthening your elbows and biceps and you'll risk getting tendonitis or tearing a bicep. Attempt the movement without understanding how to control the scapula specifically, and you'll be barking up the wrong tree entirely. It took me a good couple of months the first time I tried planche to realize I wasn't actually locking out my arms. You'll also need a fair degree of wrist mobility and strength.

---

92 For those wondering, I cannot do a full planche but can currently perform an okay-ish straddle planche. I'm still going after the full planche, but I'm pretty chuffed with the straddle to be fair!

To reach this point, you must train gradually through progressions. These will typically start with frog stands and crow poses, along with the pseudo-planche push-up. In the former, you'll be balancing your weight on your hands, first with a slight bend in the elbow, and then with arms locked out. Pseudo-planche push-ups are push-ups where the hands are placed further down the body (next to the hips), and you are encouraged to lean forward into the movement as you go through full range of motion. At the top of the move, you must be sure to lock out the elbows and protract the scapulae. This places a significant strain on the biceps and can be a useful form of prehab for those not interested in learning show-stopping calisthenics skills.

Eventually, you'll be ready to attempt tuck planche and tuck planche push-ups, where you are in planche position but with your knees tucked in. From there, you might move into straddle planche, which uses a split leg position to shorten the leverage on the hands. With months or even years of practice, you should be ready to attempt full planche.

This system of using "progressions" is the equivalent of using progressive overload in regular weight training, and it is one of the ways we can achieve progressive overload in calisthenics.

Pistol Squat

Single-leg strength is another overlooked aspect of strength training that is well-covered by calisthenics. While vertical jump from a standing position is highly sought after in athletic training, the truth is that we rarely need to perform this kind of movement in an actual sporting event. In reality, we are far more likely to need to jump from a single leg. Likewise, we push off one leg when running or changing direction.

The actual mechanics of this kind of movement are significantly different. Not only do you need to generate power from just one leg rather than two, but you also need to shift your weight to ensure you are correctly balanced. Hip, ankle, and knee stability become more important to prevent injury and to maximize power output. Proprioception becomes essential to maintain balance.

The pistol squat is fantastic for developing this stability, strength, and mobility. It is a full squat on just one leg, while the other leg sticks out straight in front and hovers above the ground. This is an extremely difficult move that requires excellent ankle mobility to ensure you can lean forward enough to avoid toppling back when in the bottom of the squat. Ideally, this should include minimal rounding of the back as compensation. Ankle mobility can be a limiting factor and cause of injury for many people, so this is a great way to develop and test that ability.

You'll also need significantly more strength to lift yourself through the full range of motion with just one leg. And you'll need a strong core and great proprioception to maintain balance.

Like the other calisthenic moves on this list though, the pistol squat is also just an awesome looking move that makes for an excellent party trick once mastered. These skills are so cool as to be worth learning for their own sakes!

More Examples

For those who enjoy this type of training, there are many other advanced calisthenics moves to pick from. Great examples include:

- 🏅 **The V-Sit:** Resting on your hands with your legs up directly in front of you. This requires scapular depression (lowering the shoulders), as well as compressive strength to bring the legs up that high. An easier variation is the I-sit, while the top athletes can work toward something called "manna" where the legs actually point behind as you look upward. Here you also want scapular depression—pushing through the shoulders.

- 🏅 **Front lever:** Hanging from a pull up bar, you will use straight arms and scapular retraction while bringing the lower body up to be parallel with the ground. Scapular retraction is another example of scapula control that this time means pulling the shoulder blades back and together.

- 🏅 **Muscle up:** Perform a pull up but then transition past and over the bar into a pushing movement so that you can press your body over the bar to a locked-out position. This is another rare example of a movement that is at once a pull and a push and that features a transition between those positions. The best technique involves a specific grip called the "false grip" which will allow the athlete to perform the movement with control, rather than relying on momentum to move through the transition.

These are just a few of the amazing movements calisthenics athletes are capable of, however. Other amazing feats include the human flag, and lesser known "dragon press." Using these movements as a foundation, it is possible to transition from one position to another (V-Sit to handstand to planche), or to progress to even more incredible variations (like the one-handed handstand or planche push-up). There are videos on Instagram of people performing planche on their fingers, suspended from ropes![93]

Street workouts are a popular evolution of calisthenics that feature a lot of the same movements, typically performed in playgrounds and outdoor training facilities. These include a lot of movements like handstand push-ups and muscle ups, but also a huge variety of exciting, freestyle movements on bars. Groups like Barstarzz draw huge crowds switching from front levers, to muscle ups, to explosive pull ups where they spin 360 degrees in the air before catching the bar, to back levers (like front levers but with the arms behind the athlete). They also use a wide variety of slightly simpler pull up variations, such as the archer push-up, typewriter, and headbanger.

Of course, many of these movements have their origin in gymnastic strength training and aerial arts,[94] and you can likewise combine them with flips, handsprings, and other more explosive acrobatic movements. These movements require a surprising amount of explosive core strength and power to perform, along with body awareness and precision. Spend a day training on back flips and you may be surprised at just how sore your abs are the next day!

---

93   If you want to find the best tutorials and explanations, I recommend seeking out Gymnastic Bodies (and Coach Sommers), Simonster Strength, Official ThenX, FitnessFAQs, and Austin Dunham.
94   Aerial fabric, aerial hoops, and other gymnastic moves!

Plyometric Training for Explosive Performance

Another type of advanced calisthenics is plyometrics. Plyometrics are explosive movements, utilizing the stretch-shortening cycle and engaging more fast-twitch muscle fiber. We've discussed this in relation to medicine balls and kettlebells already, but in calisthenics plyometrics typically involve launching yourself into the air in some way.

Popular examples include:

- Clapping push-ups
- Clapping pull ups
- Squat jumps

The stretch-shortening cycle refers to the body's apparent ability to "store" elastic energy when the muscle is lengthened. In the last chapter we discussed the serape effect and how stretching the body could generate more force, but what's also key is the speed at which this lengthening and shortening occurs, also known as the "rate of loading." The less time between these lengthening and shortening stages, the more power is translated into the final movement.

We see this when looking at the squat jump versus the countermovement jump. In a squat jump, you simply explode *out* of that bottom position. In a countermovement jump, you first swing the arms up and stretch, then squat, and then thrust back upwards again.

The reason this happens appears to be due to the longer "active state" for the muscles. This may increase something called "cross-bridging." This in turn refers to the attachment of acting and myosin inside the cell, which allows for the telescoping shortening of the filaments. In other words, using the muscle longer allows it to gain more traction. This allows for a significantly higher vertical leap as compared with the standard squat jump.[95] In short, this isn't about storing elastic energy at all.

If you want to take this concept further, then you can also employ "shock training." Here, you will not only perform a countermovement, but will do so while absorbing an impact. The best example is the depth jump, which involves dropping from a short height, landing, and then springing back up with maximum force. For the most benefit, the optimum starting height is 42 inches, and you should spend no more than 0.2 seconds on the ground. Only advanced athletes should attempt to drop from greater heights, seeing as a drop from more than 42 inches actually constitutes somewhere between three to four times the athlete's bodyweight.

This additional element appears to be beneficial as it engages the myotatic reflex, the natural reflex to forcefully shorten any muscles that stretch suddenly. The myotatic reflex is why your leg jerks up when a doctor taps it with a hammer, and it's what helps you to catch your balance without thinking when you start to fall.

The myotatic reflex is "monosynaptic." This means it only requires two connections, see Chapter 3 for more detail.

This type of training can lead to *permanently* greater explosive power over time. That's because it trains the

95   Maarten F. Bobbert et al. (1996) "Why is countermovement jump height greater than squat jump height?" *Institute for Fundamental and Clinical Movement Sciences.* 28(11):1402–12.

central nervous system to anticipate the sudden powerful shortening when it enters the stretched position. In one study, volleyball players using a depth jump program were able to increase their jump height by a massive 14 percent!

Bodyweight training is in many ways the "default" mode of training. Nearly everyone on the planet knows how to perform a push-up and a pull up. That doesn't make these movements less valuable however, in fact they continue to be among the most important tools available to us. They not only develop amazing relative strength, but thanks to their closed-chain nature and relatively light load, they are also perfect for training high volume.

But our bodies are capable of so much more. By changing the lever, switching to one-sided movements, and adding explosive force, calisthenics teaches us to defy gravity and truly amaze.

And once again, this type of training provides missing pieces of the puzzle when it comes to *complete* functional performance. This can be used to develop single-leg strength, straight arm strength, balance and proprioception, and more in ways that other forms of training simply neglect.

We are gaining the ability to move quickly, explosively, and dynamically. Of course, movement that allows us to manipulate our own body is the precise type of movement we use more than 90 percent of the time, during our daily lives *and* in sport.

Next, we're going to take these ideas further and explore something new and exciting. Something that has been exploding across the internet. Something that looks entirely different from anything else you may have encountered in the gym before.[96]

---

[96] Keep in mind that true plyometric training does not mean lightly bouncing! Rather, this means exploding with maximum force, which means you must be fully recovered between sets to properly train the nervous system. Rest periods should thus be longer for plyometrics, usually somewhere between three to five times the length of the sets themselves. Also: note that tendon hysteresis plays a big role in returning energy to the ground when running and jumping. Building thicker, tougher tendons should be a priority for those athletes.

CHAPTER 9

(Re)Learning to Move

If I'm honest about what originally attracted me to physical training, I'd have to answer Sonic the Hedgehog. That may sound odd; on the surface there is little similarity between a heavy bench press and a computer game starring a superfast, anthropomorphic, blue hedgehog.

But it was the speed and freedom of movement depicted in those games that I found so exhilarating. A good *Sonic* game is designed to feel like a giant playground, where you can test your skill and mastery of the physics, in order to pull off incredible feats and explore new areas.

This is likewise what attracted me to fitness training, although I didn't know it at the time. It's why I was similarly awestruck by Jackie Chan when I first saw the film *Who Am I*, and subsequently went on to buy every DVD of his I could get my hands on. It's also why I loved Spider-Man comics. Spider-Man moved unlike any other fictional character.

Why do we possess strength and mobility? I believe the answer is locomotion. We aren't strong so that we can lift extremely heavy things (how often would primitive man have needed to do that?) and we aren't endurant so that we can last in a fight (most fights are over in minutes—and natural selection does not reward constant brawling). Thus, our muscles must be for running, climbing, crawling, and swimming.

> Our muscles must be for running, climbing, crawling, and swimming.

With greater mastery over your body, you gain greater mastery over your environment. You can move more freely through it and manipulate it more easily too.

The stronger and fitter you are, the more options you have when it comes to your movement, the fewer obstacles you will face. Strength is movement, and movement is freedom.

Using your body this way can and should be a joy.[97]

Perhaps then, it should come as no surprise to learn that there is now a growing interest in making movement *itself* the priority. This growing trend has taken the world of fitness by storm and is changing what we mean by terms like "strength" and "health."

It also has huge implications for what we traditionally consider to be "functional."

Training Movement

As we saw in Chapter 1, most of us barely move our bodies anymore. We use a fraction of what our bodies are capable of because we spend most of our time sat in one position. We have designed our environments around us to the point

---

97   Who knew that a section that started talking about *Sonic the Hedgehog* would end on such a pretentious note?

that we barely even need to stoop at any point during the day, let alone run, climb, crawl, or swing.

> **We barely even need to stoop!**

These are all things that our bodies are designed for. Things we should be more than capable of.

Building more muscle is meaningless if you cannot move. And the hyperspecialization of sports training is no antidote.

These views are echoed by the king of "movement culture," Ido Portal. Ido is a figure who has risen to prominence online and amassed a huge and devoted following. He is perhaps best known for coaching MMA's most recognizable face, Connor McGreggor. You may also have seen his incredible "floreio" sessions on YouTube.

> **The hyperspecialization of sports training is no antidote.**

The basic idea behind Ido's philosophy is for the movement to be viewed as the primary goal, not a means to an end.

Instead of working on muscles, Ido works on movements and skills. He is not interested in how defined your abs are, or how big your bench press is, but rather on whether you can perform a planche, back bridge, or lizard crawl.

The movements and skills he teaches are drawn from a huge variety of sources, ranging from martial arts (especially Capoeira), to dance, to calisthenics, and to yoga. These are then strung together in seamless "flows," through graceful transitions and progressions. In practice, it looks like a form of slow, controlled dance, with Ido moving gracefully around the ground, contorting into all manner of positions.

There is no denying the power and physicality that Ido displays. Many of his adlibbed sequences include movements like one-handed handstands and handstand presses but with slow and deliberate control.

Ido has not published a guide to his system, and his retreats are notoriously expensive, so we only know what we can glean from interviews and blog posts.

Animal Flow

But Ido is not alone in his reverence for movement. Many others have stumbled upon the same realization and offer similar training systems. One of the best known of these is Animal Flow, created by Mike Fitch. Animal Flow places particular emphasis on animal movements, or "travelling forms." The three staples are ape, beast, and crab, but the real beauty comes from moving in between those positions. This again leads to stunning displays of mobility and control that look like interpretive dance routines performed close to the ground.

GMB is a similar organization that offers a course called Elements. Elements likewise works with three animal-inspired quadrupedal movements. These are the bear, frogger, and monkey. Again, the transition between these movements is what then allows practitioners to develop their own "flows."

Vahva fitness is another brand to have developed a training program based around movement, called Movement 20x. This program emphasizes the importance of freestyling, collecting a huge roster of different animal-inspired movements from lizard crawl variations to duck walks, and leaping like a gorilla. Founder Eero Westerberg combines this freestyle training with more traditional calisthenics strength training for a particularly versatile physique.

MovNat meanwhile places the emphasis very firmly on *natural human* movement and is more concerned with spear throwing and climbing trees as opposed to crawling like a lizard along the ground. We'll come back to this one in the next chapter.

As with some of the more eye-catching forms of functional training, movement training has an instant aesthetic appeal. It is different and it is a unique expression of physicality that is fresh and exciting.

> It is a unique expression of physicality that is fresh and exciting.

Unfortunately, the nebulous nature of this topic makes it particularly difficult to unravel. Coaches might likewise be wondering what benefit this type of training could have for clients.

Read on!

Why You Should Crawl Like a Lizard

In general, this form of training offers similar benefits to the kettlebell flows and hybrid movements we've discussed previously. They put us in positions that we don't typically explore during resistance training. Most resistance training—even calisthenics—is predominantly set in fixed patterns, moving through repetitive movements, largely within a single plane of movement.

Kettlebell flows and hybrid exercises improve this situation a little by moving *between* rigid movement patterns, and thereby strengthening the individual in those transitional phases as well. But even here, you are still moving in a predictable sequence, often in a straight line.

That is not how we move in real life and certainly not how we move in combat or in sports.

Movement training is about improvisation, adaptation, and creative exploration. It means venturing into movement patterns that you've never experienced before and expressing yourself. It means being strong at unpredictable angles and being able to move in unexpected ways. This is where the appeal lies for someone like McGreggor, who can strike from seemingly mechanically disadvantages positions and catch an opponent off-guard. Controlling the weight at an unusual angle along the ground is great training for resisting the pressure of an opponent when grappling.

And this has benefit for the rest of us, too.

One of the surprising ways I've found this type of movement to be useful is when looking after my young daughter. Often, I'll be relaxing in one corner of the room with half an eye on her while she is playing with blocks. Suddenly, she'll run toward the kitchen or reach for a mug I forgot about on the windowsill.

At this point, I have seconds to get to where she is before catastrophe ensues. And this where a unique ability comes in handy: the ability to get up quickly from a myriad of different positions. Whether I spring up off my knees or push from my hands into a crawl that becomes a run, being ready to move from any angle is extremely useful.

> **This is a kind of physical mastery that can't come from simply curling weights.**

This is a kind of physical mastery that can't come from simply curling weights. But in order to get here, movement training needs to forget conventional concepts of progressive overload.

The athlete is encouraged to move freely between movements, following their intuition and creativity. This is liberating, but it also means that you won't get the same benefits for hypertrophy as you might from performing 3 x 8 sets of bench presses.

Animal movements and similar patterns *can* be used to develop strength. Many crawls keep the body low to the ground, requiring significant tension in the pecs, shoulders, triceps and core. Performed for distance, time, or reps, this could be programmed for developing power. Programs like Animal Flow and GMB do a good job of breaking down broader movement into repeatable chunks.

But this is not the focus of movement training. That would be to miss the point entirely.

The secret to movement training is to transition *from* the lizard crawl and into the bear, then to "underswitch" into the crab reach (to borrow terminology from Animal Flow). The power of movement training is precisely this ability to move seamlessly from one position to another.

This is a great form of "prehabilitation" that may be superior to focusing on a single aspect of your strength or mobility; it prepares you for the unexpected.

Quadrupedal Movement

There are also other *specific* benefits to training with animal movements too.

Many of these "locomotor patterns" put us in a position that is relatively uncommon for modern humans, but that our body is more than capable of: being on all fours. A common argument is that we came down from the trees not all that long ago in the grand scheme of human evolution, so we need to keep this in mind with our training.

Getting on all fours helps to take some pressure off of the hips in particular, which in turn frees them up for greater mobility. Conversely,

quadrupedal movements place much of the weight on the hands and arms, which creates a full-body challenge. It also braces and realigns the core, introducing a different kind of challenge for the spine.[98]

Quadrupedal (four limbed) movements like the lizard crawl, bear crawl, and crab—as well as other bipedal and locomotive movements—are also what we refer to as "contralateral." This means that they train the body across the X-shape that we observed earlier discussing the serape effect. Moving the two sides of the body asynchronously is cognitively demanding, and this may therefore help develop coordination and muscle control that has beneficial transfer to other activities. After all, it is through crawling activities that infants eventually learn to walk.

If we constantly move in a symmetrical manner, those neural patterns become ingrained and we lose a large number of movement options as a result. Not to mention, the "bilateral limb deficit" shows us that we actually lose some strength when using our limbs simultaneously. Because of the amount of effort involved in using two sides simultaneously, we can actually lift more than half of our one-rep max on the chest press when performing the move with one arm (when controlling all other factors, such as balance and torque).

Separating your limbs is an important way to tap into reserves of strength and agility!

---

98 This may help train the multifidus muscles and rotatores that run up the spine. These tiny muscles were once thought to be unimportant, but more recent research shows that this is far from true! These muscles contribute to extension and lateral flexion and are extremely dense with muscle spindles (proprioceptors). This is used in an anticipatory manner to help us brace for incoming movement, and they play a large role in preventing that aforementioned "movement blindness." They are also thought to contain the stiffest and strongest fibers in the entire human body! They're kind of a big deal...

Levels

The danger though, is that "movement training" becomes all about crawls and low "ground movements." At its most effective, movement training should actually incorporate climbing, hanging and swinging (brachiation), upright bipedal movements, object manipulation, and even swimming. This is something that Ido Portal understands well, and that is inherently built into MovNat. Vahva fitness also does a good job of understanding this and including a wider variety of moves than just crawls and ground flows.

This is, unfortunately, missing from some forms of movement training—even yoga. The shoulder girdle's mobility is partly evolved to facilitate hanging and swinging. It's kind of important! Focusing only on pushing movements can thus lead to imbalance and weakness.

Swinging from monkey bars is something most of us associate with young children, but it's actually a fantastic exercise that develops shoulder mobility, pulling strength, core stability, grip, and much more. Swinging around like a monkey also couldn't be *more* primal. Other excellent options include the use of gymnastics rings, or rope climbing.

Rock climbing is another extremely natural activity that has extensive, unique benefits for your health and performance.

Level changes should also be incorporated into a complete approach to movement training. This is the transition from one level to another. That's a big focus of functional training for athletes (think lunging to strike a tennis ball or dropping to crawl through a pipe during an assault course) and it should be incorporated into smart movement training, too. An ideal training environment for this type of training might resemble an assault course then, with space to crawl alongside bars for swinging on and objects to hurdle!

Parkour

There is another form of movement training that you may be more familiar with: parkour a.k.a. free running. Free runners, or *traceurs*, are those individuals who run and leap across rooftops, flip their way over obstacles, and generally move like Spider-Man through city environments.

Free running is a movement practice that is similarly embedded in its environment. The practicality is focused almost exclusively on *efficiency* of movement.

At least this was originally the case. Eventually, parkour and freerunning would evolve to become two slightly different expressions of the same initial concept. Whereas parkour is about moving gracefully and efficiently from point A to point B, free running is more about acrobatic self-expression performed in a flowing and graceful manner. To put it more simply, freerunning has flips.

This is an interesting concept I wish to explore here: evolution.

Because even as parkour has grown, it has begun to develop different styles and branches. Whereas London-based traceurs placed more emphasis on precise jumps, the "European style" spearheaded by the likes of Oleg Vorslav, placed more emphasis on creativity.[99] His videos are truly something unique to enjoy. We see him collapsing onto railings and allowing them to flip him, or running along the ceiling while supporting his weight on crutches.

---

99   This observation comes from an excellent video from YouTuber JimmyTheGiant: "How Freerunners Learnt to FLIP to Handrails."

Like a language with dialects, movement training has been influenced by environments and cultures to evolve in the space of years.

The creation of parkour itself is often attributed to David Belle, who initially described *"l'árt du déplacement"* based on the ideas of none other than Georges Hébert and the *Méthode Naturelle.* You may recall from Chapter 1, that Georges recommended the use of *"parcours"* (assault courses) for French military training. Belle's father, Raymond Belle, was trained by said French military, where he also learned efficient escape techniques, ideas he passed on to David.

Belle enjoyed playing with his friend Sébastien Foucan[100] at the age of fifteen. The two would play chase around their neighborhood, finding ways to traverse their surroundings gracefully.[101]

So, we can trace the origins of parkour back to the ideas of Georges Hérbert, whose same ideas also influenced the likes of MovNat and modern "functional training." This is what I understand by the term "movement culture."

Today, traceurs perform feats of incredible superhuman agility that would have seemed impossible to the culture a decade ago. Freerunners in particular combine kong vaults and cat leaps across obstacles, with backflips and handsprings from gymnastics, and extreme kicks from XMA. XMA or "extreme martial arts" are another expression of this movement culture that has thrived online, evolving

---

100   You may recognize Foucan from the opening chase scene in *Casino Royale.*
101   It was Foucan who would go on to differentiate his more acrobatic style under the title "freerunning" ("follow your way"). He was heavily influenced by Bruce Lee's ideas and saw free running as a means of unrestricted expression. It is unclear whether he intended for freerunning to be considered independent from parkour, and the importance of this distinction is hotly debated.

from the more showy and acrobatic kicks found in Wushu martial arts.

There is no "right way" to move or to train.

This is very much at the heart of the movement training philosophy. Don't ask how you can "learn" movement training: simply start exploring what your body is capable of and try moving in different ways. Improvise, explore, and try experimenting with tempo and level changes. Tap into the movements you've learned from your own practices, and add new ones along the way. That way, you can develop your own unique style.

Limitations

Movement training offers a huge number of advantages and is in many ways a "limitless" form of training. By being unconstrained and ever-changing, it can provide whatever strength training and mobility benefits the individual needs. It borrows the "best" movements from a variety of different training styles and glues them together into something unique and often beautiful.

But no form of training is perfect, and this style does leave some avenues unexplored.

For one, the constantly flowing and changing nature of movement training makes it slightly less suited to building maximum strength. There is nothing quite like a heavy bench press for building pushing power and even bone density, yet it's hard to see how this might be adapted into a natural movement flow other than in a form of concurrent training (i.e. training strength separately in parallel).

While Ido Portal emphasizes the importance of hanging movements, bipedal movements, and manipulation, this is sorely missing from practices such as GMB and Animal Flow. Thus, those forms of training completely neglect entire ranges of motion and musculature. There is no way to adequately train the lats and biceps using only ground-based movements (this criticism could likewise be levelled at yoga).

This is why this style of training arguably works best when combined with other methods once again. Likewise, these "other methods" can allow us to develop different traits such as cardiovascular endurance, mental focus, and explosiveness. But it also has an additional, wonderful application as a way for us to integrate and bring together many of the skills and moves we've learned.

CHAPTER 10

The Evolution of Movement

Much of what we have discussed as "functional training" so far involves moving the body as it seems to have *evolved* to move. This is not a unique take.

In his book, *The Functional Training Bible,* author Guido Bruscia describes the importance of separating the *functions* of a muscle or system, versus the actions. The action of the adductor brevis is to adduct the thigh (bring it in toward the body), however one of the key *functions* of the muscle is to provide stability when walking.

By tracing the functional origin of muscles and muscle groups, we can train them in a highly functional manner. And that often means considering the environmental challenges we face.

So, why not go all the way back? Why not simply look at the way that humans would have moved during their evolution and use that thought experiment to *reverse engineer* the very purpose of our many muscular systems?

Well, that's precisely what many groups propose we should do.

Shoes Off Please! And Why Don't You Go Play Outside?

A common argument across different forms of movement training is that you should train barefoot or in minimal footwear. I wholeheartedly agree that this is optimal for any training that could be considered "functional."

Training barefoot has *huge* benefits for our performance and our general health. Investing in a pair of minimal shoes is a very easy thing you can do *right now* to become more functional. Minimalist shoes include footwear from the likes of Feiyu and Vivobarefoot that are designed to offer the flexibility and natural foot position offered by going barefoot, while still protecting you from glass and other hazards. 90 percent of the shoes I wear now fall into this category.

Today, most people wear large, structured shoes. These shoes typically involve a thick sole that protects our feet from the pavement and any litter we might otherwise step on, along with a heel that raises our foot further off the floor.

Without meaning to be overly dramatic, this *cuts us off* from our environment, robbing us of one of the single most important sources of proprioception. That in turn leads to significant muscular atrophy (and corresponding neural atrophy), as well as a loss of strength, balance, and performance.

Were you to go running in the woods without any shoes, your feet would play a significant role helping you to balance. The toes are designed to splay and bunch together, while the foot itself bends and flexes. This allows the foot to conform to the shape of the ground, preventing the sprained ankles that are commonplace when wearing thick shoes that prevent any bending or flexing.

At the same time, all this conforming and changing shape provides data that should be sent back to your brain. Muscle spindles, Pacinian corpuscles, and golgi-organ tendons in your feet should let you know the shape and angle of the ground, helping your body align itself to get the best purchase and avoid falling.

Through your feet you'll also know if the ground is slippery, if it is hard or soft, etc. All this information changes the way you move.

It is very possible that simply switching to minimal shoes could prevent a significant number of falls among the elderly.

For athletes, training this way will create a better connection to the ground that can enhance athleticism.

And to compound this effect, you need to spend more time on *interesting* terrain, not just the static, flat ground that we find everywhere in civilized society.

Toe Training

Meanwhile, your feet will actually contribute to the force you transfer to the ground. In the interests of "training everything," I challenge you to think about developing your *toes*. The flexor hallucis longus is a muscle that connects to the big toe and to help push through the floor when running and jumping. This muscle responds to *direct training* which has been shown to increase jump height, running speed, balance, and more.[102]

102   Jan-Peter Goldmann et. Al. (2013) "The Potential of toe flexor muscles to enhance performance." *Journal of Sports Sciences.* 31(4):424–433.

Training in thick shoes prevents you from even *using* this muscle, let alone training it.[103]

The flexor digitorum longus meanwhile is connected to the four smaller toes and has a role supporting the arch of the foot. This position can help us to better engage the glutes during movement, which in turn can enhance power generation through the posterior chain. The glutes are the largest muscles in our body and potentially the most powerful, but being tipped slightly forward all the time prevents us from engaging them fully.

The toes can even be used to grip the floor, providing additional purchase and friction when running and reacting in an instant to prevent falls.

Imagine how much *more* profound this is for a *traceur* balancing along a beam.

The Tarahumara Tribe: Superhuman Runners

Thought I was done? Far from it.

Wearing traditional shoes while running actually goes as far as to alter the very biomechanics of our gait. That's because the thick heel encourages us to run with a heel strike that lets the shoe absorb most of the impact.

This overrides our natural inclination to run on the ball of our foot, which is still what we see when observing indigenous tribes. None make this more apparent in fact, than the Tarahumara tribe. Members of this tribe of Native Americans in northwestern Mexico have famously

---

103   This truly is a footnote.

demonstrated the ability to run over 435 miles in just two days![104]

The Tarahumara run barefoot or wearing very thin sandals, and it is thought that this is what allows them to properly absorb the impact of so much running and thus protect the knees. Not only does this prevent a career-ending sprain or muscle tear, but it allows the knee and the ankle to bend like a spring as those joints remain aligned directly under the center of gravity during impact. This is especially effective as the Tarahumara are pros at keeping their center of gravity aligned.

Of course, these superhuman efforts can also be attributed to a lifestyle that *revolves* around running long distances. But the body evolved to run long distances barefooted, and heavy shoes understandably interfere with those natural biomechanics.[105]

The same thing happens in the gym performing a variety of other movements. For instance, squatting with a big heel in your shoe is almost an *entirely different movement* compared with squatting barefoot. This becomes even more apparent when attempting a pistol squat.

Performing a pistol squat in shoes with padded heels is significantly easier than doing it without any. The reason for this, is that the angle of your foot leans your body forward when wearing heels, meaning that you actually don't need as much ankle mobility to avoid toppling over backward. This also shifts a large amount of the effort onto the quadriceps rather than the glutes.

---

104   Christopher McDougall (2009) *Born to Run: The Hidden Tribe, the Ultra-Runners, and the Greatest Race the World Has Never Seen.* Profile Books.
105   In fact, some anthropologists even believe long-distance running was the primary "skill" of ancestral man: that our tracking abilities combined with cardio endurance were what allowed us to catch much faster and larger animals as our prey.

The Benefits of Training Outdoors

So, training barefoot and in natural environments creates a richer sensory experience that stimulates the nervous system while also developing the stabilizing muscles in the feet, ankles, and legs.

But those benefits extend throughout the entire body, not just to the feet.

Take climbing a tree for instance. This is a brilliant way to develop lat, bicep, and grip strength. Performing pull ups from a tree branch is infinitely superior to performing pull ups from a pull up bar. Every single set is completely different from the last when performed on a branch. That's because each branch has a slightly different thickness, random changes in height, and varying angles. One hand might be higher than the other, wrapped around a lumpy knot, while the other might be bending under your weight.[106]

This makes it impossible to adapt to the movement, such that every single workout challenges the body in a slightly different way. Now if you ever *do* need to pull yourself over a rocky cliff-edge, you'll be far better prepared for that unpredictable situation.

The same is true for lifting logs and rocks, or for scrambling up and down hills. Even if you don't have access to a forest or park where you can train, you can mimic this unpredictability at home. Using a towel and a pull up bar for instance, you can experiment with different grips as well as different cadences. I challenge you to find fifteen different ways to perform a pull up the next time you try.

---

106   This is what Nicolai Bernstein refers to as "repetition without repetition." This may help to form more robust mental models by varying the movement to make it more generalized. This is also another benefit of training with, say, a sandbag.

You'll find that once you switch to this way of thinking, the possibilities are endless.

Then there are all the other potential benefits of training outside. Being exposed to sunlight for instance will aid the production of vitamin D. This has a *huge* number of profound benefits throughout the body. Not only does vitamin D help to strengthen the bones by aiding the absorption of calcium, it also has a plethora of other benefits: increasing testosterone production, strengthening the immune system, enhancing blood flow, and more. Vitamin D acts like a master-key for hormone regulation and may explain why it seems that those "outdoorsy" types of people you know never seem to get sick or feel down.

It also explains—at least partly—why we modern "indoorsmen" have such low average testosterone compared to men from even a few decades ago.

Daylight also helps us to regulate our biological clock. Daylight is an "external zeitgeber"—a cue that tells our body what time it is. Most of us spend all day cut-off from the outside world and exposed to artificial light, which makes it extremely difficult to sleep later at night.

But what if it's not sunny? Turns out that's good for us too! Cold exposure is a stressor that places a strain on the immune system in the short term, but which can actually *train* us to be more resilient in the long-term. In other words, by exposing the immune system to acute stress, it may actually be possible to toughen it against future assaults. In one study,[107] regular cold showers were shown to reduce the number of sick days taken by participants.

---

107   A. Buijze et al. (2016) "The Effect of Cold Showering on Health and Work: A Randomized Controlled Trial." *Plos One*. 13(8):e0201978.

Cold exposure triggers the release of testosterone, raises metabolism, enhances thermoregulation, and may even offer a form of "discomfort training." We have become so accustomed to being just the right amount of fed, and just the right amount of warm, that we struggle with even the slightest inconvenience. Doing push-ups in the snow, or running through thick mud, can help to introduce some much needed "hardiness" back into our psychology. We'll explore this more in an upcoming chapter.

Jumping into a cold lake can supply a huge dose of cold exposure, provide a full-body workout (in the form of a swim), and trigger the "mammalian diving response."[108] Here, dousing the face with cold water actually interacts with specialized receptors that reside there. This lowers the heartrate by 10 to 25 percent and increases blood flow to the vital organs. The spleen contracts to release a greater amount of blood and changes your internal pressure.

You can "hack" this response quite simply by splashing your face with cold water. This is great for waking up when you feel brain fog starting to set in, and can even help you to sober up quickly should the need present itself after a few alcoholic beverages.

But more importantly, this reflex shows us that our body is *designed* for this kind of thing. We have built-in features that are going entirely unused because of our modern lifestyles.

Even the lush surroundings may have benefits. It turns out that simply being exposed to nature can help to lower blood pressure and stress, while enhancing creativity and

---

108   W. Michael Panneton (2013) "The Mammalian Diving Response: An Enigmatic Reflex to Preserve Life?" *Physiology.* 28(5):284–297.

FUNCTIONAL TRAINING AND BEYOND

problem solving. This is likely due to the association with resources and shelter during our evolutionary history.

MovNat

This type of natural movement grounded in the environment is precisely the focus of another system of movement training: MovNat. MovNat was founded by Erwan Le Corre and is of course a portmanteau of "movement" and "natural" (or rather "movement naturel" as it is in French). Inspired once again by the training methods of Georges Hébert, Erwan developed MovNat to be a:

> School of physical competency based on natural movement, which includes the locomotive skills of walking, running, balancing, crawling, jumping, climbing and swimming, the manipulative skills of lifting, carrying, throwing and catching, and the defensive skills of striking and grappling.

He believes the most important principles of natural movement to be "practicality and adaptability."

Erwan also trained in parkour for many years before developing MovNat as his own style. Once again, we see evolution in movement and multiple interpretations of "functional" performance.

MovNat has philosophical similarities to Ido Portal and the likes of Animal Flow, but focuses less on the seamless movement "flows" and more on climbing onto tree branches and throwing stones. There is less interest in mimicking animal movements, and more in exploring the natural options available to humans.

In practice, MovNat involves a lot of climbing up onto tree branches, jumping into pools of water, and throwing sticks to a partner while running. This may not be quite so artistic or expressive as the training used by the likes of Ido Portal, but it is great for developing such things as hand-eye coordination, proprioception, and useful movement patterns like mounting and balancing on beams.

Natural Human Mobility

A huge aspect of movement training, and one of the biggest advantages, is the effect on mobility.

Mobility as a concept is often misunderstood and is *not* necessarily synonymous with flexibility. Whereas flexibility refers to your ability to get into a position with or without an external aid (such as pushing your leg against a beam in order to stretch), mobility refers to freedom of movement. What positions can you get into through your own strength and control alone?

Mobility is one of the key factors that will lead to a controlled and beautiful looking movement "flow." This, along with strength, is a limiting factor for many people just starting out.

> How do you develop mobility? Simply by moving.

Mobility includes aspects of muscle control and of strength. When performing the V-Sit for instance, a gymnast must call on significant "compressive strength" in order to bend their hips and torso to raise their legs as far as possible. You could be highly flexible and still unable to raise the legs like this!

How do you develop mobility? Simply *by moving*.

Through moving gently into different positions, you gradually train the body to feel more comfortable there. It thus becomes easier to move into those positions in the future, and to go deeper into the movement.

This makes sense, given that our mobility is largely limited by our own nervous system. Through decades of barely moving, we have learned to move only within limited ranges. When you attempt to touch your toes, or get into a deep squat, it is not physically "short" tendons or muscles that prevent you from doing so. Rather it is your body *tensing up* to try and prevent injury. Just as the myotatic stretch response can prevent you from falling over, so does this instinct seek to avoid excessive range of motion.

This is expertly explained in Pavel Tsatsouline's book *Relax into Stretch*. A dramatic opening example from this book asks the following: if you can raise (abduct) either leg 90 degrees to the side, why can't you do both at the same time and achieve the full splits? Consider that no connective tissue ties the two legs together.

The *only* reason you can't get into the full middle splits position is that your body contracts out of fear in order to protect you from potential injury.

Thus, forcing yourself into uncomfortable positions and trying to hold there is not particularly productive. Far better to move naturally into those positions as part of a more complex movement pattern, to breathe through the movement, and to focus on self-expression rather than the searing discomfort. Martial artists and dancers are able to maintain impressive mobility because those positions are naturally incorporated as the end-ranges in many of their often-repeated movement patterns. So it should be for movement practitioners.

Of course, this is how we develop and lose movement ranges based on our environment and external pressures. This is how prehistoric man learned to climb and run. And it is how you learned *not* to stand up straight.

You should also focus on using active stretches that don't incorporate external resistance. For instance, simply raising your leg as high as you can while standing in a controlled manner will help to develop strength in those muscles and to move through those ranges of motion *with control*. Adding a little bit of weight—such as holding a light kettlebell while attempting a middle split—can help you to gain just the right "nudge" in the desired direction.

Passive stretching is also a useful tool, simply spending time in a stretch at the point where it is only slightly uncomfortable. This helps the body get used to that position and overrides some of the reflexes that are acting against it.

You can enjoy the benefits of passive stretching by changing your position while working or reading. Just employ a minor stretch and then try to focus on the task at hand.

According to people who have trained with Ido Portal, one of the first drills he will provide new pupils with, is to incorporate "dead hangs" (simply hanging from a pull up bar) and deep squats into daily routine. As a starting point, he recommends that pupils try to hang for seven minutes a day, and squat for thirty minutes. This is something that has tremendous value, and that anybody can do.

The Resting Squat

The resting squat is the perfect example of a movement that humans should possess and yet do not. Even if you can get into an ATG squat (ass-to-grass) at the gym under a barbell, that does not necessarily mean that you can drop into a full, deep squat—heels on the ground—and stay there while chatting to your friends on the phone.

But this is precisely the movement that we would have used for preference when relaxing in the wild. There were no chairs back then! We've already seen the significant harmful implications of spending too long seated, and squatting is the ideal solution.

Not only does squatting keep the core engaged (a "second best" option is to remove the back from your chair) but it also prevents the unnatural curvature of the spine that sitting encourages. Squatting allows us to breathe much more deeply as it doesn't compress the abdominal cavity meaning that the diaphragm can drop down lower. It has even been suggested that squatting should be the preferred position for using the toilet. This allows the bowels to evacuate more fully, potentially avoiding a number of health complications down the road.

In a world designed for sitting, you can't be expected to squat all the time without being considered completely insane (reading my books has that effect on people). However, you can certainly integrate squatting into your routine by occasionally choosing it when reading, gaming, or talking.

Passive active stretching are useful tools (and look up PNF stretching too), but simply moving deeply and exploring the limits of your range of motion can be enough. What's more, is that performing a crab walk is significantly more enjoyable for most people than holding an overhead stretch for two minutes.

Note: You should avoid using static stretches prior to strength training. Most experts now agree that this can actually decrease performance and even increase the likelihood of injury by impairing protective mechanisms![109]

Training the Fascia

To me, the true aim of a fully functional, compound training program, should be to move the body as though it were "one muscle." That means using every part of the body in unison, toward one biomechanical goal.

---

109   L Simic et. al. (2012) "Does Pre-Exercise Static Stretching Inhibit Maximal Muscular Performance? A Meta-Analytic Review." *Scand J Med Sci Sports.*

Well guess what? This conceptualization may be more literally accurate than you previously imagined!

While we have separate muscles, they are in fact contained by a *single* connective "sheet" called "muscle fascia" or "myofascia." This is just one form of the fascia that is found throughout the entire body.

If you have ever prepared a joint of meat and noticed that it is covered in a thin "film," well that right there is the fascia! This shrink wrap was disregarded by fitness and medical experts for hundreds of years—thought of as just some inert "stuff." In fact, it was rarely seen, seeing as the fascia is largely made up of water and practically disappears when the body is dissected. That didn't fool da Vinci though, who actually included fascia in his anatomical sketches.

An elastic sheet of connective tissue made from collagen, the role of fascia is to enclose and support muscles and organs within their cavities, along with bones, cells, and practically everything else. It doesn't just fit around the outside of the body like a catsuit. It weaves in and out and around of muscles, organs, and cells, even morphing into distinct elements like tendons and aponeuroses.

This viscous membrane network provides tension throughout the entire body that helps keep everything in place. This property defines it as a "tensegrity structure," which also applies to the body at large; think about the way that a tent holds itself up by maintain constant, opposing tensions. This design may also allow the fascia to dissipate impacts and energy across the entire surface, thereby minimizing the damage caused by a fall.

The flexibility of the fascia therefore contributes *greatly* to the flexibility of an individual as a whole with tightness in one area affecting far-flung parts of the body. But that's not all.

The muscle fascia contains large amounts of elastin fiber to help provide elasticity and can actually supply additional energy rebound when running or jumping.

But what is truly remarkable is that the muscle fascia contains blood vessels, smooth muscle cells, and even sensory receptors. In fact, fascia may be equal or even *superior* to the retina in terms of sensory nerve receptor density.[110] It has between six to ten times more nerve endings than muscle.

In short, it seems that the fascia may play a key role in the expression of strength, along with improved balance, and agility. One of the important ways this happens is via fascial force transmission. It appears that the fascia facilitates communication between distant muscle groups, such that contracting one area encourages another to contract too.[111]

What's more, training seems to alter this force transmission. Fibroblast cells act like architects, travelling through the fascial system and producing the necessary collagen, collagenase (which breaks down collagen), and other chemicals to help build and reform the fascia. According to Tom Myers, this process allows the fascia to strengthen itself in response to specific stress and pressure signals. In other words, the fascia can get stronger across specifically lines to connect muscles that are often used in tandem.

It is also thought that an additional function of the muscle fascia may be to act as a kind of communication system helping electrical signals to spread between muscle

---

110   Much of this information comes from *Anatomy Trains* by Tom Myers.
111   Frieder Krause et. al. (2016) "Intermuscular force transmission along myofascial chains: a systematic review." *Journal of Anatomy*.

groups and nerve endings. This could even go some way to explaining the "irradiation effect" (the fact that consciously contracting one muscle tends to result in the reactive tension of surrounding muscle). Although that could also be due to the close proximity and interlinking between neural maps in the brain.

The fascia might in fact be one of the oldest features of the human body, allowing us to move and evade predation even before we even possessed a nervous system.

We are only just beginning to scratch the surface of the muscle fascia and what it is capable of.

We simply don't know enough for me to provide practical advice on how to "train the fascia" right now. Whatever the case, what everyone can agree on is that the fascia responds extremely well to training with a wide variety of different movements. The more you move, the more pliable and flexible the fascia will be and the less tension you will carry and the greater control you will have over the entire body. The fascia works best when hydrated, which keeps it spongey and resilient. Continually moving it in different directions seems to facilitate this suppleness, whereas a lack of movement may cause it to become rigid and stiff.

Likewise, moving in multiple "vectors" can potentially train and strengthen this tissue in angles that aren't described in a traditional "muscle-tendon-unit" model of human anatomy. We must train the entire system, not individual muscles.

The fascia is *everywhere* after all and can move in ways that our fixed muscle-tendon-units cannot. The fascia has potential for endless variety and adaptability. If you remain in purely fixed movement patterns like curls and squats, then the surrounding fascia will be extremely underdeveloped compared with the fascia that sits right next to it. It's not a huge leap to suggest that this may lead to discomfort and limited strength development.

In *Fascia Training: A Whole-System Approach*, authors Bill Parisi and Johnathan Allen even suggest that fascia training may partly be responsible for the "farmer strength" we encountered previously. Farmers are strong from labor work because they have strengthened the connective tissue at angles that are otherwise ignored, through submaximal loads with non-repetitive movement.

Likewise, the fascia will *thank you* for performing each pull up differently. Movement training that takes you through countless, unpredictable movement patterns is ideal for "fascia training." If research into fascia continues down this promising path, it is very likely to offer increasing support for these less rigid forms of training.

Finally, the fascia shows us once again just how truly adaptable the human body is. Training with specific movements may do more than building the necessary muscles. It may also develop tissues *between* those muscles to make us better at using them in a coordinated manner. As Myers puts it: "the body responds to demand."

"Supernatural" Movement

As this chapter has hopefully demonstrated, many of the limitations in our physicality are a result of the predictable and "safe" nature of our environments. By providing the body with more varied, chaotic, and *living* input, we can challenge it to grow in more ways and take advantage of its in-built adaptability.

But with that said, we must also be careful not to fall into the "natural is best" mode of thinking. We mustn't romanticize the lives of our ancestors at the expense of our current way of life.

Because adaptability is the key word here.

There isn't one correct way to move; we have adapted to different types of movement throughout our evolution. We came down from the trees, we lived in mountains, we swam, and now we sit at computers. This is not a flaw in our biology, it is an incredible example of optimization. Our bodies are remarkably adaptable, as are our brains.

Just take a look at the Moken people. This is a tribe that gets the vast majority of its food from the Andaman Sea. The children of this tribe have adapted to be able to see clearly underwater by actually *bending* the lenses in their eyes to counter the refractive properties of water. They can additionally narrow their pupils to the very limits of what is humanly possible. Moken people of all ages are capable of amazing free diving, which is a trait they share with the Bajau "sea nomads" who make similarly incredible free dives across the Philippines, Malaysia, and Indonesia. The Bajau regularly stay underwater for as long as thirteen minutes, diving to around two hundred feet. This is due to remarkable adaptations of the spleen.

But this is just another adaptation that is no more or less "correct" than our current one. We don't have amazing spleens because we *don't need them*.

The nervous system, it would seem, is designed to adapt to whatever "scenario" it finds itself in. That is to say that you could take your nervous system and place it into the body of a different animal, and it would adapt to the musculature, size, and weight of that animal to an extent.

(This is just a thought experiment, such a transplant would in fact be messy and terrible.)

A piece of evidence for this comes from studies that wire monkeys' brains up to robotic limbs. Given time, the monkey learns to move the robotic limb as though it were their own. New neural maps form, and they eventually start using the limb to peel oranges and pick up objects.[112]

The question is what inputs you want to feed the nervous system in order to produce the optimal results. The problem is that most of us don't feed the nervous system anything new. But that's not to say that we should be limited only by what has come before.

If we only focus on "Paleolithic man" then we would rarely lift anything heavier than 50 kg. We certainly wouldn't have needed to bench press 150 kg. And to be honest, there isn't really any natural pressure I can think of that would require us to walk on our hands.

To me, the remarkable fact that we *can* adapt to such varied demands is where the real excitement and potential of physical training lies. What else might the body be capable of?

I'm not purely interested in moving naturally, I'm interested in moving *supernaturally*. Taking cues from our history where appropriate is one small part of that.

---

112   Meel Velliste et al. (2008) "Cortical Control of a Prosthetic Arm for Self-Feeding." *Nature.* 453(7198):1098–1101.

In Defense of Modern Humans

I'd also like to take this moment to point out that modern humans aren't *all bad*.

We like to point the finger at our relative lack of movement, our shockingly bad diets, and our stressful lifestyles. I did it in the first chapter, in fact. There is certainly much we could improve on and we're pretty easy targets in that regard.

But there's another side to this story.

Imagine driving a car down the motorway. This is an *extremely* complex task that requires you to be fully aware of your surroundings at all times while simultaneously operating the steering wheel, pedals, and gear stick. Your brain needs to adapt to the unnatural high speeds and remain focused sometimes for hours on end.

Computer games, believe it or not, provide a similar challenge.

When we play sports like football, we challenge ourselves both physically and mentally, combining numerous different skills at once in a competitive environment. Meanwhile, athletes at the top of their games are shattering records on a constant basis, running faster than ever before, jumping higher, and swimming further.

More and more people are taking up physical hobbies and pushing their bodies in incredible ways. Free runners regularly post videos of themselves flipping across rooftops, while others lift weights in their spare time that would have been new world records a hundred years ago.

Thanks to the internet and the cumulative nature of collective human knowledge, we are better educated than ever before across multiple topics and fields. Thanks to travel, we have a huge wealth of experience. We juggle larger social networks and carry massive amounts of information about the world.

We have greater understanding of our bodies and access to the medicine to extend our lifespans far beyond what is natural. We survive diseases and injuries that would have been fatal only decades ago. Many of us supplement our diets with powerfully beneficial nutrients and adopt diets and lifestyles that benefit brain and body alike.

Sure, we sit too much. And we eat sugary foods. But it's not all bad; we are *bossing it* in many ways. The key is to take the very best from then *and* now, thus bringing out our fullest potential.

CHAPTER 11

The Mind-Body Connection

What does training mean to you? To me, it is the systematic application of challenge in order to develop desirable traits or skills.

To that end, it is truly baffling to me that so few of us actively train our cognitive abilities in the same way that we train our physical ones. Following from the ATSP system that I outlined in Chapter 2, it is *very* apparent that we could improve our ability in sports, as well as in our daily lives by developing mental traits and attributes.

Especially in an age where brain frequently trumps brawn, why do we insist on spending thousands of dollars on gym memberships and spending countless hours curling weights, only to do *nothing* to train our mind in the same way?

Why do you have a "legs day" but not a "brain day?"

You can train your memory in just the same way that you train your strength. You can train focus in the same way you can train mobility. And you can develop emotional intelligence just as you can learn to stand on your hands.

These skills will take you further in life than nearly anything else you can develop. You can build your brain like an impossibly intricate muscle.

Just think what might be possible!

Embodied Cognition—How Movement Shapes Your Mind

What's more, is that training your body and training your brain are *inseparably* linked. It hardly makes sense to do one without the other.

It is my belief that as long as computer scientists focus on creating disembodied programs to try and develop a true "general" artificial intelligence, they will be unsuccessful. The solution, I imagine, will come from giving that artificial lifeform a body to inhabit and an environment to explore—even if those things are virtual.

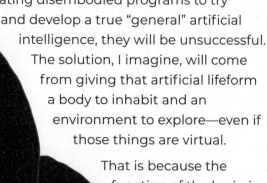

That is because the function of the brain is seemingly *inseparable* from the function of the body. And if this is correct, it provides us with vital insight that may help improve our cognitive abilities and further explain why we should.

Perhaps the best demonstration of how the mind and body connect, comes from the relatively new-yet-popular theory of embodied cognition. This theory suggests that many aspects of our cognition are in fact *grounded* in our physical experience. The topic is broad and comprised of many smaller ideas, but what I'm particularly interested in is embodied language processing, and the implications this has for broader cognitive processes.

This is a difficult idea to convey, but ask yourself for a moment how your brain "understands" language. When you learn a new language, you do so by using the original language as a reference—you *translate* the new words. But before you learn that initial language, what basis for reference is there?

If English is the "programming language," then what is the *machine code*?

To put it another way, how do people who have never been able to learn a language *think*?

At one point, philosophers and psychologists referred to this hypothetical base code as "mentalese." This was a "stand-in" for a working theory that would explain how we gave words meaning.

Embodied cognition provides another explanation. We gain our understanding of words from our experiences and interactions with the world. From our sensorimotor experience.

This means that when someone tells you a story about how they walked through the woods, you actually "experience" that story to an extent by relieving your own experience of being cold, of walking through woods, or of feeling the crunch of twigs underfoot.

Much of this might be described as visualization but it can also take a proprioceptive form or an auditory form.

Of course, this doesn't mean you need to have seen something or done something to understand it. Our brains are sophisticated enough to construct novel experiences out of our varied references.

This theory helps to answer a lot of questions. For instance, it explains why we so vividly picture the novels we read.[113] It explains why we use metaphor so frequently when describing abstract feelings and concepts. It may even explain how and why we gesticulate the way we do!

We can even see how this evolution may have occurred when looking at the origins of languages. According to author Daniel L. Everett's "sign progression" theory of language, the first written languages initially began with indexes, which developed into icons, which were followed by symbols. From this point, you only need add grammar and syntax to form a language.

An index is simply a sign (natural or otherwise) that provides additional information to a scene (for example, smoke is an index of fire). An icon takes this one step further as it can represent something that may not have been physically present and does so by imitating that thing—such as a drawing of a person. And finally, symbols can encode objects or concepts with no obvious link between the appearance or sound of the symbol and what

---

113   Brain imaging shows that we use the motor cortex when understanding words relating to motor actions | Victor de Lafaente & Ranulfo Romo (2004) "Language Abilities of Motor Cortex." *Neuron.* 41(2):178–180.

it is supposed to represent. This makes the symbol far more powerful.

When trying to communicate with someone in a foreign language, what do you turn to? Most of us will either point at objects or attempt to *mime* our meaning.

Words are symbols, but in order for symbols to *mean* anything, they need to *represent* something.

So, even when dealing with seemingly abstract concepts such as greed or math, our understanding might still be *rooted* in our physical experience. Could you understand math with no first-hand experience of quantity?

The ability for us to add these layers of abstraction is of course what separates us as uniquely human, and it is predominantly handled by the more recently evolved prefrontal regions of the brain.

There is plenty of evidence for embodied cognition. When we read or hear language, we see activation in sensorimotor parts of the brain almost as though we were personally carrying out or experiencing what is being described.[114]

This could also explain why we are increasingly seeing an important role for the cerebellum in a range of cognitive tasks. The cerebellum is a small part of the brain that translates to "little brain" (named by none other than Leonardo DaVinci). As you may recall from chapter three, this small part of the brain is responsible for taking in proprioceptive information, and then using that to help us prepare for movement.

---

114   Hauk O., and Tschentscher, N. (2013) "The body of evidence: what can neuroscience tell us about embodied semantics?" *Front. Psychol.* 4:50| Innocenti, A. et. al. (2014) "Understanding of action-related and abstract verbs in comparison: a behavioral and TMS study." *Cogn. Process.* 15(1):85–92.

The fact the cerebellum is involved in cognition, suggests that even when we are grappling with higher level concepts such as philosophy, morality, or theoretical physics, we are still relating everything back to our own physical, embodied experiences.[115]

We also see the premotor cortex light up during numerous cognitive tasks. Note that this is also the seat of our intuitive "physics engine." Like video game worlds, humans have an in-built understanding of physics that allows us to predict the movement of objects in the world. Of course, this understanding of physics has adapted from our own interactions with the world, which is probably why kids love knocking down Lego towers even more than they love building them.

Likewise, we gain a better understanding of physics and biomechanics every time we swing on the monkey bars, go down a slide, or do a cartwheel. That information is then used to help us make judgement calls when running to catch a ball on the field, or even when thinking of seemingly unrelated abstract concepts.

Or so it would seem. Note that I'm extrapolating a lot here, and this line of thinking is based on early theories. But still, it makes a lot of intuitive sense and explains an awful lot. I personally believe there is sufficient evidence to suggest that a *lot* of our thinking is related to our bodily experience.

---

115   Catherine J. Stoodley (2012) "The Cerebellum and Cognition: Evidence from Functional Imaging Studies." *Cerebellum.* 11(2):352–365.

FUNCTIONAL TRAINING AND BEYOND

How to Train the Brain: Neuroplasticity

This theory is interesting, but it also provides some insight as to how we might then train the brain to achieve greater focus, processing speed, and computational power.

Thanks to a phenomenon called neuroplasticity (or brain plasticity), this is possible.

Adaptability is our superpower as a species. A human baby is extremely vulnerable and underdeveloped compared with animals of other species. They can barely see inches in front of them, and they will take months if not years to learn basic movements like walking.

Why is this? It is often postulated that the answer is that we are so intelligent we need that extra time to bake. Our brains and therefore our skulls would be far too large to give birth to if we were born ready-made.

But this is only one explanation (after all, evolutionary forces could always just have enlarged the opening and brain size only somewhat correlates with intelligence). Another is that we are born relatively underdeveloped so as to be given the opportunity to adapt to our surroundings. This makes a human baby uniquely capable of rising to meet the unknown challenges that will face it. And it makes the human species uniquely capable of significant cultural change and development.

Think about it: your brain and body are nearly identical to those of a prehistoric human's. The only difference is the environment you were born into, an environment that was able to mold you into something far more intellectual, but in many ways less physically capable. And with this molded brain, you in turn gain the capacity to alter the environment around you!

What else could you have chosen to be?

Infant humans are then able to pick up language at an incredible pace, learn to walk, and familiarize themselves with countless concepts and ideas. My seventeen-month-old daughter, Emmy, seems to learn new words every single day, and it blows my mind! We have to be extremely careful what we say around her.

> **What else could you have chosen to be?**

This plasticity is a feature of the human brain that will continue into adulthood—albeit at a slower pace—and that will continue to set us apart from any other animal.

This also means that if we wish to grow and strengthen our brains, we can do so by practicing certain skills. The amazing thing is that this adheres to the precise same rule as training the body: the SAID principle.

If you want to become better at math, practice math.

If you want to improve your focus, practice focusing.

This is why London taxi drivers famously have more hippocampal gray matter. The hippocampus is the brain region where we store routes and other geographical information; by driving the huge network of roads every single day, those drivers literally *bulk up* that brain region like a muscle.[116] We see similar effects over and over again across disciplines. Cello players for instance, have increased

---

116   Eleanor A. Maguire. (2006) "London taxi drivers and bus drivers: A structural MRI and neuropsychological analysis." *Hippocampus.* 16(12):1091–1101.

representation in their neural maps corresponding to the fingertips of the left hand.

Just as swinging a baseball bat can develop traits and physical attributes that can then be useful in other sports, so too can developing brain regions specific to one task ultimately assist in others.

For instance, we now know that music training can have a huge number of broad benefits for visual abilities, cognitive processing speed, and more.[117] Playing high-paced, first-person shooting games like *Call of Duty* meanwhile can boost decision making and visual acuity.[118] Quickly deciding which enemy needs your attention first and remembering to switch weapons can prepare you for making *other* high-pressure decisions out in the real world.

The exciting implication of all this is that we can actually "choose" the brain we want to a degree, by focusing on specific skills and the corresponding brain regions that we want to develop. You can design your own brain!

You can design your own brain!

Complex Movements: Catnip for the Brain

Throughout this book, I have been looking for "bang for your buck" exercises that would develop the maximum

---

117   Anna Carolina Rodrigues et al. (2010) "Musical training, neuroplasticity and cognition." *Dementia & Neuropsychologia.* 4(4)
118   Vikranth R. Bejjanki. et al. (2014) "Action video game play facilitates the development of better perceptual templates." *PNAS* 111(47):16961–16966.

number of physical traits and attributes. While I'm going to save my conclusions for the final chapter, suffice to say that this list will consist mostly of compound and *complex* movements.

We can apply the same logic to brain training. What types of training will yield the very best results? What are the best "value" brain-training exercises?

Guess what: it turns out the precise same complex movements are very high up on the list.

This makes a lot of sense. We've just seen that the brain is built-upon physical interactions with the world. And we've seen that practicing certain skills can enlarge the relevant brain regions. It follows that practicing complex movements will enhance our ability to process and understand concepts.

Complex movements such as the lizard crawl, juggling, dance choreography, martial arts, and more all require a *huge* amount of information processing. These are multisensory experiences that require our full attention and awareness. They are like catnip for the brain! Refining your golf swing, your planche, or your roundhouse kick each require fine tuning of neural maps, through constant trial and error, and a cascade of plasticity-enhancing chemicals.

Perhaps this was one of the key factors that *influenced* the human brain to evolve as uniquely as it has. By raising ourselves up onto two feet and opening up countless new ways to use our limbs, we created an incentive for greater plasticity. As others have observed, human beings are the only animals capable of mimicking nearly every *other* animal.

Varied Exercise for Varied Cognitive Benefits

It has long been known that aerobic conditioning (going for long runs or walks) is extremely good for the brain. This increases BDNF which in turn triggers greater brain plasticity. This makes some sense, given that running will provide greater blood flow to the brain. From an evolutionary standpoint, a long run might be an opportunity to map new locations for later reference. An ability to cover large distances and thus experience varied terrain might have been *another* factor that stimulated brain development.

But studies *also* now show us that weight training can increase other cognitive abilities, including associative memory and executive function.[119] This may be due to an increase in IGF-1 (Insulin Like Growth Factor) that contributes to both hypertrophy *and* the formation of new brain cells and connections. Combining aerobic exercise and strength training provides dual benefits.

But it seems that the most profound growth comes from complex movement. Exercises that incorporate balancing, asynchronous limb movement, and manipulation all appear to increase the size of the basal ganglia, which may have direct effects on focus, visual-spatial processing, and more.[120]

Research from study authors Tracy and Ross Alloway shows that climbing trees, crawling on beams, and *running barefoot* all significantly increase working memory. It seems that MovNat has the right idea! And note how these

---

119   Teresa Liu-Ambrose et al. (2010) "Resistance Training and Executive Functions: A 12-Month Randomised Controlled Trial." *Archives of Internal Medicine.* 170(2):170–178.
120   Becker L et al. (2016) "Exercise-induced changes in basal ganglia volume and their relation to cognitive performance." *Journal of Neurology.* 1(5):19–24.

are all things that we *loved* doing as children and would *naturally* do in the wild.[121]

The benefits may arise as they require us to process information in the cerebellum and motor regions in parallel with the prefrontal cortex.

It appears that combining these two types of skills is particularly important for the most profound changes. Tasks that combine proprioception with planning, orientation, and calculation provide an excellent mental workout that sitting in front of a computer and typing just can't match. Another excellent example according to Alloway is surfing, as this requires you to not only balance on the board, but also to think about the incoming wave and getting yourself into the best position to catch it.[122]

Remember when I told you not to completely discard those balance boards? Perhaps they are better for your brain than they are for your ankle stability. Juggling while balancing might be one of the closest things to catching a wave that you can do from the comfort of your own home.

That said, you may be fine sticking with lizard crawls and bear crawls. It turns out that quadrupedal movements of this nature are fantastic for "cognitive flexibility" as well as "joint repositioning"[123] all on their own.

---

121   Ross G and Tracy Alloway (2015) "The Working Memory Benefits of Proprioceptively Demanding Training: A Pilot Study." *Percept Mot Skills*. 120(3):766–775 | Claudia Voelcker-Rehage (2013) "Structural and Functional Brain Changes Related to Different Types of Physical Activity Across the Life Span." *Neuroscience and Biobehavioral Reviews*. 37(9 Pt B):2268–2295.

122   *New Scientist The Collection: The Scientific Guide to an Even Better You* | This might also explain why author Steven Kotler experienced his first flow state while surfing.

123   Martyn J Matthews et. al. (2016) "Quadrupedal Movement Training Improves Markers of Cognition and Joint Repositioning." *Hum. Mov. Sci.* 47:70–80.

(Another of the very best complex skills you can develop to trigger significant growth in numerous brain areas is juggling. This is supported by countless studies.)

The bottom line? Our entire nervous system is built to facilitate complex movement through a challenging and chaotic environment—where danger and opportunity are around every turn. Sitting in front of a computer and repeating the same monotonous tasks, heady though they may be, simply can't compare.

If you want a young, limber brain, then you will benefit from using your body to its fullest potential.

Fine Motor Control

That said, it would be remiss of me not to point out that there are other forms of "complex movement." Not all of them involve leaping and crawling about like Spider-Man. Case in point: cursive.

That's right. The dying art of handwriting is the *perfect* example of an extremely complex movement that goes well beyond the scope of what an animal might be capable of. Just think of the countless neural pathways necessary to form each letter and connect it to the next in a seamless flow of movement. Think how precisely the tiny twitch muscle fibers in the forearms must contract to apply just the right amount of pressure, at just the right angle and trajectory. And consider that we do all this unconsciously while simultaneously writing the prose in our mind's eye!

This is fantastic training for the premotor cortex, which in turn is critical in a number of different tasks. We've already seen how this brain region is used when making physics calculations, but it is also key in speech and even language comprehension.

Consider the case of a young boy described in the book *The Brain That Changes Itself* by Norman Doidge. This unnamed child suffered from poor language comprehension, awkward handwriting, and muddled speech. He attended a special school called the Arrowsmith School, set-up by Barbara Arrowsmith-Young, where he was tasked with tracing detailed images. This training quickly enhanced his ability to speak in longer sentences, communicate effectively with others, and generally demonstrate greater verbal fluency.

It is a great loss then, to think that children throughout the world are no longer practicing fine, articulate movement. Even fewer adults engage in these practices, with most of us preferring to type instead.

Playing piano, coloring, sewing, or playing *Operation!* could all be useful practices.

As could writing with your nondominant hand.

An Argument for Ambidexterity Training

Ambidexterity is something that very few people spend time developing these days, and yet I believe it can have tremendous benefit.

In sports, being ambidextrous will give you more options. You can throw with either hand or throw a powerful hook from either side. In the gym, ambidexterity can help you develop a more balanced physique, as you are able to exert equal control (and thus strength) when curling/pressing/pulling on either side.

Being ambidextrous can be useful when handling objects with both hands.

The very act of developing ambidextrousness might also help to boost plasticity (as this is an extremely demanding physical skill to develop), while also thickening key brain regions such as the corpus callosum.

The corpus callosum is a thick bundle of nerves that bridges the two hemispheres of the brain and may thus contribute to "whole brain thinking." Studies examining Einstein's brain found that he had a thicker corpus callosum, which may have facilitated greater creativity.

While it is circumstantial evidence at best, many famously creative individuals were known to be ambidextrous, including Ben Franklin, Leonardo da Vinci, and Albert Einstein. Nikola Tesla apparently trained himself to be ambidextrous, saying:

"I am ambidextrous now, but then I was left-handed and had comparatively little strength in my right arm."

The belief that ambidexterity could be useful was once popular. In fact, in the early twentieth century, the Ambidextral Culture Society was established by Hughlings Jackson to promote "two-braindness" and contribute to the betterment of mankind.

Jackson wrote:

> Each hand shall be absolutely independent of the other in the production of any kind

of work whatever...if required, one hand shall be writing an original letter, and the other shall be playing the piano, with no diminution of the power of concentration.

I concede that this is a controversial subject still. Some people fear that training ambidexterity can actually lead to a number of issues. However, this concern (I believe) is based on the incorrect reading of studies that link ambidexterity to developmental issues such as stuttering. It is more likely that in some cases, developmental issues lead to both ambidexterity and other dysfunctions.

There is evidence for this, as stated by Johanna Barbara Sattler in a review of the literature:

> Systematic investigations of the second group of subjects always revealed perinatal cerebral disturbances. This paper discusses the thesis that insufficient oxygen supply to the brain in the perinatal period of life mainly affects the function of the dominant cerebral hemisphere that is responsible for the congenital handedness.

In short, it is highly unlikely that developing ambidexterity will lead to cognitive deficits. Quite the opposite, in fact! Speaking from personal experience, I have been practicing ambidexterity for over a decade now with no severe side-effects.

(What was I writing about, again?)

How do you train for ambidexterity? I recommend practicing cursive with the nondominant hand. This will, at the very least, provide the benefits of any highly demanding motor skill, while also giving you the opportunity to engage in fine motor movements. You could get added benefit too, from practicing something that would be inherently beneficial such as journaling.

Does this practice transfer to other skills? I was surprised to learn as a new parent that toddlers aren't able to brush their teeth themselves effectively until they have learned to write. It is that practice that helps them develop the fine motor control, so I would say yes!

(And of course, this also highlights another option for developing ambidexterity—brushing with the nondominant hand.)

Visualization

Another awesome study that highlights the importance of physicality as it relates to cognitive performance showed how athletes (wrestlers specifically) would approach a task differently from non-athletes and with better results.

When asked to mentally rotate physical objects, elite wrestlers appear to use their motor regions more than the control group (who presumably relied more on visual processes). By using this strategy, the wrestlers were capable of significantly superior mental rotation![124]

124   David Moreau (2012) "The role of motor processes in three-dimensional mental rotation: Shaping cognitive processing via sensorimotor experience." *Learning and Individual Differences.* 22(3):354–359.

But this is not to say that there are not scenarios where superior *visualization* is also an asset. In fact, many tasks require us to visualize objects and manipulate them in our mind's eye. Likewise, we use visualization in problem solving, navigation, and more. Much of our daydreaming and creativity takes the form of visualization.

We have already discussed Einstein's brain in relation to the corpus callosum, but there are some other interesting differences. For instance, Einstein had particularly large inferior parietal lobes. These are brain regions associated with spatial and mathematical reasoning and may have helped him with his imagining.[125]

This concurs with what we know. The famous story goes that Einstein had the breakthrough that led to his theory of special relativity while working in a patent office. This kind of repetitive work is known to activate a network of brain regions referred to as the "default mode network" or the "imagination network."

Einstein describes visualizing an idea, and intuitively understanding from that how the universe worked:

> If I pursue a beam of light with the velocity c (velocity of light in a vacuum), I should observe such a beam of light as an electromagnetic field at rest though spatially oscillating.
>
> There seems to be no such thing, however, neither on the basis of experience nor according to Maxwell's equations.
>
> From the very beginning it appeared to me intuitively clear that, judged from the standpoint of such an observer, everything would have to happen

---

125   This blending of sensory modes to make sense of the world can be referred to as "cognitive-semantic blending.

according to the same laws as for an observer who, relative to the Earth, was at rest. For how should the first observer know or be able to determine, that he is in a state of fast uniform motion?

One sees in this paradox the germ of the special relativity theory is already contained.

I personally *love* the idea that our brains are so powerful as to allow us to intuit laws that determine the movement of planets and stars.

Note that although the reasoning attached to this is occurring in the default mode network and frontal, more recently evolved brain areas, it is being *fueled* by activity in the sensorimotor regions.

But this also shows how a different approach to thinking can sometimes be more suited to a specific problem. In Einstein's case, a kind of visual, mathematical intuition.

The good news? You can actually develop your visualization skills. Playing computer games can help you to develop greater spatial awareness, whereas "image streaming" is a technique that may be able to do the same.

This practice involves closing your eyes and then allowing your imagination to conjure up whatever image it likes. Don't try and force it, just let it come. Now *describe* what you are seeing out loud and continually describe the scene as it changes.

(If you find nothing comes to your mind's eye at first, you can give it a little nudge by consciously choosing the first image, or by "interpreting" the patterns that form in front of your eyes.)

This strategy was invented by Win Wenger PhD and has helped many people to successfully improve the vividness of their "mind's eye." Developing improved working memory can also help, which we will discuss shortly.

There are other strategies that work well too. You can practice mental rotation of objects for example, by looking for items in your current field of view and then imagining what they would look like from different angles.

Big Idea Meditation

If you are going to spend time bulking up the sensorimotor parts of the brain, it also makes sense to dedicate some attention to the higher-order functions at the front of the brain. Our prefrontal cortex is what gives us the ability to plan, reason, and juggle complex ideas. It allows us to add abstract layers, and to juggle and combine information. Unfortunately, much like the rest of our brains, we often neglect to use these skills.

One solution I enjoy from the book *Deep Work* by Cal Newport, is to use a form of meditation called "productive meditation." This involves dedicating a set period to solving a specific problem. This isn't traditionally what we think of as the restful practice of meditation (more on this in the next chapter) but is rather a directed effort to focus the brain and utilize its problem-solving capabilities.

I also propose a similar-yet-distinct approach that I call "big idea meditation." The aim here is to grapple with a concept that is huge, creative, and potentially even impossible to fathom. You are literally stretching the capabilities of your brain and learning to think way outside the box. This is something I have been practicing since I was very young, and it's actually a fun form of brain training.

So, for example, I will often try to think of explanations for problems I read about in New Scientist, or come up with what I think might be satisfactory answers to the birth of the universe or the nature of consciousness. Of course, I am not usually particularly successful! But sometimes I find myself scratching against the edge of what my brain can grasp, and that is where I believe there is a possibility for growth.

This trains you to "think big" in other areas, and to make far-flung connections. This has led to some of the ideas in this book.

As a programmer, I often enjoy taking on hypothetical programming challenges ("how would I build this app?") which is particularly rewarding, as it provides a framework for my thinking.

Other times, I might be less grandiose. I enjoy thinking about how I would write my own James Bond film. I have about a hundred issues of Iron Man planned out in my head![126]

---

126   In case any Marvel executives are reading: Iron Man's next armor should have a combat drone that follows him around. Also, he should design an "Iron Man Buster" suit that is designed to be able to take *him* out if he ever goes rogue. Of course, this armor is stolen and used against him. BY HIS ILLEGITIMATE SON. This stuff is gold, right?

Working Memory

In most cases, the brain will use a combination of visual, auditory, and motor experience in order to form a cohesive picture that you can use to reason, imagine, and problem solve.

This is also how memory likely works. The hippocampus stores most of our memories in what can be thought of as an index. Highly connected to many other regions of the brain, encoded memories play out by reigniting the senses as they were at the time of the event, or in the sequence that they were learned. When you remember the classroom you spent time in as a child, your brain lights parts of your visual cortex, your piriform cortex (which identifies smells), and more.

This ability to call up information and manipulate it in the "visuo-spatial scratchpad" is referred to as our working memory. Working memory contains the information we are currently manipulating and working with. Hence the name!

Likewise, working memory is what allows us to remember a phone number while we look for a pen to write it down, or to carry over numbers when performing sums in our head. It is also the working memory that we use to store all the positions of the chess pieces on a chess board while playing chess, or the positions of our teammates on the pitch when playing team sports. Working memory allows us to move fluidly through the environment, maintaining a mental model of our surroundings without us necessary being able to see everything.

But working memory is limited to only a few bits of information. This is generally written as 7 +/- 2. That is to say that someone with a poor working memory would be able to retain only five numbers while looking for that pen, whereas someone with a good working memory could manage nine. There are ways around this though, such as repeating the numbers back (to help them last longer) or "chunking" numbers together. For instance, you might only be able to remember five letters, but you can remember many more by remembering five *words* comprising of letters. Likewise, you can store a six and a three as a single unit: 63. Area codes don't count, seeing as we can retrieve them from long-term storage. We've rehearsed those strings often enough that the neural pathways have been reinforced.

When you consider the multisensory nature of working memory, you see that this explanation is not quite sufficient. After all, if we create a representation of the world by combining senses, how do you define a "bit" of information anymore?

To illustrate this, consider games of "blindfold chess" in which players will actually play chess without seeing or touching the pieces. They are thus required to maintain a mental map of the entire chess board! Not impressed? How about people who can play *simultaneous* games of blindfold chess at once! One player, Alexander Alekhine, played twenty-six games of blindfold chess, wining sixteen, drawing five, and losing five!

Sherlock Holmes, eat your heart out!

We've already seen that you can train working memory with quadrupedal movements and balancing tasks, but games like chess provide another excellent way to strengthen this skill. Another option is a form of brain training known as "Dual N-Back Training."

Dual N-Back is one of the only forms of brain-training game that is backed by a considerable body of research.

The task involves watching for sequences of numbers or letters as they appear in a grid and identifying repetitions of either the letter or the position. The catch is that you aren't looking for immediate repetitions, but rather repetitions that occurred "N" number of moves ago. Was the position or letter the same two times ago? Three times ago?

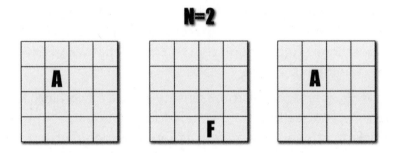

Working memory is closely linked with attention and focus, where the ability to concentrate on the mental experience may be the limiting factor. This may explain, at least to some extent, how the effects are then able to crossover into a range of different activities.

Amazingly, this actually *includes* physically demanding tasks. Not only could working memory help you to split the bill, not only could it help a footballer to keep track of teammates, it could also lead directly to improved physical mastery. In one study, it was shown that training focus and working memory through a video game called *Musical Catch* could actually improve the walking speed of participants aged sixty to eighty.[127]

I cannot guarantee you'll be able to play twenty-six simultaneous games of blindfold chess, however.

---

127   Nagamatsu, L. S. et. al. (2013) "Mind-Wandering and falls risk in older adults." *APA PsycNet.*

CHAPTER 12

Enhancing Plasticity for Skills and Intelligence

Brain plasticity shows us that the brain can adapt to demands just as the body can. In fact, the brain is far *more* plastic than the body; we likely haven't even scratched the surface of what is possible. It is this adaptation that gives blind individuals heightened hearing as neighboring brain areas grow to compensate for the atrophied auditory cortex.

More incredible still are hemispherectomy patients, individuals who have had half of their brain removed, only to retain most of their cognitive function. This is possible as the remaining half adapts to take on the responsibilities of the missing. Entire functions of the brain are migrated to the remaining half of the brain as huge amounts of rewiring take place.

This plasticity is what makes brain training a worthy pursuit. It means we can sculpt our brains like our bodies. But the question then is: what to do with this potential? How do we make our brains *more* plastic, and how can we ensure that our training affects our brains the way we want it to?

Defining and Increasing Intelligence

There are two predominant schools of thought when it comes to the nature of intelligence. For many years, inspired by the ideas of psychologist Howard Gardener, it was believed that there were multiple "types" of intelligence. A person could therefore be intelligent in math, but not so good linguistically. Gardener's original list also included some dubious factors, such as "naturalistic intelligence."

Either way, this led to the creation of many intelligence tests that focused on just a single one of these domains. What was found though, was that there was a definite *correlation* between scores on these tests. That is to say, someone who was good at math was also more likely to have better linguistic skills. The conclusion this time was that there must be some overarching *general* intelligence that feeds down into each of these subdomains. This "general intelligence" was thus referred to as the "G-factor" and is what many intelligence tests measure today.

There is plenty of evidence both for "modular" intelligence *and* for general intelligence. We can see that certain skills reside in specific brain regions, supporting a modular approach. But likewise, we know that the integration of these disparate areas is also extremely important.

So, who is right?

And moreover, what *is* "G?"

I believe that the following answer satisfies both camps:

G = Plasticity + Training

If you are fortunate enough to have a highly plastic brain, you will have been better able to grow the individual brain areas *and* the connections between them. You *could* be better at one type of thinking than another, but if you are exceptionally talented in that one area, chances are that you have the capacity to learn and develop—thus you will more than likely be above average in other areas too.

Thus, we see a correlation between different subsets of intelligence *and* the overall versatility of mental capacity.

That is why I consider "plasticity" to be a "Super Trait." This is a trait that can help you to gain other traits more quickly and effectively.

Given the right opportunity and environment, if your brain is highly plastic, then you can quickly improve both in individual skills and in general connectivity. Given the right training, you can better improve the individual areas and the efficiency of any information stored.

Tapping into Plasticity

If plasticity is a Super Trait, then what can we do to enhance it? And how can we employ the best strategies to learn new skills and reshape our brains?

The general process underpinning plasticity is simple and can be explained by a single rule:

"Neurons that fire together, wire together. Neurons that fire apart, grow apart."

This law is what allows an adaptable brain to develop the skills it needs. From this one global rule, we learn to walk and talk, and to read and write. Optionally, we can learn to program or walk on our hands.

It is a simple but extremely powerful algorithm.

If you perform one action followed immediately by another, and you continue to repeat that pattern over and over, eventually you will form a new connection between those two actions.

Likewise, if you hear a bell every time someone gives you delicious food, you will develop a physiological reaction to the sound of the bell—as Pavlov famously demonstrated.

This corresponds with new networks forming in your brain as the dendrites of one neuron reach out to the axon of the other and a synapse (connection) is formed. This is why you can't hear the letters "ABCD" without instantly thinking "EFGH." You've heard those stimuli in that sequence so many times, that the entire pattern of neurons fires without any conscious effort on your part.

This is how we learn new skills: through repeated rote performance of movement patterns that link the necessary neurons. These new neural patterns will be transcribed via your DNA, and the procedural memory will be stored.[128]

If you continue to repeat that action some more, the connection will become stronger and stronger. Myelination will occur—meaning that the axons will be insulated by a myelin sheath that provides protection and allows signals to travel faster. Eventually, you can perform that entire dance routine almost instinctively. As Bruce Lee would say: "It hits all by itself."

---

[128]   This same process explains why the motor cortex is arranged the way it is—like a map of a tiny person. That's because the parts of the body that are anatomically closer to one another are more likely to be used consecutively or simultaneously. Again: neurons that fire together, wire together.

FUNCTIONAL TRAINING AND BEYOND

But if you stop practicing, eventually the connection weakens. Eventually, you might forget the movements entirely. The neurons that fire apart *wire apart*.

This is also how we form unwanted habits (called negative plasticity). It explains some limitations in our movement, too. Move your arms symmetrically over and over again, and eventually you start to wire representations of the two sides of your body together. This makes it harder for you to then untangle that web and move the limbs powerfully, independently. This is "negative plasticity."

This process is further enhanced by the action of chemicals called neurotransmitters. These are released into the brain from neurovessicles (tiny "sacks" of chemicals) found at the axon terminals (the end point of the neuron). When an action potential jumps from one neuron to another across the synapse, chemicals are released from these tiny sacs that then affect the surrounding networks. These neurotransmitters modulate the behavior of nearby neurons by interacting with them via receptor sites that receive and react to specific chemicals.

Other chemicals can also interact with neural networks this way, including hormones produced throughout the body, and nutrients/drugs that we consume orally.

We'll discuss more about neurotransmitters in the next chapter, but for now, know that certain chemicals act as rewards for positive experiences and therefore help to encourage the formation of new connections in the brain.[129]

---

129   Very negative experiences can also drastically increase the likelihood of a long-term memory/connection being formed, which is why we often remember where we were when we received bad news. Psychologists refer to this phenomenon as a "flashbulb memory."

Dopamine is one of the neurotransmitters that is most responsible for this process.[130] This "reward hormone" is closely linked with motivation. It is produced in vast amounts when we are working toward a goal (which keeps us motivated) or when dealing with novel and interesting stimuli. When things go to plan, dopamine helps to encourage the formation of new connections. Dopamine is closely linked to BDNF, which we know is a key modulator of plasticity.

This plays out each time that we perform an action. When you prepare to perform your golf swing, you do so first by visualizing how you want that swing to go. You then execute the swing. If the performance matches or exceeds your expectations, then positive hormones are released and the neural pathways that led you there are strengthened.

But if you miss the shot, then a different neurochemical and hormonal cocktail is released. This is a prediction error, and here the cascade of chemicals actually increases your attention and alertness, thereby helping you to perform the movement more efficiently next time. The neural pathway that led to the incorrect swing is *not* cemented so strongly.

This is why practicing something you're already good at is so rewarding, whereas practicing something you find challenging can feel frustrating. But stick with it and over countless repetitions, you forge deeply embedded neural networks that have been endlessly refined to perfection.[131]

---

130   Hongjoo J. Lee et. al. (2006) "Role of Substantia Nigra-Amydala Connections in Surprise-Induced Enhancement of Attention." *J. Neurosci.* 26(22):6077–6081.
131   The same process is what helps us refine that physics engine I talked about in the last chapter. The brain is often described as a "prediction" machine, especially by the Bayesian brain hypothesis, where one of its main functions is to predict what will happen next.

Imagine a small child learning to stand. He or she will fall over thousands of times and each time, the brain will save that data. Every small twitch of a muscle fiber that helps prevent them from falling will move them a little closer to success the next time.

This neural basis explains the "Process of Learning Motor Skills" that was postulated by P. Fitts & M. Posner in 1967, and that is still popular in sports psychology today. The model describes three distinct phases:

- Cognitive

- Associate

- Autonomous

Essentially, each new skill requires a lot of conscious effort and attention to begin with—before those neural maps exist—but they eventually become second nature once the correct pathways have been formed.

Skill Acquisition

Raising plasticity can help us to boost intelligence across multiple domains. However, understanding that plasticity also provides us with an advantage when it comes to learning new skills. How do we use this information to improve our performance in sports, in the gym, and in life?

Firstly, the mechanisms of neuroplasticity highlight the importance of being mindful of our practice. The rewarding chemicals won't be as strong if your mind is elsewhere. It also shows us the usefulness of an *immediate* feedback loop when attempting to learn a new skill. Once again, this demonstrates how the brain *loves* to learn, and why computer games are so inherently addictive.

It also emphasizes the value in what Pavel Tsatsouline refers to as "greasing the groove." This practice involves rehearsing a movement over and over again, in order to refine the neural pathways.

Pavel views many strength exercises as skills. That includes seemingly simple movements like pull ups. By refining neural pathways, you can perform more efficient repetitions, while also recruiting the optimal motor units for the job at hand.

Traditional strength training that involves breaking down muscle fibers and incurring muscle damage reduces the amount of reps you can put in. If you go extremely hard and need a whole week to recover, you add in as many repetitions.

But what if you flipped this concept on its head and simply performed three to five pull ups multiple times throughout the day? By the end of the week you could have racked up hundreds of repetitions without incurring any muscle damage.

This strategy has even more benefit when applied to more complicated movements that are challenging to learn and master. A perfect example is the handstand. I have been practicing this movement multiple times a day, every single day, except when injured. As such, my body has been able to carefully refine the way it handles proprioceptive input when I'm upside down. Over time, I've been able to better align my center of gravity and stack my joints, as well as to detect slight imbalances and adjust for them using tiny contractions. (It's still not perfect!)

This also shows us another tool we can use for training: visualization. In the last chapter, we saw that using your mind's eye could light up brain areas as though you were actually engaged in any given task. It follows then, that you can actually strengthen connections simply through mental rehearsal. Indeed, that is what the evidence strongly suggests. By mentally rehearsing dance choreography or a golf swing, we can actually reinforce the neural networks responsible for those movements and improve memorization.

Author Norman Doidge points out some fascinating examples of this being put to good use. For instance, he tells the story of Anatoly Sharansky, a human rights activist who was falsely imprisoned for spying in 1977. Sharansky spent a lot of time in isolation, and to avoid going insane, he played blindfold chess against himself. Upon his release, he had developed his skills to the point of being able to defeat then-world champion Garry Kasparov. Rudiger Gamm is likewise referred to as a "human calculator," and was able to develop those skills using nothing but mental practice.

We can even improve our motor skills by simply *observing* others performing them (like Taskmaster, for the comic nerds out there). This may be possible due to the activation of mirror neurons, neurons that fire when we observe something happening to someone else. This may even explain why we enjoy watching other people dance.

(And why I love watching Jackie Chan/Goku punch people in the face...)

Spaced Learning

If you want to get even more benefit from your skill training, you should consider spacing it out effectively throughout the day/training session.

Spaced learning is a tool that is often employed when memorizing factual information. Here, the student will repeatedly study the same content in three blocks, with two ten-minute breaks in between each segment. This significantly improves retention versus studying for the same amount of time in a single sitting[132] and appears to encourage that information to be moved into the long-term memory. That may be because the break gives the neural pathways time to return to their resting state before you reactivate them. In other words, you are studying the information *three times* rather than just once, as far as the body is concerned.

You could apply this process to a workout by electing to practice a movement such as the handstand at the start of the workout, in the middle of the workout, and again at the end of the workout.

And seeing as motor unit recruitment is key for max strength, this could even help to encourage greater strength gains. That is very much speculation though.

---

132   Paul Kelley and Terry Whatson (2013) "Making long-term memories in minutes: a spaced learning pattern from memory research in education." *Frontiers in Human Neuroscience*. 7:589.

Enhancing Plasticity

While these strategies can help us to utilize our brain's natural plasticity, it would be better still if we could actually *enhance* that plasticity such that we effortlessly encoded more information. If plasticity is a Super Trait that can be trained, how do we train it?

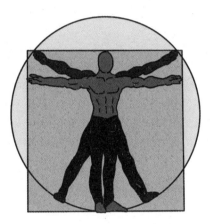

Well, like anything else, the answer is by using it.

Many things can elevate plasticity-supporting chemicals. These include a number of "nootropic" substances such as lion's mane mushroom or magnesium threonate.[133] Omega 3 fatty acid is fantastic for brain plasticity too, and sleep is an absolute *must*—a lot of brain reorganization and memory consolidation occurs when we are sleeping.[134] You can even increase plasticity by wearing tDCS headsets (transcranial direct current simulation) that run small

133   Nootropics are "smart drugs" that enhance some aspect of cognitive performance. We'll be meeting them shortly.
134   As this is a book about training and it is already rather comprehensive, I won't look into sleep in detail here. Suffice to say that those wishing to enhance their performance for sports and for life should definitely focus on optimizing their sleep.

electric currents through the brain to increase the resting potential of neurons in specific brain regions.[135] And we've seen that going for runs will increase BDNF, particularly in the hippocampus (whereas resistance training leads to more IGF-1).

But the simplest and most profound way to make the brain more plastic is simply to keep learning and keep challenging it. As we saw earlier, learning new movement patterns results in the release of BDNF which is used to form and refine the necessary neural patterns. The act of learning requires this chemical and thus it increases.

That BDNF sticks around and makes it easier to learn *other* new things. Likewise, learning a new language, learning to program, or picking up an instrument can all help you to increase plasticity, and thereby increase further learning.

Does this mean that you might find your bench press numbers go up if you are also learning a new language? As far as I'm aware, there are no studies looking at this, but it is certainly a reasonable hypothesis. That said, I imagine the strongest effect would be seen the other way around. Practicing bear crawls along tree branches could help you to more quickly study new languages.

Amazingly, playing computer games can actually increase global brain connectivity,[136] which is not all that surprising given the way it simulates being in a new environment *and* requires new motor skills as you learn the new inputs (virtual reality could someday take this to another level).

---

135   This definitely works to some degree, but there is a lack of long-term studies. And having tried using a consumer product to this end, I can also say that the practicality is somewhat lacking!

136   Diankun Gong (2015) et. al. "Enhanced functional connectivity and increased gray matter volume of insula related to action video game playing." *Scientific Reports.* 5(9763):9763.

Just like learning to balance or dance, this is a multisensory learning experience that requires constant refinement and is perfectly tailored to excite the dopaminergic pathways. The great thing about computer games is that each time you pick up a new one, you're forced to figure out entirely new skills and rules.

One day, I believe that VR (virtual reality) could take this to a whole different level by fully immersing us into new worlds with new rules to learn. VR might just prove to be the ultimate form of "brain training."

This kind of multisensory challenge could even explain the highly plastic nature of a child's brain. Some have suggested that the incredible plasticity seen in infant brains is the result of a pre-determined "critical period" with a defined cut-off point. After this crucial period, the adult brain continues to learn but at a much slower pace.

But rather than this being a hardwired window of opportunity, I believe that this plasticity is determined by the context. Imagine being born into a world where *nothing* is familiar. You don't recognize a single object around you, and nor do you even understand the concept of "objects." You have yet to learn that sounds and images are very often tied together. You can't lift your own hand to your face with any degree of reliability, and even digestion is something that doesn't come naturally yet.

Every single interaction is an extremely rich learning experience across ALL of the senses.

Is it any wonder then that the brain is absolutely *awash* with chemicals that enhance learning?

Perhaps the adult brain could be just as plastic, if only we were able to unlearn everything we know about our environment, physics, and our own bodies.

Again, maybe in the future we could use VR to plunge ourselves into equally unfamiliar worlds and see huge changes in our brain plasticity. Until then, the best thing we can do is to keep learning, keep exploring,[137] and keep *moving*.

Learning High-Level Skills

In the previous chapter, I discussed the roles that the cerebellum and motor cortex—brain regions typically associated with movement—play in higher-order thinking. We saw that our experience of moving through the world is what underpins our ability to reason, and that practicing complex movement could actually enhance working memory and even creative problem-solving. The cerebellum has even been hypothesized to contribute to ideation and planning, thanks to its ability to predict and refine patterns of behavior. This crucial role could help to explain why the cerebellum has roughly sixty-nine billion neurons, as compared with the roughly sixteen billion found in the cerebral cortex.

But of course, we can also improve specific higher-order skills by training in those things. Practicing a particular skill can "bulk up" associated brain regions, which can in turn make us better at said skills. To return briefly to the ATSP Hierarchy, this shows the specific physical attributes that underpin our traits and skills. It's more nuanced than "music skill lies in one brain area, art in another." Rather,

---

137   Exploring and encountering unfamiliar environments is a key factor in brain plasticity. It has been suggested by many that the sense of awe you feel when coming across a truly spectacular scene is actually your brain attempting to recalibrate for the sheer amount of sensory information and your realization as to your relative *smallness* in the grand scheme of things. This might be why we get a similar sense of awe when watching documentaries about space (just me?).

FUNCTIONAL TRAINING AND BEYOND

music ability is defined by many traits such as creativity, rhythm, pitch, each of which resides in a specific brain area. The size and efficiency of that brain region is the *attribute*. We can thus supplement music practice with other activities such as rhythm or pitch training.

What's more fascinating still, is that this can actually change the way we think. The sheer range and variety in the way people think may surprise you. I was shocked to learn that not everyone has an internal monologue, for example, whereas mine never shuts up! Similarly, while I recall the positions of items in room by recalling a visual "snapshot" of that room, a friend of mine achieves the same thing by referring to something akin to an "associative array." That is to say he has memorized the items as a list, along with where each item is in relation to another.

Perhaps these differences are somewhat genetic. Perhaps they've been *reinforced* by my years of writing 10,000 words a day, and his training in mathematics through university. Studies show that writing activates brain areas associated with language (Wernicke's area and Broca's area) along with visualization. The writer pictures what they want to say and then narrates it.[138] It has been hypothesized that this leaves a writer more likely to narrate their own experiences, too.

Developing skills like writing, speaking, programming, and math could have profound implications for the way we think too. That's because tools like language, programming, and math provides us with the means to abstraction. The ability to codify abstract concepts and manipulate more data than we otherwise could. Programming involves

---

138   Martin Lotze et al. (2014) "Neural Correlates of verbal creativity: differences in resting-state functional connectivity associated with expertise in creative writing." *Frontiers in Human Neuroscience.* 8:516.

speaking to the computer in a language *it* understands, in order to be able to shuttle data around physical switches, resulting in an application. Math allows us to wonder about the birth of the universe.

One amazing study shows how this is possible. Here, chimpanzees were taught to use plastic tags to represent sameness and difference. Cup-Pear would gain the different tag, Cup-Cup would gain the sameness tag. Only once the chimpanzees learned to use this symbolic representation, were they then able to consider *higher-order* relationships. For example, they could correctly identify that two pairs (Cup-Cup and Cup-Pear) were also different from one another.[139]

As Professor of Cognitive Philosophy, Andy Clark, put it:

"Experience with external tags and labels thus enables the brain itself to solve problems whose level of complexity and abstraction would otherwise leave us baffled."

Could taking up a habit of writing, programming, or learning math help you to think more deeply? To engage in creative problem solving? Or to think about future outcomes and how to prepare for them? I would certainly attribute most of my own success as an online entrepreneur to this type of thinking.

Alternatively, practicing other skills could have alternative benefits. For instance, a study published in *Neuropsychologica* found that trained musicians demonstrated superior speed and accuracy in the Stroop task and Simon task, suggesting improved cognitive processing.[140] There is a *huge* amount of anecdotal

---

139   From *Mysteries of the Human Brain*, New Scientist.
140   Ines Jentszche et al. (2014) "Improved effectiveness of performance monitoring in amateur instrumental musicians." *Neuropsychologia.* 52(100):117–124.

evidence from polyglots who feel they can think "differently" in different languages.

Perhaps we should all think about the types of cognitive skills we admire and would like to display, and how we could train them. Learning music, writing, art, languages, and math might have more far-reaching benefits than we suppose.

The best part is that this kind of learning is easier than ever thanks to the huge number of resources available to us online. Literally anyone can take an online course or try learning through an app like Brilliant. And thanks to powerful tools that now allow a single person to accomplish a whole lot more, it's actually possible for individuals to contribute significantly in a number of fields. Consider, for example, how game engines and freely available 3D assets now allow solo "indie developers" to release highly successful games that compete with blockbuster efforts developed by huge studios. 3D printing, powerful editing software, crowdsourcing platforms, and countless other tools have similar effects in a variety of different fields. In short, we may be seeing a return of the "polymath." *Digital* polymaths.

Learning new skills will not only provide you with useful new abilities, will not only keep you plastic and learning, but also give you new tools for *thinking*. And this could have exponential benefits for cognitive performance.

What Happens When We Stop?

With an understanding of the crucially connected nature of the mind and body—and of how this fuels our plasticity—it becomes extremely apparent just how potentially damaging a lack of movement can be.

Likewise, a lack of learning *in general* may present a serious issue. In fact, it could explain *many* of the problems we currently associate with aging.

Remember the baby whose brain is awash with chemicals as they attempt to make sense of the world around them? They continue to learn at an accelerated rate for many more years. Even once they have mastered the basics like walking and talking, they still need to figure out the nuances of social dynamics. They will go to school and learn about math and science, and they will go on holidays and see new countries and climates for the first time.

They'll play football, take karate classes, and be forced by parents to learn a language or an instrument.

As teens, they might have less to learn in any given subject, but they will continue building on the knowledge they've gained. And they'll continue to have new experiences, whether that's learning to drive, falling in love, or moving away from home. They might join the university rowing team or discover a passion for dance.

This continues after we graduate and land our first jobs. But eventually, we will likely fall into a particular job or industry and stay there. We might take on more responsibility over time, but our day-to-day work starts to become fairly rote.

Parenthood is exciting and new at first, but for many of us that will be the last big life change we experience until those children leave home. And we're too tired to keep up the rowing or the dance classes. We move homes for the last time in years. And we choose to stick with the friends we have, rather than make any new ones.

Evenings are spent on the sofa. Our New Years' resolution to learn German falls by the wayside. You know the drill.

It's at this point that we become more set in our ways. It becomes harder to learn new skills. And it becomes harder for anyone to change our opinions on anything—even if it would be for the better.

But it gets worse as we get older. That old rowing injury is really acting up now, and over the years it has led to compensatory movement patterns. Years of sitting at a computer has left us hunched over, and thoughts of squatting are a *very* distant memory. Eventually, we start to actively minimize the amount of moving we do. And as our friends and relatives become older too, we gradually stop socializing.

The amount of information coming into the brain is sorely diminished as our eyes get weaker.

Eventually we retire, and unless we actively seek out new challenges, our lives become perilously "comfortable."

Is it any wonder that you start to lose your keys? Or aches and pains start to pile on top of each other? That you struggle to stay awake after lunch?

But it's not too late for you! Start by moving your body, and you can regain the plasticity that you once had. Start learning again, and you can reawaken your mind to new possibilities.

Don't stagnate—keep moving.

CHAPTER 13

Self-Mastery and Physical Intelligence

You can be the smartest person in the room or the greatest athlete in the world, but if you go to pieces on the night, you won't be able to tap into that massive potential.

Learning to control your response to a given situation is key then, and this is once again where neurotransmitters come into play, along with various autonomic functions of the human body such as breathing and heart rate.

Once more, we see the interconnectedness of brain and body, as the physiological state hugely influences the mindset.

And when you understand this—when you recognize the way that your body affects your mind and performance and elect to *take back control*—that is when you have attained "physical intelligence."

Physical intelligence is described by authors Claire Dale and Patricia Peyton as the ability to detect and change chemicals and other physical factors that might dictate mental state, mood, and efficiency. It is closely linked with the concept of "interoception," which is the ability to "sense" one's own bodily state.

But this is a practice that has been going on for centuries under many different guises. And it may just be the path to unlocking hidden potential and gaining total self-mastery.

Fight or Flight Versus Rest and Digest

At any given time, the human body falls somewhere on a spectrum between two opposite states: fight and flight, or rest and digest. These two states are also referred to as sympathetic and parasympathetic, as they are induced by the sympathetic and parasympathetic branches of the autonomic nervous system respectively.

Fight or flight is a state of physiological arousal that occurs during moments of intense stress. We often think of the stress response as a negative thing, but in fact acute stress can be a highly valuable tool. In a dangerous situation, the body will increase production of catecholamine neurotransmitters such as dopamine, norepinephrine (noradrenaline), and epinephrine (adrenaline), along with others such as cortisol.

> Acute stress can be a highly valuable tool.

These chemicals are "excitatory neurotransmitters" which means that they *increase* the likelihood of neurons firing. Thus, the brain becomes alive with increased electrical activity, and we experience an increased awareness, along with racing thoughts focused on potential dangers. While activation of some brain areas increase, higher cognitive processes handled in the prefrontal cortex will largely be shut-down. After all, this is no time to be daydreaming about summer vacations or planning your next presentation!

Those neurotransmitters likewise make you more likely to remember the events that occur next, seeing as they may help you to avoid danger in future.

Meanwhile, signals are carried along the vagus nerve that increase the heart rate and breathing to deliver more blood and oxygen where it is needed. Blood pressure changes will send more of that blood to the muscles and brain, while the digestive system and immune system will be temporarily suppressed.

Blood viscosity actually increases to encourage clotting in the case of an injury. The pupils will dilate to let in more light, though we will subjectively experience a sense of "tunnel vision" (that will be important later). Time may even seem to slow down slightly.

In fact, what we think of as stress or fear is in many ways a superpower.

Or as Doctor Who puts it in one episode:

> Let me tell you about scared. Your heart is beating so hard I can feel it through your hands. There's so much blood and oxygen pumping through your brain, it's like rocket fuel. Right now you could run faster and you could fight harder, you could jump higher than ever in your life. And you are so alert it's like you can slow down time. What's wrong with scared? Scared is a superpower. It's your superpower. There is danger in this room and guess what? It's you. Do you feel it?

Then there's the rest and digest response. This is the state that we enter when there is *no* apparent danger.

At this point, the heart rate and the breathing slow down. Brain activity is reduced and becomes less focused. We are more likely to daydream and to activate the default mode network as we wonder about our day. The body gets to work repairing tissues, building muscle, and digesting food.

While the primary neurotransmitter produced by the parasympathetic nervous system is the excitatory acetylcholine, parasympathetic states are also likely to occur alongside "feel-good" hormones such as serotonin, melatonin, oxytocin, and anandamide.

Muscle tone is reduced, and you might just feel like taking a long afternoon nap.

But it is a mistake to think of these states as being binary or mutually exclusive. These are not states that are intermittently "switched on" in response to forest fires or big sandwiches. Instead, countless factors continuously push us slightly more toward one end of the spectrum or the other.

In fact, one of the greatest maladies facing a great number of us today is chronic stress. The fight-or-flight response that we just discussed is a powerful tool for combating *immediate threats*. During our evolutionary history, that would have meant overcoming things like predators, rivals, and dangerous climbs.

Today though, many of the threats we face are low-level and slow burning. Think about financial debt, an overbearing boss, a job you find degrading, or troubles in your relationship. Even a slightly untidy kitchen!

All these things trigger low-level stress which mean that you are unlikely to fully enter the rest and digest state. And remember what stress does to your body: it suppresses digestion and immunity. It increases blood pressure. And it encourages anxious thoughts. When this stretches for days, weeks, and months, it can lead to serious health risks.

Then there are the physiological factors that can slightly nudge you in any one direction.

For example: eating.

When you eat a plate of carbs, you will raise your blood sugar and introduce an amino acid called tryptophan into your system. The tryptophan, found in most carbs, can't be digested and so instead makes its way through the blood-brain barrier where it is converted to 5-hydroxytryptophan by the tryptophan hydroxylase enzyme. This is then converted into serotonin by the aromatic amino acid decarboxylase enzyme.[141] Serotonin, you may recall, is the "feel-good hormone." This helps you to feel cheerful and happy, but also acts as an inhibitory neurotransmitter, reducing the amount of activity throughout the brain (eventually serotonin becomes melatonin—the sleep hormone—which is why we often feel so tired after we eat). In short, we are more parasympathetic when in a "postprandial" state (meaning "fed").

Conversely, when you have very low blood sugar, this triggers the release of cortisol, which leads to a stress response. From an evolutionary standpoint, it makes sense that being hungry would encourage food-seeking behavior.

---

141   Dawn M Richard et. al. (2009) "L-Tryptophan: Basic Metabolic Functions, Behavioral Research and Therapeutic Indications." *International Journal of Tryptophan Research*. 2:45–60.

This is why we often find ourselves feeling anxious and nervous when we haven't eaten for a while. It's also why people get "hangry."

Countless other small things can factor into the way we feel, as well. For example, the time of day has an impact due to the influence of sunlight which increases cortisol (the lack thereof induces melatonin) and adenosine that builds up in the brain throughout the day and reduces activity to prepare us for sleep. Caffeine actually makes us more sympathetic by binding to the adenosine receptors and thereby "blocking" that inhibitory effect.

Likewise, social cues can alter our neurochemistry, as can the temperature, sounds, hydration, foods, gut bacteria, and more.

One aspect of "physical intelligence" is simply understanding that there might be a *reason* that you are feeling stressed, angry, or sad that has little to do with your *perceived* explanation.

Before you panic and make a poor decision, or before you shout at your partner for a perceived wrong, ask yourself whether you might just be overtired, over hungry, or anxious about something unrelated. Then ask how you can *fix* that by altering your chemistry and getting back to an ideal equilibrium.

(Likewise, when someone shouts at you, consider whether the hot weather might be making them more short-tempered.)

This also demonstrates the close link between physical intelligence and emotional intelligence. Emotional intelligence is a term used to describe our awareness of our own and others' emotions. It has been described as being equally important as IQ, and in many ways even *more* important.

After all, a high emotional intelligence will help you to persuade others, to sell to them, and to win them over. It will help you to maintain a stoic mindset through times of trouble, and it will give you the ability to stay calm during interviews or intense competitions. It's also an extremely valuable skill that lets us help *others* to deal with difficult emotions, and to bring out the best in everyone. Great leaders are masters of emotional intelligence.

The Anabolic Mindset

Bodybuilders and strength athletes might be familiar with similar concepts: catabolism and anabolism.

Catabolism is a state in which the body burns fat and breaks down tissue to use for fuel. We are highly catabolic during a training session for instance and first thing in the morning.

Anabolism, on the other hand, is the state of rest during which time the body *rebuilds* muscle tissue, facilitating hypertrophy. Muscle building is therefore a biphasic process: breaking down muscle tissue is insufficient without dedicating equal time to build it back up. There must be an equal and opposite reaction. We briefly touched on this in Chapter 3.

These states are largely determined by AMP-activated protein kinase (AMPK) and mTOR. Activity creates adenosine monophosphate (AMP), a byproduct of the energy process which we shall examine in an upcoming chapter, which activates the enzyme AMPK. AMPK reduces protein synthesis by *inhibiting* mTOR. mTOR conversely is Mammalian Target of Rapamyacin and is responsible for elevating levels of IGF-1 and other anabolic compounds that support protein synthesis. These substances are likewise regulated by other factors, such as what we eat.

Other processes also connect anabolism to our sympathetic response and vice versa. For instance, low blood sugar not only increases cortisol but also myostatin, which is a substance that leads to the breakdown of muscle. Cortisol also has a negative correlation with testosterone, which is to say that the more cortisol you have in your system, the less testosterone will be circulating at any given time. Insulin, which is spiked by high blood sugar, *promotes* muscle building and is an anabolic hormone in its own right.

Catabolic states are sympathetic, anabolic states are parasympathetic. Sleep is the "most anabolic state" that there is.

Bodybuilders and athletes will spend a lot of time trying to be as anabolic as possible during their downtime, with spikes in catabolism during actual training. They do this largely by manipulating diet, sleep, and training variables to avoid drops in blood sugar, ensure sufficient rest, and even to carefully time meals.

But what is often forgotten is the *mental game* and the importance of controlling the stress response. There is a big debate as to whether "overtraining" is truly a term that can apply to noncompetitive athletes other than military personnel. After all, if a pro athlete can train five hours a day, how can you be "over-trained" from your one workout a week?

Some have suggested using alternative terms to describe this burnout such as "under-recovery" or "over-reaching." But whatever you call it, it all makes perfect sense when you consider that the average person experiences a huge amount of chronic stress during their day-to-day lives. (Whereas the pro athlete also *rests* like a pro!)

If you are constantly getting injured at the gym, if your training only seems to be making you *more* tired, it's probably because you aren't genuinely relaxing and allowing yourself to recover. If you train at the gym but *also* have a busy commute, a stressful job, and a long list of chores to do when you get home, you need to consider all those factors *together*. Likewise, if you spend your evenings playing intense video games, that isn't going to help!

And if you can't get to sleep because your mind is racing, that will only cause further harm. Even the light from your mobile phone triggers a release of cortisol right before bed, just when your brain should be awash with inhibitory neurochemicals and anabolic hormones.

This is one of the reasons that Shaolin warrior monks use meditation practices such as Qi Gong to try and restore their energy and fully recover the body outside of training sessions. They see it as a careful balance of yin and yang.

We could all benefit from a similar perspective.

How Our Thoughts Determine Our Physiological State

It is not always external physical factors that triggers certain moods and mental states. Just as important is what we choose to focus on and what we think about.

In previous chapters, I discussed how our thoughts and understanding are grounded in our physical experiences. Thus, when you think about something bad happening, it is almost as though that bad thing is *already* happening, as far as your physiological response is concerned.

Danger doesn't have to be present for the idea of it to impact on your mental and physical state.

To demonstrate this, imagine for a moment that you are camping in the middle of a thick jungle, sitting around a campfire. Unbeknownst to you, there is a tiger in the bushes waiting for its moment to pounce. You hear a rustle and instantly your focus homes in on the noise. Everything seems to fall silent; your hairs stand on end.

In one scenario, you correctly identify this as a tiger. Cue the biggest fight-or-flight response of your life as your heart leaps into your chest and your feel sick with fear and panic (that would be your digestive processes losing their blood supply and your blood becoming more acidic due to rapid breathing).

But in the other scenario, you assume that this noise is just your friend coming back from washing their clothes in the river. There is no panic response.

The physical situation in both these scenarios is the exact same. The only difference is in your head! But the physiological difference is huge.

> We often imagine tigers where there are none.

There are also countless nuances in that response. You might have a milder fight-or-flight response if you believe there is a tiger but also believe that it won't attack you. You might have a worse one if you happen to have a *serious phobia of tigers*.

No, I don't know why you would be camping in the jungle in that case!

The point is that we often imagine tigers where there are none. And as such, we find ourselves in constant states of panic. People who are particularly prone to anxious thoughts might find themselves imagining the worst-case scenarios throughout their lives, and thus living in a state of constant physiological arousal.

Which is not to say that this type of low-level stress is *always* a bad thing. Just the right amount of "eustress" (the term of positive stress) can actually be a positive motivating force that encourages us to finish our projects on time and pay our bills.

As with most things in the human body, it's about balance and adaptability.

Cognitive Restructuring

Understanding these mechanisms gives us the power to take back control. One psychotherapeutic strategy increasingly used by psychologists is cognitive behavioral therapy, or CBT. The aim of this intervention is to teach the individual the power of their thoughts, and how they can control them in order to overcome limiting beliefs and even anxiety disorders such as phobias or OCD.

Many of these strategies fall under the heading of "cognitive restructuring." This is an example of "metacognition" (thinking about thinking) that aims to remove negative thought patterns and install more positive coping mechanisms. Two strategies that are commonly employed to this end are:

- Thought challenging

♛ Hypothesis testing

Let's say that you have a fear of public speaking. You might start by making a note of the kinds of things you think in those situations:

"I'm going to choke!"

"Everyone will laugh at me!"

"I won't be able to breathe."

"I don't have anything worthwhile to say."

Thought challenging would now involve assessing the reality of that situation, as well as just how devastating it would really be.

For example: do people really laugh at speakers that are having a hard time? Most people are compassionate enough to politely wait for you to finish. If they *do* laugh, does it really matter? Why would you be bothered about impressing someone so petty?

Do you really have nothing to say? Because if not, why have you been asked to talk? Did you find value in the information you're about to share? If so, then there is a likelihood that it will be useful to at least one person, in which case you have done something positive.

Hypothesis testing takes this one step further and suggests that you actually go out there and face your fears. More specifically, you face the *worst-case scenario*. In other words, you stand on the stage and give a talk, but you also *intentionally* stutter and fail. Try waiting for two minutes in between sentences and you'll see that the reality isn't half as bad as you think it will be and the repercussions will likely be zero.

(Of course, hypothesis testing is not helpful for a fear of heights.)

This is an extremely powerful tool. Many of us fail to fulfill our potential due to social awkwardness and shyness. By starting up conversations with strangers and being as cringey as possible, you can eventually desensitize yourself to this fear. Imagine how charismatic and confident you could become!

CBT is often treated as almost a form of programming, where heavy focus is placed on the phrasing and content of the thoughts as sentences. However, I believe that CBT can benefit from an embodied perspective, that it can be even more powerful when we employ a multisensory representation of the situation and really allow the emotions to be felt. Without actually needing to go on stage, you can "live" in that moment and feel that it really isn't that bad, especially as you remind yourself of all the counter arguments you have prepared.

> **Samurais would meditate on the concept of death.**

Using visualization can even be an effective tool for desensitizing yourself to extremely stressful ideas and concepts. For example, samurais would reportedly meditate on the concept of death in order to overcome any fear of it.

Next time someone asks what you're thinking, tell them you're meditating on the concept of death like the ancient samurai.

Badass points—one million.

You can use visualization in order to overcome a fear of heights, practicing standing out on the ledge and realizing that people don't *just fall.*

Athletes and those with demanding jobs have a huge amount to gain by using these types of strategies, and potentially they can help us tap into any desired mental/emotional state.

Breathing and Meditation

Returning to a more physiological approach, another way that we can take back control is through practiced breathing and meditation.

For example, the "fourfold breath" (which goes by many other names) is a technique that is used in yoga as well as by Navy SEALs to induce a state of calm under pressure. To perform the technique, you:

- Inhale for four seconds
- Hold that air in for four seconds
- Exhale for four seconds
- Hold your breath for four seconds

Wim Hof

When it comes to taking control of the autonomic nervous system, no one comes to mind as readily as Wim Hof. Wim Hof is an individual who developed a breathing technique combined with visualization and cold exposure in order to trigger a highly sympathetic nervous response. This response enables him to demonstrate feats of superhuman strength, overcome pain, and endure extreme temperatures. To demonstrate this, Wim has broken numerous world records, including one for climbing 22,000 feet to the top of Mount Everest wearing only shorts and shoes. He has another for running a marathon across the forty degrees Celsius Namibian desert without drinking a drop of water. He and his students have submitted themselves to studies where they have been injected with bacterial toxins and been able to prevent the emergence of cold and flu symptoms.[142]

The fascinating part is that anyone can learn the Wim Hof method, which involves a form of controlled hyperventilation followed by a deep exhalation then breath hold.[143] This works by lowering CO_2 and thereby raising the pH level of the blood. This, in turn, prevents the cells from offloading their oxygen stores, creating a state similar to hypoxia and thereby triggering a stress response, which also happens to facilitate the release of anti-inflammatory cytokines to combat cold symptoms and swelling. The following breath hold restores CO_2 and allows the blood to return to normal.

---

142   Matthijis Kox et. al. (2014) "Voluntary activation of the sympathetic nervous system and attenuation of the innate immune response in humans." *PNAS.* 111(20) 7379–7384.

143   Don't try this without guidance from someone who knows what they're doing and certainly don't attempt it in the bath or anywhere that you would be unwilling to pass out!

Amazing as all this is, Wim isn't the first person to use similar techniques. In fact, a major source of inspiration was the existing practice of Tummo meditation, which practitioners can use to raise their body temperature at will.

There are countless variations on this theme, but they all work because of the "two-way" nature of the communication between physiology and psychology. Just as you can change your thoughts to affect your breathing via the vagus nerve, so too can controlling your breathing change your mindset. The best results come from doing both these things at the same time.[144]

This of course, is where meditation comes in. I've already discussed some "alternative" forms of meditation such as "big idea meditation" and the samurai concept of contemplating death, but for most people, the term is more synonymous with practices such as mindfulness meditation, transcendental meditation, or breath awareness meditation.

Here, the objective is to focus the mind on something. In transcendental meditation, you focus on a "mantra" and simply repeat the same word or sound over and over. In mindfulness meditation you can detach from your thoughts and observe them in a nonjudgmental manner, or alternatively perform a "bodyscan" by progressively relaxing each muscle. Breath awareness meditation involves focusing on the breath.

---

144   Note that splashing the face with cold water as described in a previous chapter is another example of "hacking" the vagus nerve to stimulate a specific physiological response—this time with the reverse goal in mind.

I personally have had the most success with various forms of gazing meditation. This is a category that involves focusing on some outside point, such as a candle, a tree blowing in the wind, or a babbling brook.

Other forms of meditation, such as Tai Chi (which can serve as a meditative practice as well as having martial and other applications), involve focusing on movements. This is a type of "kinesthetic meditation."

All these are examples of directive meditation, meaning that the goal is to focus the mind or to clear it. Either way, this exercises mental discipline which we've already mentioned can help to strengthen the anterior cingulate cortex, the part of the brain responsible for directing attention and sustaining focus.

This has huge benefits because it means that we can simply *choose* not to focus on negative thoughts or distracting outside factors. Meditation can thus help you to focus on a task for longer, to be more engaged with a sport or exercise, or even to rise above physical pain or emotional turmoil.

Many people find meditation practices to be relaxing because they are typically combined with natural scenery, calm breathing, and relaxed postures, all of which help to encourage a relaxed state of mind and restful neurochemical cocktail.

But if you're most interested in developing focus and emotional control, you can actually get that from *any* consistent practice that involves sustaining attention; especially when attention is directed inward.

For example, practicing "mental math," has been suggested several times in this book already, and can actually benefit emotional control and even combat depression! It does this while developing the dorsolateral prefrontal cortex which plays a key role in working memory[145] and executive control. In other words, like other forms of meditation, this teaches practitioners to choose how to engage with emotions and how to direct their attention internally. The researchers comment that this opens up entirely new intervention strategies for treating emotional disorders, and it follows that this could *also* be useful for sports psychologists to consider.

Not to mention the rest of us.

The same is likewise true for big idea meditation or Newport's productive meditation. As they both involve focus, they may similarly be useful for gaining more conscious control over the content of the mind.

Directive forms of meditation can likewise lead to a host of other profound changes throughout the brain, including boosted IQ scores[146] and increased whole brain connectivity.

At the other end of the spectrum are nondirective forms of meditation. These include attempts to simply relax the mind and allow any thoughts to come and go. In other words, letting the mind wander freely. One such example is Acem meditation, which was developed in Norway in 1966 and has been shown to activate the default mode network (which I'm sure you remember is the imagination network), more so than simply relaxing or engaging in monotonous tasks. Acem meditation combines a meditative sound with a "free mental attitude."

---

145   Matthew A. Scult et al. (2016) "Thinking and Feeling: Individual Differences in Habitual Emotion Regulation and Stress-Related Mood Are associated With Prefrontal Executive Control." *Clinical Psychological Science.* 5(1):150–157.
146   Robert W. Cranson et al. (1991) "Transcendental meditation and improved performance on intelligence-related measures: A longitudinal study." *Personality and Individual Differences.* 12(10):1105–1116.

It turns out that letting the brain follow its own neural pathways via free association actually helps to organize thoughts and memories—a similar process to that which occurs during dreaming. This could result in a better structured organization for the hippocampus and other brain areas, and thus more neural efficiency and improved ability to make novel connections between disparate ideas.

People who use this free-form meditation style[147] have actually been shown to exhibit greater creativity and goal-oriented behavior. And I suspect we are just scratching the surface of what "alternative" methods of meditation like this could be useful for.[148]

---

147   Directive and nondirective meditation are also referred to as focused meditation and open meditation, or focused-attention and open-monitoring meditation. We can also consider some forms of mindfulness meditation to be examples of open-monitoring meditation: mindfulness is very often treated as a kind of catch-all for meditation.
148   Lorenza S. Colzato et al. (2012) "Meditate to create: the impact of focused-attention and open-monitoring training on convergent and divergent thinking." *Frontiers in Psychology*. 3:116.

CHAPTER 14

Ultimate States of Human Performance

You can use meditation, breathing, and CBT to gain control of your mental state and emotional state. But if this is true, then what should be the goal of this practice? What is the "ideal" mental state, if such a thing exists?

Many people would argue that the answer should be the flow state. Indeed, this is arguably the holy grail for sports psychologists and performance coaches.

Getting into Flow

The term "flow state" was first used by psychologist Mihaly Csíkszentmihályi in 1975. It describes a phenomenon most of us will have experienced at some point or another, the feeling of being 100 percent engaged with a task, to the extent that all other thoughts and distractions seem to melt away. This can happen during sporting events, at which point you might feel as though time slows to a crawl and you are able to move with unusual grace and precision. It also happens when we're writing and completely lose track of time, focusing for hours on end without coming up for air. It can happen during musical improvisation where it feels almost like we are "channeling" the music as it comes from outside of us.

When we look inside the brain, what appears to be happening at this point is that the prefrontal regions of the brain largely go quiet such that only those brain areas responsible for momentary decisions are active. This is referred to as "transient hypofrontality." This is widely regarded as the pattern necessary for flow by many prominent writers on the subject.

However, I feel that this explanation may be a little bit over-simplistic. I don't believe that there is a single pattern of brain activity that is responsible for flow, but that it is rather just the most efficient pattern of activity for any given task.

In fact, we *need* the prefrontal cortex for various forms of flow. Rappers in flow, for example, show activation in the medial prefrontal cortex. This is needed for the "internal generation of ideas."[149] It follows that the brain regions active in a rap flow would be very different from those active when surfing. It may be that the prefrontal cortex only seems to be quiet because such a small percentage of it is being used for the given task. But it is actually just being used highly *efficiently*.

By now, we all know that stories of being able to "unlock 100 percent" of our brain's potential are pseudoscience. No aspect of our brain is "locked."

But it is true that we don't use the whole brain at any one time. We have roughly the energy reserve to activate 3 percent of our brain matter at any given time. This is a finite

---

149   Siyuan Lui et. al. (2012) "Neural Correlates of Lyrical Improvisation: An fMRI Study of Freestyle Rap." *Nature.* 2:834.

resource then, and if it is spread across twenty different activities, we're going to see a drop-off in performance.[150]

This is something important to understand about the brain in general. When we talk about neurotransmitters and brainwaves (which are simply patterns of electrical activity), we are talking about effects in *specific brain regions*. You might hear about meditation experts entering a "theta brain state" but that just means certain areas of their brains are in that state.

Many writers have described flow states as the "ultimate state" of human performance,[151] and it is easy to see why. When you drive while talking on your phone hands-free, you might think that you're able to drive just as efficiently as you did before. In truth though, you are actually four times more likely to have an accident, as not all of your attention is directed to the current moment. In a flow state, you are 100 percent engaged, and you are thus able to direct every resource available to the matter at hand.

When we aren't talking out loud, our inner monologue and distracting thoughts and stimuli can have the same deleterious effect, which is why we don't always perform our very best.

Not only do flow states allow us to perform at the very peak of our capabilities, but they also feel almost meditative. Because you are entirely focused on one thing, you can experience a sort of "ego death" where you appear to exist only in that very moment. Many people find this to be an almost euphoric experience.

---

150   Csíkszentmihályi himself suggested that we can attend to 110 bits of information per second, where decoding speech accounts for 60 bits.
151   *The Rise of Superman: Decoding the Science of Ultimate Human Performance* by Steven Kotler.

How do you enter a flow state? There are several strategies and tips. One is to ensure that the level of challenge you are facing is *just right*. If the perceived challenge is small, then you won't be sufficiently motivated to focus on it. Conversely, if it is too *high* then you might feel deflated and give up entirely.

An actual flow chart...get it?

This is why the perfect computer game is one that has a steady difficulty curve—that perfectly matches our own progress as we gain new motor skills and understanding of the game's rules and mechanics. This is the "sweet spot" when it comes to rapid learning and optimum performance.

At the same time, flow states are more likely to occur if the task is inherently rewarding. Again, we see this in computer games which utilize rewarding sound effects and action-packed scenes that entirely engage our attention. It is *much* harder to enter a flow state while filling out a boring spreadsheet!

Flow states often sit on a knife-edge between stress and calm. This is simply because stressful and dangerous events *demand* our full attention. Adrenaline and cortisol help to engage us with our surroundings or tasks as we have seen when learning, but they can also cause racing and anxious thoughts. In high-stress situations, we need to be able to take advantage of the heightened state of arousal while simultaneously remaining calm and fully aware.

The effect we *don't* want to trigger is a full-on fight-or-flight response that will result in *complete* shut-down of the prefrontal cortex. This is the effect that makes us choke when we're up on stage giving a speech, that causes us to forget our lines in a play. This is sometimes referred to as a "self-prefrontal lobotomy." (It's also why I don't believe transient hypofrontality paints a full picture.)

Instead, we are trying to experience the benefits of intense focus and drive, *without* the negatives of anxiety and mental collapse.

This can be facilitated with techniques such as the aforementioned fourfold breath, as used by Navy SEALs. Other psychological and physiological strategies might also prove effective. Dr. Andy Morgan from Yale Medical School conducted research on men trained in mental toughness under extreme stress and found that they produced higher amounts of neuropeptide Y (NPY) and dehydroepiandrosterone (DHEA). DHEA is interesting because it can buffer the effect of cortisol on the hippocampus, meaning that even under high stress, you have access to your memories and ideas. DHEA is also a "neurosteroid" that increases neuronal excitability. NPY helps to minimize the effect of norepinephrine on the prefrontal cortex.

Owl Eyes

One of my favorite strategies for staying calmly focused is to use "wide angle vision." Referred to as "Owl Eyes" by Native Americans, or "splatter vision" by some survivalists/servicemen, this is the practice of becoming aware of the peripheral vision. It's also used in several martial arts.

If you stop focusing on just one spot and instead try to take in the entire scene, this expands the amount of visual information coming in and may thereby increase the amount of processing that is devote to the "here and now." This also facilitates a minor parasympathetic response (as we tend to be highly focused when we are in danger with the reverse also being true) and thus helps us to stay calmer.

Engaging wide angle vision creates an impression of time slowing down—just like the flow state itself. That's partly because you have a wider field of reference (just as you feel like you're driving slower in a wider space) and partly because input from the peripheral vision actually reaches the brain 25 percent faster than input from the focal point. Peripheral vision even helps with balance and proprioception, by providing us with a sense of "place." You may even hear more by widening your field of attention, seeing as our senses are closely bound together in the brain.

Try using wide angle vision the next time you're sparring or playing tennis and see if it helps you to engage your calm reflexes. You can also use a form of meditation to practice this, known as *hakalau* meditation.

But again, we must remember the importance of not romanticizing a single "brain state." It seems to me that an attempt has been made to commodify the flow state and sell it as a panacea, a solution for everything from depression to poor sports performance. Remember, it is eustress that motivates us to pay off debt. Moreover, it is being in a relaxed state of mind and allowing our thoughts to wander that can lead to breakthroughs (as it did for Einstein) and that can help us to see better organization of thoughts, memories, and ideas.

Losing your sense of self doesn't address issues, it just avoids them.

Every mental state has value, and a truly optimized brain is one that can easily switch *between* these states to enjoy optimum performance for the given situation.

(Another fascinating example of how a brain state can affect our physiology is seen in the hypothetical "hysterical strength." If you've ever heard stories about mothers lifting cars off of their trapped children, that's possibly because huge surges of adrenaline have allowed them to recruit *drastically* more muscle fiber. In fact, this may even explain legends of Norse "berserkers.")

Mental Toughness

Another goal of all this interoception and physical intelligence is to increase mental toughness and resilience.

In other words: when the going gets tough, do you give up, or do you push through?

> It may have been the Spartan mindset, as much as anything else, that gained the army such a fierce reputation.

We can consider this to be another "Super Trait"—a trait that can help to develop many *other* traits.

After all, it is by pushing through discomfort that we are able to train to our fullest and achieve our highest potential. Developing this mental toughness is thus one of the main focuses of many militaries and especially for Navy SEALs. SEALs are infamously put through grueling challenges such as "hell week" which involves training for consecutive days in harsh conditions and with barely any food or sleep.

The idea is that if you can persist in these circumstances and even continue to exhibit a degree of physical prowess, then you will be ready for whatever challenges you may face in real-world combat scenarios.

This was also a key focus of Spartan training, which involved training barefoot, hungry, and on minimal sleep. It may have been the Spartan mindset, as much as anything else, that gained the army such a fierce reputation.

Ex-Navy SEALs like author David Goggins preach the importance of mental toughness for all of us, and many ex-military personnel have shared the mental strategies they were taught to get through the toughest challenges. Such strategies include breaking challenges into digestible chunks ("eating the whole elephant"), for example, or entering another powerful mental state referred to as "nonreactivity."

But a large part of this is simply training yourself to be able to do the things you don't want to do and to be able to control your own will when your physiology is asking you to stop. The fact is that most of us now live extremely comfortable lives, especially compared with our wild ancestors. We rarely have to deal with so much as a slight disturbance in temperature. Imagine tracking prey in a thunderstorm, naked, and barefoot!

Is it any wonder that we've become so sensitive?

Just like our fat pets, we have been domesticated.

While you don't need to go totally feral, there may be some benefit in occasionally getting out of your comfort zone *just a little*. This is an additional benefit of training outdoors or taking cold showers—just another reason to consider those practices.

Imagine if being a little cold, hungry, or uncomfortable *didn't bother you*.

Nootropics

In the interests of hacking mental states, a growing number of people have begun experimenting with a class of drugs referred to as "nootropics" or "smart drugs." These are cognitive enhancers that act like "steroids for the brain" but which may range from harmless nutrients found commonly in food (such as omega 3) all the way to Class A drugs (such as microdosing LSD). Word has it that a large number of Silicone valley superstars and top performing CEOs secretly use smart drugs such as the prescription narcolepsy medication Modafinil.[152]

Modafinil is one a few substances considered to be the closest thing to a "real life" NZT (from the film *Limitless*). Its mechanisms of action aren't fully understood, but it appears to act through the wakefulness-modulating neurotransmitter orexin, and dopamine.

> **Many Silicone valley superstars and top performing CEOs secretly use smart drugs.**

In short, Modafinil is a kind of stimulant that behaves a bit like a next-level caffeine, though it can also enhance attention, reflexes, memory, and wakefulness. Many other stimulatory nootropics are discussed on forums and in wide use on college campuses, such as Adderall and Piracetam. We can even consider caffeine itself to be a nootropic of sorts.

There are other classes of nootropic. For example, many people prefer to use substances that trigger the release of *inhibitory* neurotransmitters. This way, they hope to reduce feelings of anxiety, while heightening creativity. Examples include the likes of L-theanine (found in green tea alongside caffeine) and the much more potent 5-HTP (a precursor to serotonin).

Do these strategies work? While they might give you a slight boost in focus and endurance in the short term, they are ultimately—I believe—an empty promise. Apart from the significant moral and socioeconomic implications (smart drugs create an unfair advantage and encourage us

---

152   And some not-so-secretly, such as prominent "biohacker," Dave Asprey, who talks about this openly on his blog and in interviews.

to work at a level that is likely unsustainable—to name just two issues), I also believe that the use of such substances is *misguided*.

Remember, there is no ideal brain state. And nor are neurotransmitters so simple as "dopamine = focused, serotonin = happy." All of these substances have a myriad of secondary and tertiary effects. You cannot increase serotonin, for example, without also increasing melatonin, resulting in lethargy and sleepiness.

Likewise, increasing dopamine will usually also increase cortisol and norepinephrine, potentially leading to anxiety while also causing digestive issues. And there are no doubt *countless* neurotransmitters and hormones that act on the brain that we have yet to identify.

There is no one "optimal" brain state. You can take Modafinil to enhance focus, but that will almost certainly *reduce* creativity. And then what do you do? Pop some inhibitory chemicals to loosen yourself up again? It hardly seems like an optimal or healthy cycle.

Each of these chemicals has different effects depending on the part of the brain they are acting on. I liken this to trying to fix a delicate watch with a hammer—we just don't have enough knowledge, nor precise enough tools, to effectively micromanage brain chemistry this way.

Again, this is before I even address significantly more concerning issues. How about the fact that many of these substances are likely to lead to tolerance and dependence as the brain up or downregulates receptors for those neurotransmitters? Then there's the *huge* risk involved with buying controlled substances online from shady sources, which is the only way to get some of them.

Are there other ways to enhance brain function with supplementation? Absolutely! And some can be highly effective. But these nootropics focus on supporting the natural functions of the brain and are generally available from natural sources.

For example, omega 3 fatty acid has a nearly *endless* list of incredible benefits for brain health. So much so that it's almost madness *not* to use it.

Omega 3 is incorporated into the walls of brain cells, which helps to improve cell-membrane permeability. This can help to speed up synaptic transmissions. Omega 3 also acts to balance out omega 6, which in turn reduces inflammation. This may have a profound effect for some people in reducing brain fog (and possibly even mood disorders), which may in some cases be caused by inflammation in the brain.

Omega 3 improves myelination,[153] which you may recall is one of the key processes in neuroplasticity (helping to protect neural pathways). Omega 3 is also neuroprotective.

Or how about combining lutein and zeaxanthin? This combination can increase the efficiency of mitochondria, raising energy levels. But it turns out that it also increases plasticity in infant brains. What's more, is that supplementing with a combination of lutein and zeaxanthin has been shown to increase visual processing speeds. In fact, supplementation was able to enhance

---

153   J.M. Bourre (2004) "Roles of unsaturated fatty acids (especially omega-3 fatty acids) in the brain at various ages and during ageing." *The journal of nutrition, health & aging.* 8(3):163–174.

visuo-motor reaction time by as much as 10 percent.[154] This could provide a huge competitive advantage for athletes!

This combination also has positive effects on spatial memory, reasoning, and more.[155] The exciting thing about these studies is that they were conducted on young, *healthy* participants. The lutein and zeaxanthin intervention did not just correct back to normal levels but helped to bring people up to "supernormal" levels.

Creatine, which is normally taken by gym rats to boost strength endurance, has also been shown to improve cognitive performance. There are countless nutrients that appear to support greater neural plasticity.

But chasing after every nutrient with potentially encouraging studies behind it is not my goal either. This reductionist approach can be something of a wild goose chase, not to mention getting expensive quickly! While you might choose to supplement with some of these suggestions, you would benefit greatly from simply seeking out the most varied and nutritious diet possible.

If you're hoping to pop a pill and suddenly understand the workings of the cosmos (or perhaps the stock market) then you will be sorely disappointed. But effective nootropics should not "feel" like anything other than you on your best day.

And effective brain performance means being able to elegantly slip from one mental state to another, as the situation demands. There are no quick fixes, but a better

154   Emily R Bovier et al. (2014) "A Double-Blind, Placebo-Controlled Study on the Effects of Lutein and Zeaxanthin on Neural Processing Speed and Efficiency." *PLoS One.* 9(9):e108178.

155   Lisa M Renzi-Hammond et al. (2017) "Effects of a Lutein and Zeaxanthin Intervention on Cognitive Function: A Randomized, Double-Masked, Placebo-Controlled Trial of Younger Healthy Adults." *Nutrients.* 9(11):1246.

understanding of the brain combined with smart practices can make a big difference.

Perhaps with training and greater understanding, we'll someday be able to switch from the heightened strength and physical prowess of a berserker, to the calm serenity of a Shaolin monk at will. In the meantime, a little more focus and calm will do a world of good.

CHAPTER 15

Energy: The Ultimate Force Multiplier

Were you some kind of overachiever, able to employ every single training method suggested in this book so far, then you could theoretically become faster, more creative, more focused, stronger, more agile, and...just *more*.

But even with all that being true, and even *without* accounting for technique and experience, there is still no guarantee that you could outperform anyone else in a given challenge. That's because there is one last vital ingredient to consider: energy.

Energy is the ultimate force multiplier. You can hit hard and fast, but you will lose any fight if you burn out after the third punch. Incredible focus is fine, but it's useless if it can only be sustained for two minutes.

Energy is therefore another Super Trait, and one that we need to dedicate some of our training to.

Understanding the Energy Systems

To tackle this energy problem, we need to make one more voyage into biology and science. This time, we're looking at the body's energy systems.

Broadly speaking, there are three different energy systems employed by the body. These are:

- 🏅 The ATP Creatine System (a.k.a. the Phosphocreatine System)

- 🏅 Glycogen Lactic Acid System (a.k.a. Lactic Acid System, a.k.a. Glycolytic System)

- 🏅 Aerobic System

The first two of these are anaerobic in nature, meaning that they do not require oxygen. The last one is aerobic, meaning that it does.

One common misconception about these systems is that they are mutually exclusive (as we have seen, this is generally a misconception about *many* processes in the human brain and body). In fact, your body is using all three of these systems constantly to power different processes.

But it can be useful to consider them on a spectrum, as this is how they are employed to fuel vigorous movement.

So, let's say you set off sprinting. At first, your body will utilize the ATP Creatine system. This will involve breaking down ATP stored in the muscle. ATP is "adenosine triphosphate," which is the "energy currency" of life. The body can convert this fuel into usable energy by breaking it down into ADP and Pi (adenosine diphosphate and an individual phosphate—a three becomes a two and a one), releasing energy in the process.

This process is extremely fast and provides an immediate burst of energy that is ideal for supplying the fast-twitch muscle for bursts of rapid, forceful movement. However, there is only a limited supply of ATP stored in the muscles, which will run out after around three seconds of exertion.

Fortunately, the body has the ability to recycle some used Pi and ADP back into ATP. To do this, it uses phosphocreatine, which is developed primarily in the kidneys. By utilizing creatine, the body is able to exert maximum power output for a further eight-to-ten seconds. Of course, this is why we supplement with additional creatine!

But what happens if you keep running after those eleven to thirteen seconds are up? At this point, the body will switch to the lactic acid system in order to keep providing energy. This system is slightly slower and less efficient at supplying energy, but is still suitable for fast, powerful movements.

The lactic acid system works through glycolysis by splitting glycogen (stored in the muscles and liver) into glucose, then pyruvate, and then again into ATP. It can also use glucose in the blood. This produces a number of byproducts such as lactate and hydrogen ions. Previously, it was thought that lactic acid (i.e. lactate) was what created the sensation of "muscle burn" during intense activity. However, we now know that this sensation is more likely the result of hydrogen ions which inhibit anaerobic ATP production and thus interfere with muscle contraction while increasing blood acidity.

The poor scapegoat that is lactate is actually useful for us, as it gets converted back into pyruvate and then glucose in the liver. Training can even make this process more efficient. This process is slow though, and thus we see lactate build-up in the blood as exertion continues. But although lactate build-up *correlates* with muscle soreness, it is not the cause. Increased acidity is also what makes us feel sick when we push ourselves hard.

Eventually, after around thirty seconds to three minutes, the build-up becomes too much, and the body is forced to revert to another system, at least for a period of time. Enter, the aerobic system.

The aerobic system is the slowest of the three energy systems and is not suited to explosive movements. However, it is capable of providing sustained energy over a long period of time because it is the most efficient.

The aerobic system works by using energy stored as fat. This needs to be transported to the muscles and broken down by oxygen. Thus, breathing becomes heavier, the heart gets to work, and we slow into a steady pace for the rest of the run. The aerobic energy system supplies the slow-twitch muscle fibers predominantly and can be used indefinitely. This is what you will use while running a marathon for instance, but it is also what your body uses to remain upright throughout the day, or to help you bring your spoon to your mouth when eating your morning cereal.

Training Each System

Different types of training will thus be useful for training different energy systems. Long distance running and other endurance activities are what we refer to as "LISS" or "Low Intensity Steady State Cardio." These typically involve activity at around 70 percent of the maximum heart rate or below.

You may have already noticed that there is some correlation between the three energy systems and the three types of twitch muscle fiber. Indeed, aerobic activities tend to utilize primarily slow-twitch fibers and vice versa.

Those looking to burn fat often aim to remain in the 70 percent "fat burning zone," seeing as the aerobic system uses fat as its fuel source and thus burns it directly. This strategy has since been challenged however, with many coaches now suggesting that "high intensity interval training" may be superior.

In high intensity interval training, the individual will engage in bouts of anaerobic, intense exercise, followed by periods of active recovery. A great example of this is the popular "Tabata protocol" which sees athletes go all out for periods of twenty seconds, followed by ten second breaks. For instance, you might perform a kettlebell swing at max velocity for twenty seconds then rest for ten, or you might sprint for twenty seconds, and jog for ten.

Another example of a high intensity interval workout might be to run full speed for thirty seconds and then jog slowly for one minute.

This type of training is excellent for fat loss, because the bouts of high intensity deplete the readily available energy in the muscles and bloodstream. That in turn means that the subsequent energy expenditure must rely exclusively on fat stores. Moreover, the glycogen needs to be restored following training, which is what creates the "afterburn effect" that you may have heard of. In short, your metabolism remains elevated for a period *following* a round of HIIT, which means that your total daily calorie burn will be higher than it would if you had used only aerobic training.

Restoring the body to its "pre-exercise state" actually requires energy in itself. This increases metabolism too via a process referred to as EPOC or "post-exercise oxygen consumption" (that's an acronym that takes liberties if ever I saw one).

That said, it's important not to overstate the power of this afterburn effect. It only lasts for around two to three hours following exercise[156] and this is unlikely to make a huge difference to your body composition.[157] From a weight loss and aesthetic point of view, the real advantage of HIIT is that it can offer similar benefits to LISS in a shorter timeframe. That said, this all depends on a wide number of factors (including the intensity of the sessions). And it's important to recognize that HIIT is *brutal* when performed properly. You're ultimately weighing up the difference between a lengthy run and a nausea-inducing sprint.

But high intensity interval training is also effective from a functional standpoint. That's because it has been shown to increase the density of mitochondria in the body, thereby

156   Kyle J Sevitis et al. (2013) "Total Daily Energy Expenditure Is Increased Following a Single Bout of Sprint Interval Training." *Physiol. Rep.* 1(5):e00131.
157   Wesley J Tucker et. al. (2016) "Excess Postexercise Oxygen Consumption After High-Intensity and Sprint Interval Exercise, and Continuous Steady-State exercise." *J. Strength. Cond. Res.* 30(11):3090–3097.

helping you to produce more energy more efficiently.[158] This process may reverse some negative changes associated with aging, with some pronouncing that HIIT is a "fountain of youth." Both forms of endurance training will achieve this, but HIIT is optimal.

(HIIT was also found in one study to be beneficial for numerous cognitive skills, including hippocampus-dependent learning and memory—similar to aerobic training.[159])

Both LISS and HIIT will improve VO2 max.[160] This is a measure of how much oxygen a person is able to use in one minute relevant to their body weight. A high VO2 max will result in greater aerobic capacity, as you will be able to deliver energy where it is needed.

Lung Training

A less obvious method for improving endurance and VO2 max, is to train the lungs themselves. You can do this by working the intercostal muscles and diaphragm that together help to expand and contract the lungs. This can be done as simply as practicing breathing through a straw or using IMT (inspiratory muscle training).

158   Li-Hua Wu et al. (2017) "High-intensity Interval Training Improves Mitochondrial Function and Suppresses Thrombin Generation in Platelets undergoing Hypoxic Stress." *Scientific Reports*. 7(1):4191| Matthew M. Robinson et al. (2017) "Enhanced Protein Translation Underlies Improved Metabolic and Physical Adaptations to Different Exercise Training Modes in Young and Old Humans." *Cell Metabolism*. 25(3):581–592.
159   Min Chul Lee et al. (2018) "New insight of high-intensity interval training on physiological adaptation with brain functions." *J Exerc Nutrition Biochem*. 22(3):1–5.
160   Carl Foster et al. (2015) "The Effects of High Intensity Interval Training vs Steady State Training on Aerobic and Anaerobic Capacity." *Journal of Sports Science & Medicine*. 14(4):747–755.

Training masks can also offer a similar effect.[161] All these tools make it slightly more difficult to breath during training, which in turn means your lungs have to work harder. This can then encourage adaptation, meaning that your lungs become more efficient at bringing in oxygen when you aren't wearing that apparatus.

Of course, wearing masks during training will limit your ability to lift heavy weights and ultimately reduce the intensity of your workouts, so this is a technique that should be used sparingly. Alternatively, you can practice IMT when you're not working. This may even be beneficial for cognitive function, as you improve your ability to supply the brain with blood throughout the day.

Another potential benefit of reducing oxygen intake during training, is that it may encourage the body to become more efficient when utilizing it and to better tolerate the build-up of CO_2 in the blood. This can also be achieved through other practices such as breath holding. Author Patrick McKeown[162] recommends that certain athletes practice exhaling and then holding their breath when running. This process causes a significant build-up of CO_2 and decrease in blood oxygen saturation. This may be useful for athletes such as sprinters in particular, where oxygen supply could realistically be a

---

161   Training masks came under a lot of fire for being marketed as "altitude masks" when in fact they did not simulate training at high altitudes. However, this doesn't mean they are useless, as they can still offer a kind of resistance for the lungs.
162   *The Oxygen Advantage: The Simple, Scientifically Proven Breathing Techniques for a Healthier, Slimmer, Faster, and Fitter You* by Patrick McKeown.

limiting factor, though it's certainly one of the more unusual methods of training. This type of training may also be able to raise erythropoietin (EPO) and red blood cell counts, although this is a short-term adaptation that is quickly reversed.

Breathing exercises such as "Minding the Gate" from yoga can also be a useful tool for improving CO_2 tolerance. This involves taking extremely shallow breaths that don't fully expel air from the lungs.

LISS is particularly effective meanwhile for strengthening the heart and developing "Qmax" (quantified maximal cardiac output). That's because training the heart rate at a lower pace ensures that it will have time to fully relax between beats, which in turn means you are able to grow it like any other muscle.[163] Using high intensity training on the other hand causes the heart to behave in more of a "twitching" fashion, which doesn't stimulate hypertrophy in the same way. In short, focusing on sustained performance at under 90 percent maximum heart rate (MHR) is the best way to build a stronger heart, which will lead to a lower resting heart rate. This is because each stroke is able to mobilize more blood around your body.

If you want to build heart strength using interval training, you take advantage of a property called "inertia." When you stop training, your heart rate doesn't *immediately* drop back down to its resting state but takes a while to reach an equilibrium. Thus, if you exert yourself at 85 to 90 percent of your MHR and then go for a walk, you'll find that you

163   Rebecca E K Macpherson et al. (2011) "Run Sprint Interval Training Improves Aerobic Performance but Not Maximal Cardiac Output," *Med. Sci. Sports Exerc.* 43(1):115–122.

spend a while with your heart rate somewhere between 65 percent and 80 percent, which is well-suited to improve heart strength. Using longer rest periods during HIIT can therefore offer some additional benefits.

A lower resting heart rate has a ton of health benefits. Not only does it result in lower blood pressure, but it can also help us feel calmer throughout the day. You should now realize that this is thanks to the link between our physiology and hormones/neurotransmitters via the vagus nerve.

Almost everyone it seems has problems with energy these days. They wake up tired, they feel too exhausted to exercise, and they struggle up the stairs. To solve the problem, they look for whatever hacks they can find. Often that means popping pills.

But what they so often forget to try is simply *improving their physical fitness*! If you become more efficient at delivering oxygen and energy to the parts of the body where it is needed, then you will feel constantly more energetic. And with a brain that is supplied by more oxygen and blood too, you'll even find that you feel more awake, more alert, and better able to focus.

Given the varied benefits of LISS versus HITT, I personally believe that, once again, the optimum solution for most people would be to *combine* the training methods. That way, you can enhance mitochondrial density, VO2 max, and resting heartrate, and prepare the body for any kind of endurance challenge. Incorporate varied protocols in your training, and challenge your energy systems in different ways.

Indeed, this is precisely the approach that is becoming increasingly popular among endurance athletes. In particular, "Polarized Training," involves splitting aerobic training regimes such that they are comprised of roughly 80 percent low intensity, and 20 percent high intensity. A little bit of threshold training is then added for good measure.

Anaerobic Threshold Training

For those interested in tapping into even greater performance, one area of focus is the "anaerobic threshold."

The anaerobic threshold is where the switch happens from primarily aerobic to primarily anaerobic processes. The point at which this happens is directly linked to the number and efficiency of mitochondria in your cells. The great news is that you can train your anaerobic threshold to the point that you will be able to run much faster and *sustain* that exertion OR hold up the roof of a collapsing building long enough for everyone to get out (this is the kind of scenario I find myself imagining often; I don't know what's wrong with me).

Doing this is simple. You find your anaerobic threshold and you run or otherwise exert yourself at that level. Running at this pace is sometimes referred to as a "threshold run" and it's a fantastic way to develop greater endurance.

While you can use a grueling process to calculate your current anaerobic threshold (which involves completing as much distance as possible over thirty minutes of exertion, then finding the average speed), you can generally assume that the anaerobic threshold will be the point at which talking becomes very difficult (this is the "talk test" used by fitness coaches throughout the land).

"Lactate threshold" or "lactate inflection point," is a term that is often used synonymously with anaerobic threshold. In fact, it is slightly different as it describes the point at which lactate build-up begins to overtake the rate at which the body can take it away. Functionally, the two are very similar, however. What is useful to reiterate here though, is that the body doesn't use just one energy source at a time. Think of this more like a spectrum, wherein the energy processes will become *gradually more* anaerobic. At a certain point, this will become too much to bear.

In fact, different types of exercise even have differing lactate inflection points! This is due to the differing ratios of muscle fiber in different muscles. You might have a higher lactate inflection point when running versus swimming.

Threshold training will not only help you to increase your ability to generate energy efficiently, but also to deal with fatigue-inducing metabolites. Ultimately, this raises the performance standard that you can sustain indefinitely.

However, many people now think that training using *predominantly* threshold training is a mistaken approach. Runners sometimes refer to this as "blackhole training"—which is training at just one speed and putting in as many "junk miles" as possible. Writers such as Ben Greenfield,[164] suggest that this method is mistaken due to its fixation on just one energy system. Many believe that it can lead to overtraining and long-term health issues. Indeed, there evidence that this type of training can cause numerous issues over time.

This is why polarized training explicitly consists of training primarily above and below this "goldilocks zone." The LISS should be purely aerobic and easy on the individual to allow

---

164   Ben Greenfield (2018), *Beyond Training*. Victory Belt.

rapid recovery. This is especially important if we want to combine cardio with strength, power, and mobility training (as we do). A good target "ratio" for this threshold training is currently suggested to be around 5 percent.

Likewise, training too much HIIT might also be overly taxing on the body. This is a case where "more" is not always more. This is another criticism that can be levelled at activities like CrossFit.

You may have noticed that all these different forms of training benefit from being able to observe your own heart rate. If you really want to tap into the full advantages of LISS for weight loss, or HIIT and threshold training for performance, then using some kind of heart monitoring device is advisable. To this end, chest-worn straps are considerably more accurate and thus desirable as compared with wrist-worn solutions which are easily affected by such things as muscle contraction.

Ultimately though, this is another example of interoception being a valuable tool for performance. If you can effectively manage your energy systems and identify the correct time to increase output or back off based on physiological cues, you can exert yourself more efficiently.

Work Capacity and Resistance Cardio

But what if you're not interested in running long distances and you just want to lift heavy weights for longer? In that case, you are looking at work capacity. Work capacity is your ability to continue whatever kind of output you want to focus on to put in more work during each session, while still being able to recover fully for the next one.

Your work capacity is influenced by a vast range of different factors that go far beyond pure aerobic fitness. This comes down partly to mitochondria, VO2 max, and lactate threshold. But it is also due to plenty of other factors, such as blood supply to the muscles (remember that high volume training can increase capillaries to specific muscles), glycogen stores, and psychology (such as mental toughness).

Even economy of movement plays an important role here, along with muscle fiber recruitment. When you engage the muscles, are you wasting energy by contracting surrounding muscles too much? Or by taking an inefficient path through the ROM?

Then there is the role of the muscles in actually enhancing circulation. "Skeletal muscle pump" is the ability of the muscles to act like miniature hearts, compressing veins that are embedded within the muscle, thereby applying more pressure to enhance circulation and drive more blood to the heart. Likewise, relaxation of the muscle may create enough of a pressure drop to draw more blood *into* the muscle.

There are countless variables influencing your ability to perform any given movement for a long duration. Rather than focusing on endurance as a whole, it may be useful to focus on the movements themselves. Rely on the SAID principle. If you want to curl weights for longer, then try curling weights *for longer*. In other words, instead of using progressive overload to increase the amount of weight you are moving, considering increasing the number of reps *at* that weight as you start to find it easier.

The key thing to recognize here is that intensity does *not* simply equal "speed." You can train using a high intensity for threshold training by adding resistance and maintaining maximum effort. This effectively turns resistance training *into* a form of cardio. But you need to get the weight correct in order to achieve this.

If the weight is extremely heavy, then you will likely begin to fail too quickly to challenge endurance. Were this not the case, you might invite injury by performing repetitive movements with higher impact. But with a mid-range weight, you can start to reach higher rep ranges and challenge your energy systems, increasing lactic threshold and other useful properties.

Tools like kettlebells and battle ropes are ideal for this kind of training as they provide just the right amount of resistance. Battle ropes are thick, heavy ropes that you can slam against the ground in a repetitive manner. This allows you to exert as much force as you want in a ballistic manner, or to find a rhythmic pattern that you can sustain for longer. Either way, they allow you to add resistance to an inherently cardiovascular challenge without any risk of injury.

Performing curls for high reps conversely will likely *not* train the heart to a significant degree, seeing as the demands placed on the body are significantly smaller when using a lighter weight and isolating only a few muscles (which is one reason a marathon runner will have a lower heart rate as compared with a bodybuilder). Push-ups and other compound, closed-chain bodyweight movements are more effective however, as they force the heart to work harder to push blood around the entire body. Extremely high-volume push-ups or sit ups *can* be used as a form of cardio.

Keep in mind that this will also vary the way that blood is supplied through the body and *which* muscle groups are working hardest. Seeing as certain metabolites and pooling blood can contribute to hypertrophy, this can be an excellent tool for enhancing endurance while *also* supporting muscle growth. Varying the types of cardio you perform can ensure that you have high work capacity across a range of exercises.

For instance, you could perform a workout focusing particularly on the shoulder muscles, only to then follow that up with a battle ropes "finisher" that will pool blood in the area while also burning calories and increasing your work capacity.

There is a potential issue of increasing slow-twitch fibers in an area where you want explosive power, but we'll discuss this in the next chapter.

Metabolic Conditioning

This brings us nicely to metabolic conditioning which uses movements like press-ups and kettlebell swings in a circuit with brief intervals to achieve even greater endurance and weight loss benefits. The aim is simply to introduce insufficient recovery; the heart rate remains elevated and various energy processes are challenged.

In short, while performing a hundred push-ups is a strength task that will build work capacity and have some endurance benefits, performing twenty push-ups ten times with thirty or sixty second breaks is an even greater endurance challenge that will somewhat manage the problem of muscle fatigue. And if we switch between push-ups and a host of other movements (pull ups, kettlebell swings, tuck jumps) and try to sustain max output for thirty seconds at a time, we have metabolic conditioning.

A good "metcon circuit" can also be designed to intentionally challenge the heart even more via "shunting." For instance, we can switch between upper and lower-body movements (push-ups followed by squats), which will force the heart to drive the blood up and then down the body. The heart works harder, and the circulatory system becomes more efficient at delivering the fuel where it is needed.

And remember, the energy efficiency of specific muscles (as determined by mitochondrial density, twitch fiber, and blood supply/pump) can be trained individually. By training the *whole body* in an endurance-focused manner, we might be able to enhance our metabolism and energy efficiency in a more comprehensive way, versus training for time in just one movement pattern.

Is metcon superior to going for a long run? That is entirely a matter of preference and your own personal goals. But with that said, it's worth noting that for the purposes of SuperFunctional Training, there are additional advantages.

That's because metabolic conditioning offers a way to *combine* endurance training with movements that provide other benefits too. For example, if you create a metabolic conditioning circuit that consists of kettlebell swings, lizard crawls, and offset loaded carries, then you can train endurance while *also* developing core stability, hip hinge, grip strength, mobility, and more.

Of course, it's always important to consider the inherent risk of performing any movement *while fatigued*. Smart exercise selection is encouraged!

With all that said, training with any and all of these methods will ultimately mean you can employ *all* of the other strategies in this book to greater effect. More volume = more results. And as you are about to see, we have a lot to get through!

CHAPTER 16

Integration: Becoming SuperFunctional

So, here we are. We've discussed just about every training method under the sun. We've looked at samurais, Shaolin monks, prisoners of war, indigenous tribes, chess masters, YouTube parkour sensations, powerlifters, ice men, adventurers, old-time strongmen, and more.

Each of them has had something useful to offer, and by combining concepts from all these disparate fields, we can devise a training strategy that is *truly* comprehensive, that trains all of our most important traits and abilities. This way, we can fulfill more of our potential, and create incredible new possibilities.

But isn't that rather...a lot? How do you even begin to program something like this? When do you find any time to rest? Batman is a fictional character, after all!

And what about the dreaded interference effect?

Fear not. I have a plan!

The ATSP Hierarchy Revisited

My suggestion is not that you should be training a full day of powerlifting, followed by a full day of movement training, followed by bodybuilding, and sprinting. Though to be fair, concurrent strategies like this *could* be employed if you want to enjoy two or three disciplines with complementary (or opposite) benefits.

What I'm proposing instead, is that we simply pick and choose the very best moves from across the spectrum and combine them into extremely functional workouts. Instead of having three bodybuilding moves for our pecs, we might have a powerlifting move, a movement-oriented exercise, *and* a bodybuilding move. This would then train max power, intramuscular coordination, and strength endurance/hypertrophy—all while targeting the same area and building on what had come before.

So, we are not doing any more or any less than we were before, we're simply choosing from a broader range of options.

The next question then: with so much to pick from, how do you know which are the best exercises?

That's where the ATSP Hierarchy comes in useful again. If the aim is to improve our physical potential as much as possible, then we should aim to select the moves that will give us the most "bang for our buck." These will be the moves that develop the most traits and/or attributes.

In short, these are the most "high value" movements from various disciplines.

While there is a limitless pool of these, I have been subtly highlighting specific movements on our journey that fit these criteria. Here are some examples that could form the basis of any highly functional training program:

Primarily Cognitive	Traits
Rope climbs	Grip strength, biceps, lats, core strength, work capacity
Lizard crawls	Contralateral coordination, core stability (anti-rotation), work capacity, hip mobility
Offset farmers' walks	Grip strength, work capacity, hip stability, core stability (anti-lateral flexion)
Quasi-isometric squat	Hip mobility, muscle control, posture, mental toughness
High-repetition push-up	Muscle endurance, core stability (anti-extension),
Handstand practice	Proprioception, shoulder mobility, wrist mobility, core strength, shoulder strength
L-Sit/V-Sit with Flutters	Tricep strength, compressive strength, ab strength
Hangs	Shoulder mobility, shoulder stability, grip strength, core strength, endurance, mental toughness, joint health
Heavy squats	Bone density, posterior chain strength

Clapping push-ups	Upper body explosiveness, pecs, shoulders, triceps
Planche progressions	Straight arm strength, wrist mobility, core stability, anterior deltoids,
Bench press	Max pushing strength, bone density
Bar bending	Muscle control, pushing strength, grip strength
Bear crawling on a beam	Balance/proprioception, pec strength, tricep strength, core stability
LaLanne Push-Ups (and progressions toward)	Core stability (anti-extension), shoulder strength,
Muscle up	Upper body explosiveness, pushing/pulling strength, transitional strength
Gama cast	Core stability, shoulder mobility, grip strength, joint health
Hindu push-up	Back mobility, shoulder mobility, pecs, shoulders, core
High-repetition Indian squats	Quad strength, calf strength, endurance, leg hypertrophy
Hardstyle kettlebell swing	Muscle control, hip hinge, explosiveness, jumping height, running speed
Cartwheels	Proprioception, balance, core strength, explosiveness
Battle ropes, tabata	Endurance, mitochondrial density, VO2 max
Heavy bag martial arts	Endurance, mobility/kicking height, shoulders, pecs, core, serape effect

Medicine ball slams (diagonal angle)	Serape effect, explosiveness, stretch-shortening, intramuscular coordination
Steady state run	VO2 max, mitochondrial density, heart health, hippocampal memory
Monkey bars	Grip strength, core strength, shoulder mobility, lats, biceps, joint health
Lunge walks	Single-leg strength, glutes, quads, hamstrings, calves
Jump squats	Explosiveness, legs
Cossack squats	Hip mobility, single-leg strength, proprioception
Front lever	Scapular retraction, lats, biceps, core

Primarily Cognitive

Juggling	Plasticity, hand-eye coordination, attention, working memory
Writing with nondominant hand	Fine motor control, ambidexterity, plasticity, verbal fluency
Hakalau meditation	Peripheral vision, calm focus, recovery
Acem meditation	Creativity, rest and recovery
Mental math	Focus/emotional control, working memory
Dual N-Back	Working memory, focus
Time dedicated to learning	Pasticity, skills

I'd like to emphasize that this is just an example. This is by no means a comprehensive list. This book was already *long enough* without me going into great detail regarding every single amazing movement. And what is suitable for one person, may not be right for someone else. Still, if you can get a bunch of these in your exercise diet, you will be *well* on your way to becoming SuperFunctional.

Likewise, there is no requirement to include every exercise I've listed here. Many of these will develop a lot of overlapping traits, in which case you can pick one or the other. Likewise, you might simply decide you don't gel well with one of these strategies and thus elect to replace it with something from your own research.

Of course, we should pay particular attention to the Super Traits I've discussed. These are the traits that will allow for the development of many *other* traits and attributes. The items on this list that deal with work capacity in some form, that enhance plasticity, or that boost mental toughness should all be considered *high priority*.

Introducing: Slowcomotion—Strength at Every Angle

Slowcomotion is the name I have given to a new training method I've been using to develop strength and control at unpredictable angles, and thus utilize as many traits and attributes as possible. It is no means the last word in training, just something I've enjoyed using and had success with.

I also call it **S**low **A**nd **M**echanically **D**is**A**dvanged **M**ovement: SAMDAM.

This is *extremely slow* locomotive/freestyle movement training, designed to build mind-muscle connection, core stability, endurance, mobility, and more in a single style of training.

There are four ways to practice this (though they are not strict categories):

- Ground SAMDAM
- Bipedal SAMDAM
- Climbing SAMDAM
- Manipulation SAMDAM

To elaborate a little further, let's consider the Ground SAMDAM. Here, you're going to be performing movements like the lizard crawl but with extreme control and awareness, like a quasi-isometric. Brace throughout your core and very slowly reach forward with one hand, lower your weight onto that pillar, and then brace again while you move the other hand and leg forward, staying close to the ground at all times.

Be sure to breathe through the movement (this is not easy at first).

Your precise movement should be varied, and you'll transition to other moves like a low bear crawl or even push-up variations, while keeping tension in the working muscles the entire time.

You might perform a slow LaLanne push-up, then move into an archer push-up, all in slow motion. You could even slowly lift your body into a handstand if you have developed the strength and control.

Not only do I think this is an extremely "high value" form of training, but I also believe it is a very useful teaching tool for illustrating many of the concepts we've addressed in this book.

Here's how it works:

In Chapter 5, I discussed how old-time strongmen would develop their mind-muscle connection in order to exert greater strength, or contract individual muscles.

In the chapter on advanced calisthenics (Chapter 8), we start to see some real-world application of this level of awareness. When performing the planche for instance, you are required to protract your scapula and brace the core. Ideally, you'll have a slight posterior pelvic tilt. Ask the average person to do those things and they will look at you blankly.

There's that sensorimotor amnesia...

But this knowledge is valuable, and the ability to control your entire body can make *every* movement more powerful and more graceful. It carries over into simpler movements as you are able to perform a regular push-up without allowing your waist to sag or shoulders to collapse. The same movement is now performed with greater rigidity, working strength in more areas as a result.

That same awareness and control can carry over into countless other activities, giving you better strength, safety, and freedom of expression in *every* movement. When engaging the serape effect delivering a punch for instance, you will contract the rotational muscles and stabilizers, and actively relax the antagonistic muscles.

Slowcomotion teaches this. By slowing complex movements down and putting yourself in these more difficult angles, you require yourself to listen to your body and make tiny adjustments to maintain balance. You will strengthen yourself at weaker points in the movement and learn how to move powerfully from any position.

Of course, slowcomotion should also be performed in other positions. Or we aren't fully developing the body. While there are many ways to break down human movement, I believe that focusing on forms of locomotion + manipulation is a good way to cover everything.

- Crawl
- Climb
- Walk
- Manipulate

Climbing SAMDAM can involve lifting yourself up on a chin up bar, then holding yourself in a position near the top. Stabilize, then slowly move one hand to a different position to climb your way *around* the bar. Practice turning around 360 degrees, lowering into a hang, performing slow front levers and slow one-armed pull ups. Much of this might be beyond your current ability level, but your moves will become more ambitious as you practice.

You can also experiment with other forms of slow climbing. For instance, head over to some railings and then grab them with both hands, keeping your feet planted against the metal so as not to touch the ground. Now brace the core, and slowly reposition one hand to move up, across, or even *around* on the spot.

(Another form of ground slowcomotion can involve crawling slowly along a rail or tree branch.)

When performed correctly, this should look almost like floating. Like *supernatural movement*.

For legs, you will practice slow squat walking, duck walking (walking on the balls of the feet with the knees slightly bent), squatting, Indian squatting, Cossack squatting, and lunge walking. The aim is to move gracefully while maintain tension and moving through every range of motion.

Manipulation uses an external submaximal load, moved in graceful, controlled patterns while standing, squatting, or even sitting.

Remember how I discussed that you could train using a chair? Try holding it from the bottom of one foot, then slowly raising it in the air, pointing it forward, moving it downward, drawing large circles etc. You can do it against a wall, applying the pressure from your own body. How about while crawling along a beam?

Take it very slow and gentle with this training. Many of the muscles you'll be activating will likely have been entirely neglected for years. Expect to wake up sore! Likewise, be careful with moving into positions that may cause impingement or other issues. If you're unsure, then stick with movements that you are familiar with and transferring between those movements in a controlled manner.

But on the other hand, by moving very slowly, you should be able to limit damage to the fascia. Make no mistake, if the early ideas surrounding fascia are correct, then this will serve as a powerful way to build that kind of strength.

And by using only the bodyweight (or relatively light loads), you will likewise limit the likelihood of injury. As I stated in an earlier chapter, I believe our strength and power is primarily intended for movement. The largest muscles in our body are all muscles that are key for movement: glutes, quads, hamstrings, lats, pecs. This form of training should develop power and control at every position that you can move in. It should help to reawaken the communication with your body, and increase the amount of information coming in.

Overcoming Gravity Isometrics

To make this training style more complete, you can also try incorporating other types of movement such as explosive plyometrics (from stronger and more stable positions only) that break the slow cadence for brief spurts, or even overcoming isometrics.

To employ an overcoming isometric this way, you simply move into a position where you *can't* lift your body. For instance, you try to perform a one-handed pseudo planche push-up, or you attempt to "squeeze" the ground like a pec fly. I call these moves the "Earth Punch" and "Earth Crusher," because you've gotsta' give these things awesome names![165]

This way, you use the ground and your own bodyweight as the immovable force and can apply max effort. The best part is that you are essentially just struggling at calisthenics moves you can't perform. Eventually, this may lead to

---

165   I have not yet reached the point of shouting the move before performing it though.

the necessary adaptations that allow you to perform the movement. Try to one arm planche until you *can* one arm planche! And this flows nicely from SAMDAM.

I consider SAMDAM to be a useful "glue" that can help to train angles and positions that even the most functional movements don't manage. Using this in conjunction with the movements I highlighted can result in an even more complete physicality.

As with everything though, you should take SAMDAM very slowly and carefully, and listen to your body as you experiment with it. You are not used to hold your weight in these positions, so don't overdo it. Adaptation takes time.

The Missing Attributes

At this juncture, I'd also like to introduce another concept related to the ATSP system: "Missing Attributes." These are physical attributes that aren't commonly considered in many training programs and which don't get developed through normal lifestyle activities. Even focusing on high value exercises may not be enough to ensure that each of these is covered.

A perfect example would be lateral rotation of the shoulders. Lateral rotation is sorely missing from a large number of programs, which is *particularly* unfortunate seeing as most of us spend 90 percent of our time with our shoulders hunched forward. We spend all day typing and hunching over mobile phones, then we go to the gym and push things *forward*. If we pull things backward, we typically do so by hinging at the elbows or pulling from the lats.

So, even though a movement like the face pull is very focused and doesn't provide multiple benefits, it is still extremely valuable because those benefits are hard to find elsewhere. It's something most of us should be incorporating.

The same is true for mobility in the thoracic spine—*especially* when it comes to extension (bending backward). Again, most of us spend all day hunched over and rarely have any need to lean backward. We have a few moves like the Hindu squat on our list that will address this. But performing some back bridges certainly won't hurt,[166] and this is why I personally like Ponte[167] from Capoeira. As they say, you're only as young as your spine!

(Though Ponte is also effective for many other things, such as proprioception, shoulder mobility, wrist mobility, and core strength, to name a few!)

Another example of a missing attribute is straight arm strength, which we can address with moves like pseudo planche push-up (for those not ready for planche progressions). How about calf strength? Few movements here focus on calves specifically, which is why I also like calf jumps. Here, you practice jumping while keeping your knees and hips entire straight. All of the propulsion comes from the calves! Calf raises also work if you don't have gym access.

We could also include finger push-ups on such a list, for finger strength (although LaLanne push-ups will also train

---

166   That is, unless you ask the "back mechanic" Stuart McGill who believes moves like this cause too much spinal compression. Practice with caution if you have a history of back pain, but keep in mind that yogis and others have been practicing this for generations without ill effects!

167   "Ponte" is the name for back bridge in Capoeira, though often practitioners will roll in and out of the position from facing forward with their hands on the ground. There are some other moves on the list we haven't met yet too: YouTube is your friend!

this, as will develop the hands). Knuckle push-ups can toughen the bones of the knuckles, which is a must for fighters. Many people could benefit from using some self-resistance to train the neck.

Sequencing

Those of you with some coaching experience might be raising your eyebrows at this point. Talk about a scattershot approach! How are you supposed to provide progressive overload? How can you develop any one trait when there are *so many factors*?

I discussed this in a previous chapter. If the move is too complex, then it won't allow you to fatigue any given muscle group. The lizard crawl won't build giant pecs, because you'll fatigue before you get to the point where that is possible. Or your core will start to sag. Or your shoulders will give up.

We can't train rope climbs for high volume because that's asking for someone to slip and hurt themselves.

So, how do we begin to structure such a mess?

The answer is simple. Place the most complex and demanding movements at the start of the routine, and the simpler movements toward the end. This takes a similar approach to power building or reverse pyramid training, except that we're focusing on complexity and nervous-system fatigue rather than *just* the amount of weight (though that's still a factor).

For example, you might start your workout with a heavy movement like a squat or bench press, or with complex moves like planche progressions and crawls. You could then move toward middling exercises like one-armed push-ups and perhaps some cable flies. Then you might end with high volume push-ups, and a finisher on the heavy bag.

Anything multi-joint, multi-planar, or extremely heavy will go at the start of the workout. Anything closed-chain, light, or very isolated will go at the end and can be used with higher volume.

These latter movements will be made more difficult thanks to the early challenges, but the risk of injury will remain low. Moreover, we'll be able to challenge the body both with enriching, demanding movements, AND with the high volume and targeted challenge that elicits an adaptation.

Mechanical Dropsets

Another powerful tool is the "mechanical dropset."

If you think all the way back to Chapter 4, you may remember how we could use a drop set in order to push past failure when training with weights, maintaining constant tension on the target muscle to facilitate hypertrophy. To do so, you simply lower the weight each time you reach failure, then keep going!

Well, it turns out that you can do the same thing using multiple different movement patterns.

In a mechanical drop set, you simply alter the precise mechanics of a movement *mid-way through* a set once you reach failure. So, you might perform as many push-ups as you can then, when you can no longer perform any more, switch to push-ups on your *knees* to carry on.

If you wanted to focus on developing your finger strength but you were worried that finger push-ups wouldn't allow you to build big pecs, you could get around this by performing as many finger push-ups as possible, then switching to normal push-ups to finish up.

There are countless other examples of how this could work, and you can "drop" your way through an endless list of different exercises to provide an incredible challenge. For example:

Overcoming isometric chest press six seconds -> 80 percent Bench press -> Clapping push-up -> One arm push-up -> Lizard crawls

Perform each to failure and maintain as little pause between these movements as possible. Rest for a good three minutes, then go again. This is *intense*. I call it a "gauntlet set." It's like a circuit without rest periods, all focused on a single muscle group. The rest between rounds should be *long* (three minutes or more).

If building endurance is your top priority, then of course you can use the suggestion from the last chapter, by creating metabolic conditioning circuits that challenge multiple different traits and attributes. Why not use a few gauntlet-sets to begin with and end on some metcon circuits?

In short, there are *plenty* of ways to combine multiple traits while designing a routine that is both challenging and safe.

Splits

The next question is how to divide these workouts across the week. We've seen push pull legs, bro-splits, and full-body routines. The good news is that all of the above can be applied just *fine* using this cross-modal approach. You can choose to build workouts by selecting movements that target one muscle group (as in the above example). You can train the entire body with a little less intensity but greater frequency. Or you can separate pushing, pulling, and leg movements and use a PPL approach.

Personally, I prefer a more full-body approach for this style of training. Many of these movements are inherently compound and multi-planar, meaning that focusing on a single body part could be limiting. Just make sure you leave *ample* time for recovery and always listen to your body.

Something else I will often do, is to make a workout full-body but with a particular area of focus. It might be a full-body routine but with multiple pushing movements for example, or a full-body routine with a heavy emphasis on core stability. I call these "Prime Focus Workouts."

There are those comic bookish names again.

I will say that the extra emphasis on mental training *may* necessitate its own "day." That is to say that you can benefit from having a "brain" day of sorts. That's just one way to structure this—plenty of options work. You could likewise start your day with one of these meditation practices and a mental "task." You could also try incorporating the mental training into your workouts, juggling at the end of a session or using quasi-isometrics as a kind of moving meditation at the end of a routine. A bodyscan meditation can be a great way to set your mindset prior to training and to "check in" with the muscles, as though it were a quick diagnostic check.

Perhaps you could even try performing math problems *while* training!

Alternatively, if you occasionally take a week off from training (a recommended strategy that you can use around once every six weeks to allow for a total recovery), you can use that time to focus primarily on mental training. This also works well with mobility.

But What About the Interference Effect?

But what about the interference effect? What about specificity?

The interference effect simply states that training in different modalities will often cause one type of training to "interfere" with the other. It's a common argument used against functional training and that would apply *doubly* to SuperFunctional Training!

The most straightforward example of this is the fact that training for endurance and strength don't really go hand-in-hand.

Running long distances will cause your blood sugar to dip, which will result in an increase in cortisol and myostatin and a decrease in testosterone. This means you will likely lose *some* muscle as a result of your training. Training for endurance will also increase the ratio of slow-twitch muscle fibers in the legs, which is precisely what you *don't* want as a bodybuilder or powerlifter seeing as slow-twitch muscle is slower to contract *and* smaller in size.

Even carrying more muscle weight is counterproductive if you want to run for as long as possible without burning out.

In short, the body is trying to adapt to *two* things!

We see this elsewhere too. I referenced a study way back in Chapter 1 that swimmers actually couldn't jump as high as untrained individuals—because they had become accustomed to using their legs in a certain way.

Can you maintain two competing neural pathways? Of course! There are plenty of people who play two instruments extremely well. If the swimmers had trained as high jumpers *as well,* they likely would be extremely good at jumping.

But they might never get quite as good as someone who trains *only* as a high jumper. Apart from anything else, the dedicated high jumper will simply have more time to train that one movement.

So, we should all only train for one thing, right?

Wrong!

First: it's time for non-athletes to get out of the mindset of trying to be the best at any one thing. Being the best simply *doesn't make sense for most people*. Sure, it can be fun chasing after numbers, but the danger is that you lose sight of the big picture.

> **Get out of the mindset of trying to be the best at any one thing.**

Do you really need to be the strongest powerlifter in your gym? At the expense of everything else?

It's also worth mentioning that there are plenty of ways in which opposite training methods complement each other: even endurance training and bodybuilding!

For example:

- Endurance training lowers resting heart rate, which may make you more anabolic

- Endurance training drastically improves work capacity, helping you to train for longer

- Endurance training and bodybuilding will both increase blood supply to the muscles

- Building strength in the muscles helps you to run more efficiently, and thus run further

- Endurance training will burn fat, thus revealing more definition in the muscles

- Both types of training increase bone density, especially in the lower body

Then there are the countless adaptations from both that don't affect one another. For instance, you can improve your muscle fiber recruitment by lifting weights and that won't have any negative effect on your marathon running. We've also seen that training with high volume and moderate weight in closed-chain exercise can potentially increase mitochondrial efficiency in *fast-twitch* fiber.

In short, the body will adapt uniquely to the challenge of increased endurance AND increased muscle mass. And there is evidence to support this. Studies find that when comparing three groups assigned with endurance programs, strength programs, and concurrent programs (which combine both), the third group *still makes gains*. In one study, participants were assigned either to riding on a bicycle to build endurance, using an isokinetic device to increase torque strength, or doing both simultaneously. To begin with, the combo group kept up with the other two groups both in terms of endurance gains *and* strength gains. However, as the study progressed, they fell behind—though they continued making smaller gains in both areas.[168]

The conclusion of this study is that "simultaneous training may inhibit the normal adaptation to either program when performed alone." That's fair enough—it does! But that's not a negative consequence for the vast majority of us, because we can *still get stronger and more endurant simultaneously.*

And this is desirable! The problem with these studies is that they are generally written from the perspective of the pro athlete. But it is simply *not optimal* for the average person to develop the physique of a competitive bodybuilder. Getting that big takes you to the point where you can get out of breath climbing the stairs. Mobility is hindered by the sheer size of the muscle. And to compete, there is almost a requirement to use drugs.

But nor should the average person strive for the physique endurance athletes like Mo Farah. Farah is an incredible athlete, but he's also extremely slim and light at around fifty-eight kg. (or 125 pounds). He would likely have a hard time wrestling the average person, and his explosive speed is likely to be very low. Moreover, the sheer amount of running you would need to put in to compete at this level could risk significant injury.

You can train using concurrent methods and still be *much* stronger than the average person *and* have much higher endurance. You're ready to run for the bus when you need to, *or* to wrestle a bear when you're attacked in the woods. To me, it's a no-brainer that this should be the most desirable physique for the average person.

***

168   A. G. Nelson et. al. (1990) "Consequences of Combining Strength and Endurance Training Regimes." Phys. Ther. 70(5):287–294.

(None of this is to take away from the incredible achievements of pro athletes. They are extremely dedicated and breathtaking examples of pushing human limits in a single direction. But that is a big lifestyle decision that is certainly not for everyone!)

The authors of the concurrent training study *also* go on to say: "The extent of the interference probably depends on the nature and intensity of the individual training program."

That's the other point that I wish to make: if you design your training smartly, you can get around many of these challenges. We've seen for example that you can trigger many of the desirable adaptations gained from endurance training by using metabolic conditioning circuits, or by using resistance cardio, and that these won't seriously harm your strength gains.

This book is full of examples of people who have demonstrated exceptional skill in strength and endurance. How about Ross Edgley's marathon car tow? Or Jack LaLanne's incredible swims? How about Tom Platz's insane repetitions on the leg press? CrossFit places a huge focus on this type of training, too.

Powerbuilders meanwhile demonstrate that you can train for epic size *and* incredible strength. YouTuber Jujimufu is built like a bodybuilder yet does a variety of flips and acrobatic movements. Old-time strongmen regularly incorporated hand balancing and other various physical feats into their acts.

There are other workarounds too. For example, thanks to epigenetics, we know that achieving a certain level of strength, or endurance *once* will make it much easier to get back to that point. This means that you could dedicate several months to building size and strength, then focus on a different skill for a while. Then, when you incorporate both into a combined training regime, you should see impressive results in both categories.

Over on my website (www.thebioneer.com), I provided training programs that are designed to help readers improve in multiple areas simultaneously. I've had great feedback from those that have tried them, and I've been doing the same myself for years. If you don't know how to write a program and want something ready-made, then this can be a good place to start. That said, I do encourage experimentation and adaptation. We are all different!

And finally, there are plenty of types of training that won't have a negative impact on any others. For example, if you are a bodybuilder *or* an endurance athlete, none of the following will trigger the interference effect and, in many cases, will significantly support you in your chosen event. Yet these are all things that are typically overlooked by most athletes/average folk.

- Grip strength training
- Meditation
- Brain training for focus, working memory etc.
- Mobility
- Straight arm strength and other "untapped" forms of strength training
- Ambidexterity
- Foot strength and mobility
- Breathing
- Visual processing speed

⚱ The list goes on!

Certainly, I believe that *everyone* should spend some time training their brain. And I hope I've made a case for that here.

And for most people, I hope that I've made the case for training like a "performance polymath." For picking and choosing from disparate areas of fitness and training, to become the precise person you want to be, and to drastically extend your potential in the process.

Training should not be limited to a few big lifts or trying to build big muscles for show. I believe that training has the ability to drastically extend human capabilities.

CHAPTER 17

What Will You Become?

In this book, I have tried to illustrate that any distinction between training the body and mind is really an arbitrary one. It is all nervous system training; it is all training one big plastic *thing*.

Thus, it makes sense to approach any training regime in a more cohesive manner, treating brain training and mental training as effectively one and the same.

And likewise, I recommend that you consider your training program as part of holistic lifestyle transformation.

This is where a lot of attempts to "get into shape" fall flat, viewed as a separate endeavor we can just bolt on to a packed and hectic lifestyle. I've lost track of how many people have enthusiastically asked me to write them a training program, only to completely forget about it weeks later. Unless they're paying me, I actually now tend to *assume* this is what will happen.

Why? Because there was a reason they weren't already in shape! That reason was that they were extremely overtired, overstressed, and overburdened. If you are coming home and crashing on the sofa every night in front of the television, it's because you have no energy.

Time isn't the issue here as many people think (unless you can honestly tell me you haven't watched any TV boxsets this year). The issue is that energy is a finite resource. You can't keep adding new activities without eventually running out of juice.

So, if you're already too tired to train, what makes you think that you can simply *start* training an additional four hours per week? Add the commute to the gym on top of that, the showering, the washing of gym kit, even the energy it takes to *mentally convince* yourself to work out.

If you really want to commit to becoming a healthier version of yourself, you need to look at your current routine and *make space*. That might mean removing a commitment, or even quitting a hobby.

Alternatively, you could consider the "super trait" that is energy. How could you improve your sleep, or reduce stress, in order to gain more energy to apply to a training regime? You may find that meditating helps you invest time to earn more energy back.

Finally, you could *incorporate* your training into your routine in a way that would allow you to develop yourself without doing anything extra. This is the option that I believe has the most transformative potential.

Lifestyle Changes

There are thus a few tweaks that I believe we should make to our general practice and lifestyles, that could have huge benefits across our training and other activities.

- Wearing barefoot shoes is extremely advisable for most people. Ease yourself into this, especially on tarmac. But it's time to reawaken your feet!

- Training outside wherever possible is also *highly* recommended.

- Taking a cold shower can have numerous benefits.

- Enhancing sleep is a priority.

These are easy changes or "hacks" that you can make that will once again develop a huge number of beneficial traits.

We can also use the "bang for your buck" approach to considering supplementation. There is an endless number of supplements and nutrients with beneficial effects for the brain and body. Seeking out all of these—either through your diet or as pills—would be an all-consuming wild goose chase. Instead then, we can consider substances that benefit multiple attributes and traits at once.

Some examples that I consider to meet these criteria are:

- Vitamin D

- Omega 3 fatty acid

- Lutein + zeaxanthin

- Creatine

- Magnesium

- Vitamin C

- Ashwaghanda

That said, the best thing you can do for your diet is simply to eat as healthily as possible by seeking out varied, nutrient dense foods. This will have a huge impact on your energy, your recovery, and even your strength.

Micro-Workouts and Incidental Training

If you think this book listed a *lot* of things that are currently missing from your fitness regime then...*well yeah*! Our bodies evolved to be in constant motion. We would be trail running, climbing trees, throwing rocks, swimming, and fighting. We'd be playing, dancing, lighting fires, and cooking. Even when chatting, we'd be squatting. The rest of the time, we'd be asleep or at least very much at rest. We would not spend hours "sitting down stressed."

The top athletes in the world train multiple times per day. Military personnel are made to perform high reps of push-ups and pull ups from dusk 'till dawn.

Forty minutes in the gym does *not* compare with this. Neither will forty minutes in the gym undo the damage caused by decades of sitting for nine to ten hours a day. Not from a mechanical standpoint, not from a mental standpoint, and not from a metabolic standpoint.

Really, you should be *constantly* training or relaxing. Or at least, you should be constantly moving and using your brain. This doesn't have to be extremely intense. In fact, it's better if it isn't.

We have a tendency to push ourselves extremely hard at the gym because we're trying to make up for our incredibly inactive lifestyles in such a short space of time. It's like trying to pack a week's worth of movement into a few hours.

No surprise that many of us end up injured.

Unfortunately, that's the reality for most of us. Unless you have a physical job, you simply can't choose to engage in constant movement. If you become that guy/gal who squats at their desk, you'll probably be escorted off the property.

One solution is to use "micro-workouts."

Micro-workouts have been gaining more attention recently. And for good reason, as they can be more fun and practical as compared with longer workout sessions. And they are no less effective.

If you know how to trigger a response in a short space of time, you can actually get quite a good workout in just ten to fifteen minutes. A big drop set for your biceps is enough to trigger hypertrophy in the biceps. Three sets of a hundred push-ups in ten minutes will trigger growth and add to work capacity in your pecs.

Three times your one-rep maximum on the bench press with a few warm-up sets can help you increase your max pushing strength in just ten to fifteen minutes.

Tabata is a highly effective protocol for increasing endurance and mitochondrial density that takes just four minutes!

And approaching training this way has *many* functional benefits. By breaking your workouts up throughout the day, you'll actually raise your metabolism multiple times. Remember, the afterburn effect lasts for two to three hours following a high intensity workout!

This could also help to spike your anabolism and protein synthesis multiple times throughout the day for enhanced muscle growth. You'll boost your brain plasticity more times, and you'll increase blood flow to the brain.

Performing multiple micro-workouts is also perfect for improving mobility, seeing as mobility isn't something you can "overtrain" in as easily. It's perfect for greasing the groove on a low-intensity skilled movement like the freestanding handstand or juggling. And it's well-suited to quick stints of meditation or mental math.

The main issue here is showering. Doesn't training three times in a day mean showering three times in a day, too? To that I say, if you train with your top off outside, it's less of a problem. It's also less of a problem if you keep the workouts *really* short. It's also less of an issue for a mobility routine, or spot of mental math (if you sweat while performing mental math, you can probably tone it down a notch).

You might use these ten- to twenty-minute micro-workouts on top of a longer training stint, or you might use them *instead* of that one workout, performing the precise same amount of work, but broken down into smaller chunks. This gives you the added bonus of being able to fully recover between exercises and thus improve your effort and technique for each movement.

And there are many logical ways to do this. If you currently use full-body routines, then why not simply break them down into separate push, pull, and leg workouts? If you train using a big split, pick three pushing movements and train them each separately.

Pandiculation and Continuous Movement

Does this already sound tiring?

Here's the paradoxical thing: it really isn't. In fact, the more you move and the more you engage your brain, the more energy you have. Of course, that's especially true if you also combine all of this with a relaxing meditation practice, weeks off, and great sleep and nutrition.

But the simple act of continually moving throughout the day is something that can provide you with more energy than you thought possible.

Many of us plan to work out in the evening only to put it off when the time comes. Why? Because we feel tired and sluggish and the mere thought of movement seems completely alien to us. That's because you've been static all day. You haven't had need to engage your muscles or even listen to your proprioceptive feedback. It's as though your muscles have switched off and, as such, you struggle to summon the energy, strength, or coordination to bring them back to life.

The muscles actually build up a slight residual tension as a result of this neglect, and over time this is what has led to many of us completely losing conscious control over them. This is what happened to the muscle control that you should have had in the first place. Author and creator of Somatics, Thomas Hanna, refers to this as "sensorimotor amnesia."

But if you've been moving all throughout the day, this isn't an issue. It's like you're constantly warmed up. (Though a quick warm-up is still advisable to activate those pathways and limber up the connective tissue.)

You aren't starting the engine from cold every time, but instead just switching your attention to something else.

Another strategy you can use to "wake up" the muscles prior to a quick workout or incidental movement, is to perform a "pandiculation."[169]

If you've ever seen a cat or dog wake up from a long sleep, you'll notice that it doesn't start doing static stretches or warming up. Instead, it performs a long stretch and a yawn, which together form a pandiculation.

Pandiculations appear to have the explicit purpose of releasing residual tension in the muscles and simultaneously reawakening the sensory input from them. We do this when we yawn—this is actually a pandiculation of the respiratory muscles! But we can also use the technique in other parts of the body, it should feel almost like you are yawning with your pecs or your legs.

Once you get it, this is a great way to increase energy, strength, and proprioception prior to a short bout of movement. It won't replace a brief warm-up, but it can help you feel "ready to go" much faster.

---

169   Thomas Hanna (2004), *Somatics: Reawakening The Mind's Control of Movement, Flexibility, And Health*. De Capo Press.

A Modular Approach

With this perspective, you might choose to view your workouts as modular.

Instead of writing workouts, consider writing a *list of specific traits* that appeal to you. What do *you* want to work toward? What traits matter to you and your goals? Now select exercises and techniques that will train the specific physical attributes related to those traits.

Then take each of those "blocks" of moves and train them either on their own or combined into longer workouts. As long as you train each of them the optimal number of times each week, it doesn't matter how they are clustered.

Incidental Training

But I'm also interested in taking this further with what I call "incidental training." I looked for a similar approach online and was surprised not to find one.

Basically, I think that we should aim to turn many of our everyday activities into opportunities to train. Once we know all the different traits we are interested in pursuing, and all the different ways we can develop them, we might start to see opportunities cropping up throughout the day.

This effectively results in a change in *environment*, which is ultimately what shapes us. More on this in a moment.

As a very busy dad, I don't get time to start my day with a mobility routine and ten-minute meditation. Those "morning routine" videos on YouTube look very nice in theory. Instead, my morning is taken up with playing with my daughter and preparing breakfast before I start work. I love this, I wouldn't change it for the world. But it does mean I get approximately zero time to do anything else, and I start my working day with three hours of intense playing already under my belt.

But there's no reason I can't have it both ways! When Emmy wants to be chased, I'll chase her around the house in a bear crawl or lizard crawl. When the kettle is boiling and she's in the highchair, I squeeze a grip trainer. Sometimes I do a spontaneous handstand, which Emmy responds to by shouting "upside down!" and then getting into downward dog herself. (She is far more flexible than me.)

When Emmy wants me to draw a cat, I do it with my left hand. And when she wants to play Lego, I play with her while in a deep, resting squat.

And it's not just playing with children that presents opportunities like this. If you're waiting for the bus, why not do calf raises on the curb? How about doing a quick five-minute meditation in the shower? Or practicing your squat there? Why not run to the shop down the road instead of walking?

I have a five-minute nondirective meditation while standing in the shower and do a little stretching there. I always brush my teeth with my left, nondominant hand.

If you drop something on the floor, pick it up with your feet, or pistol squat to the ground to grab it. If you're sitting watching TV, why not hold a passive stretch?

My only advice here is to be slow and careful when incorporating this amount of activity to your routine. You probably aren't used to it, and trying to force adaptation too quickly can lead to injury. Start with small changes and *listen to your body.*

(This goes for everything discussed in this book. Remember that while you may see muscle changes in as little as eight days, it can take as long as two months to see structural changes in the tendons. Rush ahead, and you may invite injury.[170])

As for mental training, almost anything can be training if you apply the right mindset to it. Remember how flow states are engaged by finding the perfect level of difficulty? Well, when it comes to everyday tasks, you *set* the difficulty by deciding your own standards.

Instead of just writing some notes, how about trying to write with the most beautiful handwriting you can, as quickly as you can?

I enjoy trying to read Doctor Seuss's books to Emmy quickly, fluently, and with as few errors as possible (they aren't half tongue twisters).[171] My verbal fluency has noticeably improved as a result, especially when it comes to presenting on my YouTube channel.

This directly led to more exposure for my online business, and possibly helped me get this book written. See how training creates possibilities? And how changing your intent and environment can bring this about?

> Apply the right effort and you can learn to do anything better!

Apply the right effort and you can learn to do anything better, which will make you better at everything.

---

170   Keitaro Kubo et al. (2011) "Time course of changes in the human Achilles tendon properties and metabolism during training and detraining in vivo." *European Journal of Applied Physiology*. 24(2):322–331.
171   Tongue twisters they aren't half!

Change the Environment, Change the Organism

If you really want to transform yourself, change the environment.

Throughout this book, I hope I have demonstrated the *extreme* adaptability of the nervous system and the human organism.

Consider the Tarahumara, who are capable of running over four hundred miles in fifty hours; or the Moken children reshaping the lenses of their eyes. Consider how cognitively different modern man is compared with our prehistoric counterpart, despite having precisely the same biology at birth.

> There is no "natural man," there is only man the adaptable.

Consider the monkeys whose nervous systems adapted to integrate robotic limbs into their own sense of self. Or the hemispherectomy patients that are able to adapt to having 50 percent of their brain removed!

I put it to you then, that there *is* no "natural man," there is only man the adaptable.

Romantic notions of an optimized lifestyle for our biology I believe to be misguided. The popular idea that we should return to our roots, to a more "natural" way of life, assumes some kind of consistency in our history. In fact, we have lived in countless environments and continually been forced to adapt. We have lived in the trees, in caves, in open planes, by the sea, and now in chairs.

Not one of these environments was perfect. Nor is our current lifestyle "wrong."

But many of us are unaware of the way in which our environments are shaping us. Thus, we lose the right to *choose* what we want to be. And we inadvertently ignore so much of our potential.

If we want to do more and be more, we have to redefine ourselves. We do this by redefining our purpose.

We can do better than being "sitters."

If we want to create real change, then we should change our immediate environment, such that adaptations go beyond "training."

If we train push-ups two days in a row, we worry that we might over train the pecs. But we never worry so much about using our legs two days in a row, twenty-four-seven, to bear all of our weight. Why? Because our bodies have adapted to that demand. It has become normal.

As we saw earlier in this book, this might even explain why children have such incredibly plastic brains. They have been dropped into a completely strange and foreign world with no choice but to adapt. This triggers the most profound development of our lifetimes.

Training for just three hours a week is a poor substitute for this kind of total immersion. You might force a little bit of change, but you will remain adapted to your current environment and routine.

But make that challenge *a part* of your environment, and that's when incredible change becomes possible. What if you regularly placed your weight on your hands a fraction as often as you place it on your feet? What if you regularly wondered about the cosmos?[172]

And as we've seen, it can also be as simple as changing the intent. It can mean trying to read faster and more efficiently, trying to see more, or feeling the muscles working as you walk.

By moving *throughout* the day and by choosing to be more present and effective, by creating more challenge and resistance, you change your communication with the world around you, and the way it shapes your plastic mind and body.

(This is another benefit of slowcomotion—you can easily incorporate this into your daily routine. I'll use it when I'm brushing my teeth, when I'm playing with my daughter, or when I'm getting up from an awkward angle. It often just means taking up a more difficult position, instead of the easiest one.)

I like to imagine what a perfect environment for shaping our bodies to a higher potential would look like. Instead of designing our environments to make life *easier* for us, what if we designed them to offer more challenge, play, and opportunity for creative expression?

A standing desk is one small example of this. But what if we had a rope instead of stairs? What if the doors were designed to require significant strength to open? What if

---

172   This critical role of the environment is also explained in the "dynamical systems theory" of motor learning proposed by developmental psychologist Esther Elen and others. Here, we see that every movement pattern must account for the environment and the task, as well as the organism itself (these three factors are "constraints"). In other words, we can't learn a useful new movement without the context of the environment or the aim. Coaches that subscribe to this theory can bring about impressive changes by simply changing the nature of the task or introducing new environmental variables.

your alarm clock required that you solve mental puzzles to switch it off?

What if your doorway was low and required you to crawl through it?

This is a fun thought experiment. I like to refer to this hypothetical building as "Adaptation Facilitation Machine."[173] Such an environment would not only trigger physical changes as a direct result of its obstacles to movement, but it could also create increased plasticity simply as a result of such a novel environment.

Of course, the space would need to be constantly changing to keep us truly plastic!

I can't go to these extreme lengths because I have a wife and daughter who think I'm crazy enough as it is. But there are small things you can do such as keeping a pull up bar in your doorway, and dip bars in your home office. Little "reminders to move" can make a big difference.

And more importantly, you must change your relationship with your environment by maintaining an intent to train and explore your movement.

If you get this right, there is the potential to completely redesign the working of your body and mind. Surely that's the most authentic form of self-expression?

The question then, is what do you want to become?

---

173   Inspired by Cal Newport's "Eudaimonia Machine"—an office concept designed to facilitate the ideal mental state for productivity.

What Do You Want to Become?

In this book, we've seen humans that can swim underwater for huge stretches of time. We've seen people who have escaped from prison by bending iron bars. We've witness cannon balls being caught with bare hands. We've encountered chess masters who can play multiple games simultaneously *in their mind*. And I've barely scratched the surface. The limits of what we are capable of are truly fantastical.

I'm not suggesting that you should use every strategy and tip in this book. I'm not even saying that you should necessarily choose any more than two or three of the types of training I've addressed. Rather, the point is that you can choose *which* of these options applies to you and *your* goals.

You don't have to walk a well-trodden path. You can blaze your own trail.

Why not combine these training styles and create something entirely new?

Those are the people who truly inspire me. The people exploring what their bodies can do and finding exciting new ways to express that potential, the Oleg Vorslavs, Ido Portals, Jackie Chans, Bruce Lees, Alexander Zasses, and Harry Houdinis.

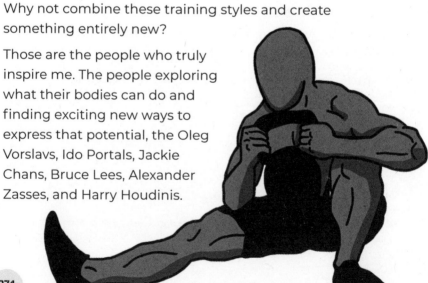

There is still potential here to do something no one has seen before.

And the limits of the mind are even *less* explored. Only now are we beginning to realize the plastic potential of our gray matter and its capacity for change and growth.

How might we change our perception, the organization of our thoughts, and our ability to focus and react? What new discoveries could we make, what new ideas could we stumble on? Studies now suggest that it might even be possible to *teach* such skills as synesthesia (the ability to perceive more than one sense in a merged fashion). What could Einstein have done with the working memory developed from games of blindfold chess?

Your highly plastic and adaptable body gives you the ability to become anything you want to be. To train like a real superhero and to explore your own limits.

I don't just want to be stronger and faster. I want to learn to move differently, and I want to think differently.

This is what "training" can do for us. It is so much more than just a way to maintain basic health or gain bragging rights on online forums. Training should be a personal tool we use to express ourselves and expand beyond our boundaries. That is what it means to be a "SuperFunctionate."

You don't have to take every idea in this book and apply it. If you want to stick to hour-long workouts, that's understandable! Most will, I imagine. But I hope that at the very least, you will consider training in more than one modality. Or that you will consider training your brain as well as your body.

Maybe you'll just reconsider what training means to you, and what *can* be trained.

And I hope this book has demonstrated just how many options are available to you. Now it's for you to pick the ones that appeal to you, and to decide what you are going to become.

That's why I believe the human body is the final frontier.

Acknowledgements

This book is dedicated to my hilarious, genius daughter Emmy, who is eighteen months at the time of writing and is a genuine ray of sunshine.

I also want to give special mention to my amazing wife, Hannah, who has supported me through the writing of this book and through all things! She is my rock and best friend. And a big thanks to Sophie Bunce, who likewise proofread select chapters for me!

This book remembers Bernard Hunt, who got me into training. I should also thank my sister, Kat Sinicki, for putting up with all the times I tried out karate moves on her after watching *Who Am I*, or playing too much *Shenmue*. I'd also like to thank my mum because she's awesome.

I'd also like to thank all the subscribers to my YouTube channel, who are genuinely amazing. I am fortunate to have what may well be the most positive comments section on YouTube! There's an amazing community there, so come and say hi (www.youtube.com/thebioneer)!

And of course, a big thank you to the extremely generous individuals who have supported the channel through Patreon.

A big shout out to Mango Publishing for making this possible, and my editor Hugo Villabona, who has been brilliant. And to Chris "Goof" Hanlon. Not for any particular reason, but it has become tradition to involve him somehow in these things!

And to you, of course!

About the Author

My name is Adam Sinicki, pleased to meet you!

You may be wondering what on earth compels a guy to write a book about training like Batman. Before we go further, I'd first like to highlight that I in no way consider myself to have achieved some "ultimate" level of fitness. Far from it! Nor do I practice everything I preach in here. That would be impossible! I drink *way* too much coffee, for starters (an irony my wife pointed out to me when proofing the first chapter of this book).

Rather, I'm just a guy who loves researching exciting and unusual forms of training, as well as cases of individuals who have pushed the limits of human performance. I have indeed adopted a large number of the principles I'll be addressing in this book, and I've enjoyed some pretty decent health and performance benefits as a result. But for me, it's as much about the journey as the results.

The aim of this book is not to prescribe anything in particular, but rather to explore ideas and get you thinking. I want to encourage you to think outside the box when it comes to your training, and perhaps introduce you to some ideas you can implement in your own routines. This book is primarily a discussion on training philosophy, and self-fulfillment in general. Albeit with plenty of practical application.

So, how did I get here?

I've been interested in what the human body and brain can do since I was a young boy. I was enamored with superheroes, action heroes, and game characters. Just a few of my biggest role models growing up were Jackie Chan, Bruce Lee, Sylvester Stallone, Arnold Schwarzenegger, Sonic the Hedgehog, Tony Stark (Iron Man), Spider-Man, Optimus Prime, Batman, and Superman. I was in awe of what these fictional characters could do, and I wondered if there was any way to achieve something close.

Inspired by Jackie Chan in particular (who really did seem to be a real-life superhero), and heavily encouraged by my Granddad Bernard Hunt (who arguably got me started down this path and enjoyed playing Mr. Miyagi to my Daniel-San), I began working out every night. At first, I had no idea what I was doing, so I'd just do hundreds of press-ups!

That said, I also enjoyed performing the exercises Bernard prescribed for me, including the likes of catching coins off my forearm before they could fall. Eventually, this developed into a fairly standard bodybuilding routine, which I trained in regularly with my buddy Goof.

I distinctly remember being in awe of hand balancers, and particularly an incredible Pirates show we saw once in Majorca. These guys were like walking Greek sculptures and could seemingly defy gravity, standing on one hand on another person's head, scaling ropes, and performing amazing acrobatics. They seemed superhuman.

After that, I didn't stop until I could walk on my hands!

I also took karate classes, Capoeira, and Tai Chi. Later, I entered Teen Bodybuilder of the Month on Teenbodybuilding.com and won! This led to a few early opportunities, including getting a website professionally built for me. Exciting stuff for a sixteen-year-old! And with the help of my friend Matt, this led to the creation of my own fitness and self-improvement site: The Biomatrix; and eventually my current website: The Bioneer.

I was also inspired by the free running documentary *Jump London* to take up parkour. My sister spent many hours diligently filming me jumping off bridges when we were out walking the dogs.

I told people I wanted to be a stuntman or action hero, but really, I wanted to be a superhero!

My favorite superhero was Iron Man though. I loved the notion that he could solve almost any problem just by thinking about it long enough. And so, in a bid to learn more about the mental aspect of training and self-development, I opted to study psychology at Surrey University. I did my dissertation on the ethics of transhumanism.

When I finished university, I decided I would make like Tony Stark and become an entrepreneur. To that end, I became a freelance writer, focusing primarily on health and technology. I also started to regularly upload fitness videos to my YouTube channel. Though those early videos were not the most polished, let's just say.

A decade later, and I'd written and read a HUGE amount about health and fitness for many clients, trained online clients, and acquired a diploma in personal training. I also used my spare time to teach myself to program (I already had some experience as a child in BASIC), which resulted in the release of a couple of successful Android apps, and landed me ongoing freelance work with a respected tech channel (Android Authority).

Seeing as I was paid per-word or per app download, many of the brain-training methods I wrote about had direct benefits for me. The faster I could output high-quality work, the more I earned! On some days I managed to write over 30,000 words! The methods I used are all detailed in this book.

All the while, I kept uploading content to my channel and to my website (www.thebioneer.com). Over time, the content morphed from typical health and fitness posts, to posts that discussed a broader range of topics. Common topics included the link between training the brain and body, or aspects of strength overlooked by most training programs. Even programming! I've talked about Einstein's brain, and the little fingers of samurai (both of which will also get a mention in this book!). I also discuss fictional characters, and how you might train like them. What training would Batman *really* need to focus on, for example? How could you run faster, like Sonic the Hedgehog? These flights of fancy help frame training in a way that I find exciting and inspiring.

And it seems this was a popular move! After nearly a decade of shouting into the void, the channel has enjoyed a substantial boom in the last couple of years. Now with 168,000 subscribers and counting! (19.8k new subscribers just this month!)

As the channel has grown, I've explored more fascinating topics, and gotten to meet and learn from some amazing people. Including channel collaborator, friend, and insanely impressive martial artist, Grant Stevens.

It seems I've captured the zeitgeist. Mine is just one of many channels exploring alternative approaches to training right now. The term "functional training" has been around for an age but has exploded on social media in recent years. The "movement training" movement has likewise blown up, and health bloggers are increasingly preaching the harm our modern lifestyles are causing to us. Biohackers are experimenting with all kinds of supplements and other strategies to enhance their health and productivity. Training is changing in an exciting way.

This book is a herald for that change and a summation of all the research I have done, both for clients, and as The Bioneer. It is the culmination of hundreds of articles and more than 250 videos. Through it, I propose that we rethink our approach to training, and tentatively provide some ideas as to what that might look like.

When I'm not obsessing over how to jump higher or climb my rope faster, I also enjoy spending time with my wife and daughter, reading comics, playing computer games, and eating tuna sandwiches. I live in Oxfordshire, and I often return to Bournemouth where I grew up. I'm very happy.

Oh, and in the interests of historical context, much of this book was written during the COVID-19 lockdown! It certainly gave me something to stay occupied.

Mango Publishing, established in 2014, publishes an eclectic list of books by diverse authors—both new and established voices—on topics ranging from business, personal growth, women's empowerment, LGBTQ studies, health, and spirituality to history, popular culture, time management, decluttering, lifestyle, mental wellness, aging, and sustainable living. We were recently named 2019 *and* 2020's #1 fastest growing independent publisher by *Publishers Weekly*. Our success is driven by our main goal, which is to publish high-quality books that will entertain readers as well as make a positive difference in their lives.

Our readers are our most important resource; we value your input, suggestions, and ideas. We'd love to hear from you— after all, we are publishing books for you!

Please stay in touch with us and follow us at:

Facebook: Mango Publishing

Twitter: @MangoPublishing

Instagram: @MangoPublishing

LinkedIn: Mango Publishing

Pinterest: Mango Publishing

Newsletter: mangopublishinggroup.com/newsletter

Join us on Mango's journey to reinvent publishing, one book at a time.